THE SCOUTMASTER

Also by
Brooks Eason

Travels with Bobby: Hiking the Mountains of the American West
Fortunate Son: The Story of Baby Boy Francis
Bedtime with Buster: Conversations with a Handsome Hound
Redemption: The Two Lives of Harry Brooks

THE
SCOUTMASTER

Lessons in Service and Leadership
from an American Hero

BROOKS EASON

WordCrafts Press

Published by WordCrafts Press
Cody, Wyoming 82414
www.wordcrafts.net

For the Scoutmaster

Lives of great men all remind us
We can make our lives sublime,
And, departing, leave behind us
Footprints on the sands of time.

From "A Psalm for Life"
Henry Wadsworth Longfellow

PROLOGUE

A man whose talents and efforts are perfectly suited to his mission can accomplish great things. My father, Paul Eason, was such a man.

Daddy worked hard to earn a living and provide for my mother, my sister, and me, but his mission in life had nothing to do with making money. His job was just a job. His mission, the calling to which he devoted thousands upon thousands of hours of his time, was to serve as the Scoutmaster of Boy Scout Troop 12 in Tupelo, Mississippi.

The Boy Scouts of America was founded in 1910 and has a long and glorious history. More than a hundred million Americans have been members of one or more Scouting organizations. Millions of them have gone on to serve as leaders in business and government and their churches and communities. Those who have attained the rank of Eagle, the highest in Scouting, include Gerald Ford, Neil Armstrong, Steven Spielberg, and Sam Walton.

For most of its existence, Scouting was universally regarded as an invaluable institution that taught time-honored values to America's youth. Boy Scouts, depicted in illustrations by Norman Rockwell, were viewed as model young men. They were as American as Mom and apple pie.

But in recent decades, changes in America have brought controversy and challenges to the Scouts. There have always been gay Scouts, but gay adolescents in past decades rarely announced their sexual preference. As more and more young people came out as gay, the Boy Scouts grappled with the issue. Openly gay youths were traditionally barred from membership, but the Scouts reversed this position in 2014. Openly gay adults were authorized to become Scout leaders the following year.

Several years later, the Boy Scouts announced that girls would be allowed to join the Scouts and earn the same ranks and merit badges that boys earn. The organization changed its name to Scouts BSA. Same-sex troops are required, but "linked" troops of boys only and girls only can meet at the same time in the same location and camp together.

The changes have been welcomed by some parents but not by all. My daughter was not pleased when she learned that a girls' troop was at summer camp for a week when her sons' troop was there. She was understandably concerned that the boys would not devote their time and attention to earning merit badges and having fun with their male friends. Hormonal teenagers camping together—what could go wrong? Some organizations also opposed the changes. The Boy Scouts were sued by the Girl Scouts for poaching their members.

The Scouts have also suffered from dwindling participation. Enrollment peaked fifty years ago and has been shrinking since then. The causes are many. There is now far more competition for the time of young Americans than in decades past. Sports and other activities have proliferated, leaving little time for Scout meetings and campouts. Many young people, regrettably, would rather stare at their screens than camp in the woods. Many parents, regrettably, indulge them. Some parents believe Scouting is too old-fashioned, others that it's not old-fashioned enough. While the Scouts walked a fine line in recent years between remaining true to their core mission and values and keeping up with the times, the pandemic exacerbated the enrollment crisis.

Worst of all, the Scouts have been besieged by a scandal involving thousands of allegations of sexual abuse. In the 1980s, the Scouts began implementing a program designed to protect innocent Scouts from abuse and innocent leaders from false accusations. The rules have been strengthened and enforcement has become more rigorous in the years since then. The program is now set out in a detailed policy entitled Barriers to Abuse. Adult leaders must be registered and trained in youth protection. At least two leaders are required at all events, and one-on-one contact between a leader and a Scout is prohibited.

But in spite of the protections in the program, claims of sexual abuse increased dramatically. The sheer number led the Scouts to seek bankruptcy protection in 2020. A total of 92,000 claims of sexual abuse were ultimately filed in the bankruptcy court. Many claimants came forward only after the opportunity was publicized by lawyers seeking to represent them. Some of the allegations were from the time before meaningful protections were in place, involved alleged abusers who were deceased, and thus could not be contested. In other cases, because records from long ago were not retained, it was impossible to determine if the claimants had even been Scouts. But many of the claims were undoubtedly valid. Until recent years, the Scouts admittedly did a poor job of identifying sexual predators and protecting young people from them. Some cases of abuse were covered up.

All this makes it appear that there is nothing but bad news these days for the Boy Scouts. But there is also good news, as there always has been. In March 2023, a federal judge in Delaware approved a settlement of the sexual abuse claims filed in the bankruptcy court. In addition to compensation, victims will receive counseling and support. A month after the settlement was approved, the Scouts emerged from bankruptcy. These developments bring with them the hope that the Scouts can put this dark chapter behind them and look to a brighter future.

In other good news, enrollment is now increasing for the first time in many years. The number of youth participants topped a million by the end of 2022. Thousands of outstanding men and women continue to give freely of their time as leaders. Through their efforts, millions of Scouts will receive the same benefits that millions of others received in the past. Scouting continues to pro- vide America's youth with the opportunity to learn skills and habits that will make them the nation's future leaders.

This book tells the good news the Boy Scouts have to share through the story of one remarkable man. Paul Eason served as a Scoutmaster for more than six decades and led thousands of boys on their journeys from childhood to manhood. One of those boys, Charles Johnston, will celebrate his ninetieth birthday in November 2023. When I interviewed Charles for the book, he told me the story of Daddy's selfless commitment to the Scouts of Troop 12 should be documented and shared far and wide. I agree. The story of the lifelong benefits of Scouting and the devoted leaders who make it a success should be shouted from the mountaintop.

Daddy became the Scoutmaster of Troop 12 when he was only twenty-five, still single, and just home from the Navy after World War II. He served in the role for more than forty-five years, not stepping down until after he turned seventy. Most men would have concluded that forty-five years was enough, but not Daddy. He continued as an Assistant Scoutmaster for nearly sixteen more, working and camping with the boys in the troop until he turned eighty-six.

For six decades, from 1947 to 2008, Daddy served as a beacon and role model for three generations of boys in Tupelo, giving generously of his time and talent as few men do. More than 350 Scouts attained the rank of Eagle during his tenure, and all of them learned lessons from him about honor, principle, leadership, and service. After he died, a friend declared that he was the best Scoutmaster in the world.

Leroy P. McCarty Jr., known to one and all as Buddy, was one of the boys who learned from Daddy and became an Eagle Scout in Troop 12. Buddy is nearly eighty years old, but he has not forgotten about his time as a Scout and his love and admiration for his Scoutmaster. After learning that I was writing this book, he sent me a long message that included a story I'd never heard:

> *My most powerful personal memory of Paul is from the summer of 1957. The only requirement I lacked to earn my Eagle Scout badge was the three-quarter-mile timed run for*

Personal Fitness merit badge. I had not yet begun my high school growth spurt, was a bit chubby for distance running, and could not run the distance in the required time of six minutes. So, for weeks on end, on Monday through Friday during that summer of 1957, Paul picked me up after he got off from work, took me to the Robins Field track, and trained me.

Weeks into the training I wanted to quit, but Paul would not allow it! He was encouraging, he was tough, he was kind, he was patient; he knew exactly what he was doing. He consistently let me know that I could succeed. He never once raised his voice and was always positive. The result? After weeks of training, I completed the run in the required time, with thirty seconds to spare!

The experience was a valuable lesson that has served me well throughout my life. I am forever grateful to Paul for teaching me much more than how to run. Thanks to Paul Eason, I am an Eagle Scout.

Paul Eason is an authentic American hero.

Thanks to the training he received in the summer of 1957, Buddy McCarty became the forty-fourth young man to attain the rank of Eagle in Troop 12 since its inception. He was the twenty-fourth under Daddy's leadership, which began a decade earlier. After completing the last remaining requirement with thirty seconds to spare, Buddy was awarded his Eagle badge on September 23, 1957, at Troop 12's weekly Monday night meeting. Sixty-five years later, he sent me the story of how he conquered the three-quarter-mile run and became an Eagle Scout.

In July 1957, while Daddy was training Buddy at Robins Field in Tupelo, I was born at a home for unwed mothers in New Orleans. Two and a half months later, the staff at the home chose Paul and Margaret Eason to be my father and mother. When the call came, they dropped everything and drove south to get me. I was placed in Mama's arms on September 19; Daddy drove us home to Tupelo the next day. Three days later, when Buddy McCarty was awarded his Eagle badge, Daddy presided at the ceremony.

Daddy is my hero. Many sons say that of their fathers, but many sons of other fathers, including Buddy McCarty, say that of mine. I rode on Daddy's shoulders as a child and stand on them as a man. Hundreds of other men stand alongside me.

I have written four books before this one. None of them is about Daddy, but he appears in all of them. My first book, *Travels with Bobby*, is about hiking trips in the mountains of the West with my best friend. I included Daddy in the book because he taught me to love camping, hiking, and the outdoors. I think about him whenever I'm around a campfire with friends.

I wrote much more about Daddy in my memoir about my adoption and discovery of the identity of my birth mother when I was nearly fifty. I chose *Fortunate Son* as the title because of how fortunate I was that the staff at the maternity home chose Mama and Daddy to be my parents. I am eternally grateful for their decision.

My third book, *Bedtime with Buster*, consists entirely of conversations between me and our beloved dog Buster, who crossed over the Rainbow Bridge while I was in the middle of writing this book. In our first talk, I told Buster all the things that made Daddy a great man. Buster agreed that Daddy was a great man, but for a different reason. He said it was because Daddy shared his ice cream with his dog. It's true; he did.

Daddy made only a brief appearance in my most recent book, *Redemption*, a novel based on the life of my maternal grandfather Harry Brooks, who was a preacher, a felon, then a preacher again. When Harry gave the invocation before President Roosevelt spoke to a crowd of 75,000 in Tupelo in 1934, Daddy was there in his Boy Scout uniform. Daddy was also in Tupelo in 1936 when the fourth deadliest tornado in the nation's history struck the city. He and Mama, who were both in the ninth grade, lived less than a mile apart. The storm passed between their homes, and the families taking refuge inside were spared.

When it came time to start a fifth book, I considered several options but ultimately decided to write one entirely about Daddy and his lifetime of service to the Scouts of Troop 12. It was a selfish choice because I love telling others about Daddy and seeing their faces light up when they talk about him. I knew that writing the book would be much more love than labor.

The book is divided into two parts. The first is the story of Daddy's life from beginning to end, from his birth in 1921 to his death nearly ninety-two years later, written from my perspective as his only son. The second part consists of summaries of interviews about Daddy. When I wrote the first draft of this prologue, I had not yet started the interviews, but I was already looking forward to them. I knew that Daddy's Scouts and his family and friends loved and respected him because they'd been telling me all my life, but I looked forward to learning stories I'd never heard, stories like the training of Buddy McCarty at Robins Field. I also wanted to hear people whose lives Daddy touched explain how he inspired and influenced them and what he meant to them.

When I came down to the kitchen and told my wife, Carrie, what I was planning, she warned me that the audience for a biography of a man who died a decade earlier and was not well known outside his hometown might be limited. She may be right, but even if the only people who read the book are those who knew and loved Daddy, I believe they will enjoy reading it, and I have thoroughly enjoyed writing it.

But it's also possible that Carrie could be wrong. We are constantly bombarded with news of men in positions of power who are immoral, unethical, selfish, and dishonest, and I believe people yearn to know the stories of men who are precisely the opposite. If I'm right, even those who've never heard of Paul Eason will appreciate learning about him. Daddy was a rare man, a gifted leader who was completely unselfish, always giving of himself, always thinking of others. He was an extraordinary role model for all who knew him, and he had a profound and positive influence on the boys of Troop 12.

We all know it's possible to be famous without being great, but it's also possible to be great without being famous. My father was a great man. He served as an inspiration to thousands who knew him during his lifetime. My hope is that he will serve as an inspiration to many more who will read about him. Daddy left us ten years ago, but we still have much to learn from him.

After Carrie warned me that a book about a Boy Scout leader from a small town in northeast Mississippi, even a legendary Boy Scout leader, might have limited appeal, she suggested that the market might be larger if the story of Daddy's life could be used to teach lessons in service and leadership. Her suggestion made me think about the qualities that made Daddy a great leader.

I became an Eagle Scout more than five decades ago, but I can still recite the Scout Law from memory. The law states that a Scout is trustworthy, loyal, helpful, friendly, courteous, kind, obedient, cheerful, thrifty, brave, clean, and reverent. Daddy possessed all those traits in abundance, though the Scouts in his troop, including me, often fell short. We failed utterly to be clean, especially on campouts. Daddy joked that the Boy Scout motto, Be Prepared, should be changed to A Little Crud Never Hurt Anybody.

The qualities that made Daddy a great leader reflect his commitment to the virtues of the Scout law. First and foremost, Daddy was trustworthy. He was a man of absolute integrity. He always told the truth, always kept his word, and always did the right thing. If he promised to do something, he did it, every time. His moral compass never wavered. And the Scouts in Troop 12 could see that. They were proud to have a man of honor as their leader. They knew they could trust him.

Daddy led by example, not instruction. He never lectured the Scouts about the leadership skills and virtues they should have. Not only would he have viewed himself as unqualified to give such a lecture, but Daddy was a doer, not a talker. When he turned ninety, my daughter, Ann Lowrey, wrote an essay about him that included a saying attributed to Saint Francis of Assisi: "Preach the Gospel always; when necessary, use words." Through his actions, Daddy preached the gospel of what a man should be and how a man should live. The Scouts saw how Daddy conducted himself, how he worked, how he treated others. They watched him, and they wanted to be like him. They may not have become as good as the original—I'm certainly not—but they became better men from spending time with him when they were learning to be men.

Nobody in the troop—neither the boys nor the assistant leaders—worked harder than Daddy. When the troop had a service project, he was the first to arrive, worked side by side with the Scouts until the job was done, then was the last to leave. If the boys were picking up garbage, Daddy had a trash bag. If they were planting trees, he had a spade. Members of an organization trust a leader who gets down in the trenches with them, and the Scouts trusted Daddy. He was a man of great stamina and self-discipline. He was steadfast.

I don't know how much of Daddy rubbed off on me, but one trait occurred to me as I was writing this. I've spent my career as a lawyer, litigating business and employment cases for four decades. When I started supervising younger lawyers and paralegals, I realized I was uncomfortable if they were working and I wasn't. If we had a brief due and I had completed my revisions, discussed it with the client, and my role was finished, I would stay at the office after hours with the younger members of the team until the brief was filed. I would offer to help as they checked the cases and statutes we'd cited, attached the exhibits, and finalized the brief. They didn't need my help and would tell me to go home, but I would stay. I didn't realize it until now, but I stayed because I'm Daddy's son.

Daddy was humble. He would brag on others but never on himself. Getting him to talk about himself was like pulling teeth. Daddy spent a lifetime serving others because it was the right thing to do, not because of the honors and recognition that came his way. He was not interested in accolades and was embarrassed when he received them. Those who knew Daddy recognized that he was an extraordinary man. He was the only one who couldn't see it. He thought of himself as an ordinary man who was just doing his part. And because he was humble, Daddy didn't assume he always had the right answer or the best solution. He sought opinions from others, including the Scouts, and he listened to what they had to say. An organization becomes stronger and its members more productive if those in charge listen to them. Daddy was a good listener. He was a leader, not a dictator.

Daddy understood the importance of organization and detail. He prepared an itinerary for every meeting and every campout. He delegated tasks to his assistants and the Scouts. As much as possible for a large group of adolescent boys, Troop 12 ran like clockwork.

Several years after Daddy became the Scoutmaster, the troop was evicted from its meeting place behind the choir loft in the First Methodist Church because the space was needed for a new organ. Members of the church's Chapman Men's Bible Class, which sponsored Troop 12, decided the troop needed a building of its own. Daddy oversaw the project and kept track of every contribution and every expense. They balanced to the penny. The cost of the new Scout Hut, which was completed in December 1953, was $5500. The troop met outside for a year while it was under construction but has had its own building ever since.

In September 1991, Daddy and I spent a magnificent week rafting the entire length of the Grand Canyon on the eve of his seventieth birthday. By then he had been planning campouts as the leader of Troop 12 for nearly forty-five years. Even though our guides prepared all the meals on the trip, Daddy kept a journal of everything we ate. Maybe he thought it would be useful in planning future campouts. It was his nature to focus on the little things that are necessary to make the big things work.

Daddy was calm and unflappable. He was even-keeled. When problems arose, as they did countless times over the course of six decades, Daddy never panicked or raised his voice. He didn't get angry, complain, or look for someone or something to blame. His focus was always on solving the problem and moving forward.

In March 1971, when I was thirteen, the troop planned a three-day canoe trip during spring break on Bear Creek northeast of Tupelo. I had broken my arm in a sledding accident in February, but I persuaded Daddy and my orthopedist to let me go on the trip and talked two friends into paddling me down the river. I sat in the middle of the canoe, a useless passenger with a plastic Wonder Bread bag over my cast.

The water was high, and many of the canoes capsized the first day. It rained during the night, and the river rose even more. Daddy took a poll the next morning. The boys who'd turned over the day before wanted to end the trip. Those of us who'd stayed dry wanted to keep going. The decision wasn't up to us, but Daddy wanted our input. After hearing us out and studying the river, he decided continuing was too dangerous. He slogged through a muddy cow pasture to a farmhouse, placed some calls, and arranged a rescue mission. Parents came a day early, picked us up, and took us home. We draped the wet tents over chairs in the Scout Hut to dry, rolled them up at the next Monday night meeting, and went camping again in April.

Daddy treated all people with kindness and respect. He did not talk down to the Scouts or treat them like children. He guided the troop with a light rein and let boys be boys, but he didn't let the occasional bullying get out of hand. He teased Scouts but didn't belittle them. He could sense which ones were struggling and needed extra attention. He was a master psychologist but would have been shocked if anyone had ever called him that.

Daddy set high standards and expected the members of the troop to meet them. He would help and encourage, but he would not do the Scouts' work for them. There was no coddling. To advance in rank and earn merit badges, the boys had to do the work. Nothing was signed off until all the requirements were done and done right. He didn't allow the Scouts to cut corners. After the training at Robins Field, if Buddy McCarty had still been too slow, he would not be an Eagle Scout.

Daddy was willing to let boys suffer from their mistakes but only enough to learn from them. Campouts were designated as either individual or patrol. On individual campouts, each Scout was responsible for his own food and cooking equipment. On patrol campouts, each patrol of seven or eight boys purchased and prepared the patrol's food. If a Scout forgot his plate or utensils or a patrol failed to bring hamburger buns or a stove, the boys suffered, learned, and remembered the next time. Daddy knew that a little misery is a great teacher. As Tolkien wrote, "The burned hand teaches best. After that, advice about fire goes to the heart."

Whenever the troop camped on Saturday night, Daddy would plan a church service for Sunday morning, often focused on the beauty of God's kingdom. He prepared a written program for the service, but the Scouts led it. One would read the message, another the Scripture, a third would lead the singing, and a fourth would say the closing prayer. The Scout Law states that a Scout is reverent. At least we were reverent then.

Daddy also made sure there was time in the schedule for fun. On Monday nights, the Scouts played volleyball and other games before the meetings. It was mostly for fun, but the boys also learned to pick teams and resolve disputes. Campouts included fishing, games of capture the flag, campfires, ghost stories, and more. Daddy recognized that the purpose of Scouting is to turn immature young boys into responsible young men, but he understood that boys will lose interest if they don't have fun. The boys in Troop 12 always had fun, and so did Daddy. He loved being the Scoutmaster.

Riding herd on dozens of rowdy adolescent boys would exhaust an ordinary man's patience. But Daddy was not an ordinary man, and his patience was inexhaustible. And he put it to use by insisting that Scouts do things that would have been much easier to do himself. The troop's officers, led by the elected senior patrol leader, ran the Monday night meetings. They learned to call a meeting to order, speak before a group, and conduct the troop's business. The younger boys watched and listened and were ready when their time came.

Every year for sixty years, Daddy contributed hundreds of hours of his time to the boys of Troop 12. If he averaged 500 hours a year, and it was surely more than that, the total would come to 30,000—the equivalent of working in a full-time job for fifteen years. And being a Scoutmaster is more challenging than many full-time jobs; a Scout executive has told me it's the hardest of all volunteer jobs. During its first two decades, Troop 12 had eleven Scoutmasters, none lasting more than three years. Then, for the next forty-five years, the troop had one.

Daddy spent his entire life serving others. During his six decades of service to Troop 12, he helped raise thousands of boys, all but one of whom were the sons of other men. All of us joined Troop 12 as boys of ten or eleven and left it four or five years later as young men, hundreds of us proudly wearing the Eagle badge on our uniforms. We came away from the experience with an enduring love for adventure and the outdoors as well as leadership and life skills we had no idea we were learning. We became better men because we were members of Troop 12 and because Paul Eason was our Scoutmaster.

PART ONE
The Life Of Paul Eason

Chapter One

1921-1939

Cliff and Margaret Eason married in Byhalia, Mississippi, in January 1921. They were both twenty-two. Their first child and only son was born just over nine months later, on November 4. They named him Paul for Cliff's older brother who was killed fighting in the Meuse-Argonne Offensive in France five weeks before the end of World War I. Cliff was old enough to fight in the war—he turned twenty in the spring of 1918—but an eye injury kept him from serving.

In the decade after Daddy's birth, the Easons had three more children, all girls—Myra; Annie Maude, who was called Puddie; and Doris. Having three strong-willed little sisters was likely one of the reasons Daddy became a man of extraordinary patience.

The Easons moved twice in the early years of their marriage, first to Belmont, then to Tupelo in time for Daddy to start first grade in 1927. In the early 1930s, Cliff and Margaret built the home on Highland Circle near downtown Tupelo where they lived the rest of their lives. Cliff spent his entire career as a banker and served as the president of Peoples Bank & Trust Company, now Renasant Bank, until he was seventy-five.

During construction of their home on Highland Circle, when Cliff decided he wanted a carport in back, the builder agreed but said it would cost an extra fifty dollars. Labor was cheap during the Depression. The home for the family of six had three bedrooms, one of which doubled as a den, and one bathroom that had a tub but no shower. An extra relative or two often lived with them. They got by.

Cliff and Margaret, who were called Daddy and Momie by their four children—and Daddy Cliff and Momie by their ten grand-children—were a fine and upstanding couple. Cliff was a respected community leader—one of Tupelo's main thoroughfares is named for him—and Margaret was a devoted wife and mother. She was always smiling, and there was always ice cream in the freezer. I have the letters she sent home to Cliff during the year she spent in a sanatorium suffering from tuberculosis, which cost her a lung. The letters were all about her family, not herself or her condition. The family was the center of her life.

Daddy referred to the house where he grew up as Momie's house. Not only was she in charge, but Cliff was rarely there. He worked from eight to five, came home for dinner, then returned to the bank from seven to nine. He kept the same schedule six days a week.

Cliff died in 1981. Margaret died seven years later, a month after her ninetieth birthday. Long after they were gone, Daddy was asked to name the most influential people in his life. He identified his parents.

I know little about Daddy's childhood because he didn't volunteer, and I didn't ask. I have a photo of him when he was three or four with his arm around a big dog, a shepherd of some sort. I wish I knew the dog's name.

But I do know a few things. Daddy was handsome but shy. He was afraid of girls and said he dated only when he was forced to. He was young for his class—he didn't turn eighteen until two months after he started college in 1939—and rail thin, 5'10" but only 120 pounds. He was a good student and a straight arrow who stayed out of trouble.

I once had a chance to speak alone to Daddy's best friend from childhood, a man named Harwell Dabbs. I asked him to tell me something bad Daddy had done along the way, some incident of misbehavior, even something minor. Harwell said he couldn't remember anything. I pressed him; surely there was something. I often misbehaved and was hoping Daddy did too. Harwell just shrugged. Maybe he was covering for Daddy, but I don't think so.

When he was in high school, Daddy worked at an icehouse on South Broadway Street that doubled as a creamery. Daddy's hourly wage was low, but the job came with a wonderful fringe benefit: all the ice cream he could eat. He said they lost money on him. Daddy loved ice cream all his life and ate a bowl every night when he wasn't camping with Troop 12. It was the closest thing to a vice he ever had. When Daddy was on hospice care in June 2013 and turned down our offer of ice cream, Carrie and I knew we wouldn't have him with us much longer. He died on the first of July.

Late, great Texas songwriter Guy Clark wrote a beautiful song about his wife Susanna entitled "My Favorite Picture of You." My favorite picture of Daddy is one that was taken by Mama on a Monday night after one of the thousands of Troop 12's weekly meetings Daddy attended. He's wearing his Scout uniform, sitting in his recliner, an empty bowl of ice cream in his lap, sound asleep. Daddy was a champion sleeper.

Daddy adopted another habit while growing up in the Depression that he followed for the rest of his life. One of the twelve virtues prescribed by the Boy Scout law is thrift. Daddy excelled at that one, and not only in his personal life. He made sure the trips Troop 12 took were inexpensive so that parents of modest means could afford to send their sons. He also spent almost nothing on himself. In the years after Mama died in 1999, his largest expenses were gifts to charity and his six grandchildren. After he stopped driving, his nephew Phil Ruff took him grocery shopping after lunch on Sundays. Phil said Daddy bought one roll of toilet paper because he figured that's all he needed. I had no idea you could buy one roll of toilet paper.

Thrift is another of Daddy's traits that rubbed off on me. Though I have made more and spent much more on myself than Daddy ever did, I hate wasting money, and spending it on extravagances pains me. Like Daddy, I've always mowed my own yard. My family and friends accuse me of being cheap. I prefer to think I'm following in Daddy's footsteps, obeying the Scout Law, and being thrifty.

On November 18, 1934, two weeks to the day after Daddy turned thirteen, President Roosevelt came to Tupelo to give a speech congratulating the city for becoming the first recipient of electricity generated by the Tennessee Valley Authority, one of the New Deal agencies created by Congress a year earlier. Before the speech, there was a grand parade through town featuring a thousand Boy Scouts. Daddy had joined Troop 12 when he was twelve and marched in the parade. Fifteen years later, he married one of the identical twin daughters of Dr. Harry Brooks, the minister who gave the invocation before FDR's speech.

Nearly a year and a half after Roosevelt's visit, a massive tornado struck Tupelo after Sunday evening church services. It was April 5, 1936, both Palm Sunday and Cliff's thirty-eighth birthday. Daddy heard the tornado but thought it was a train. After it passed, he and Cliff went out to see if there was any damage. When they turned east on Jackson Street, lightning lit up the sky. Church Street School, where Daddy went to elementary school and the podium for Roosevelt's speech was erected, was gone, swept away by the terrible wind.

Cliff and Daddy walked downtown to the hospital to see if they could help. A nurse named Roberta Dillard was brought in with a broken back. She was strapped to a door to immobilize her and screamed in pain as she was carried up a flight of stairs. On the walk home, they passed by Bob and Norma Weaver's house. A hard rain was falling, but the house was on fire. Wind from the tornado had come down the chimney, scattering coals into the house and starting the blaze. Their young son, also named Bob, cut his feet when he was passed through a broken window to safety. When the tornado struck, young Bob was four, Daddy fourteen. Twelve years later, when they were sixteen and twenty-six, Bob was the first member of Troop 12 to earn his Eagle after Daddy became the Scoutmaster.

Nearly 300 residents of Tupelo were killed by the tornado, including a couple and their eleven children. In the days that followed, funerals were conducted every hour on the hour until all the bodies were in the ground. Dr. Brooks conducted funerals for more than sixty of the victims. Hundreds of homes were reduced to rubble, and thousands of trees were blown down. The city looked like a war zone. There were no bulldozers or chainsaws then, and removing the many tons of debris took months. The old Church Street School was brick. The new one, built by the WPA, was made of concrete. Daddy said it would take an atomic bomb to destroy it.

The tornado must have left a mark on Daddy—many who survived it remained frightened of storms for the rest of their lives—but other than telling me what he saw that night, I don't recall ever hearing another word from him about it. Daddy certainly wasn't afraid of bad weather. When a tornado passed over and a river flooded on one campout, Daddy said that's exactly what boys like. I don't think Daddy was ever afraid of anything. If he was, he didn't show it.

In 1939 Daddy became an Eagle Scout, only the fifth member of Troop 12 to earn the award since the troop was founded more than a decade earlier. Harwell Dabbs was the fourth. Then, as now, a boy was not allowed to earn his Eagle after his eighteenth birthday. Daddy came home one weekend during his first semester of college and was presented with the award just before the deadline.

More than thirty years later, in 1972, I became Troop 12's 125th Eagle. Daddy had been the Scoutmaster for a quarter of a century, and he told me he considered passing the torch to someone new. But he didn't, and in the decades that followed, another 250 boys became Eagle Scouts before he finally ended his many years of service to the troop. The number of Scouts who achieved the highest rank in Scouting under Daddy's leadership is almost certainly the highest total for any leader in the history of the Boy Scouts of America. Many of Daddy's Eagle Scouts went on to become Scout leaders themselves, but none have served as long or as well as he did.

Chapter Two

1939-1946

Daddy attended college at the University of Mississippi, also known as Ole Miss. The school is in Oxford, fifty miles west of Tupelo. Daddy majored in accounting and planned a career in business. I suspect he chose not to become a banker because he wanted to chart his own course. He was not the type to seek favors or take advantage of the fact that his father was the vice-president of a major bank in Tupelo and later became its president.

In his freshman year in Oxford, Daddy joined the same fraternity I would join thirty-six years later, Phi Delta Theta. He treasured his time living in the fraternity house with a sleeping porch in back and maintained close relationships with many of his fraternity brothers long after they graduated, including future Mississippi governor William Winter. But Daddy was not a typical frat boy. He was not much for partying and, according to one of his classmates, often served in the role that later came to be known as designated driver.

In his junior year, Daddy was elected to serve as president of the fraternity. I'm certain it was not because he was the life of the party but because he'd earned his fraternity brothers' respect. They knew Daddy could be trusted to do the job and do it well.

Most college men spend their extra time and money on dates and beer, but not Daddy. If he had any romances while in college, I never heard a word about them. Rather than the usual pursuits, Daddy learned to fly. In early 1940, with twenty-five dollars saved from a part-time job, Daddy bought an old Model T Ford that came with neither a top nor a key. He draped a tarp over the car when it was not in use and started the engine by winding a crank in front. Cars no longer have cranks like the Model T, but starting a car is still called cranking the engine.

Daddy used the Model T to drive to the Oxford airport to take flying lessons, learned to fly, and loved it. He earned his private license and received academic credit to boot. Because he gave up flying before I was born, I didn't realize how much he loved it until near the end of his life. Even then, he didn't tell me. Like nearly everything I learned from him, it came to me through observation.

My first clue was the discovery of a poem in Daddy's bedroom in Tupelo when Carrie and I moved him south to our home in a Jackson suburb two months before his ninetieth birthday. The title of the poem, a sonnet, was "High Flight." The author, John Magee, a young Royal Canadian Air Force pilot, was killed on a training flight over England four days after the attack on Pearl Harbor. He was just nineteen. The poem is about the joy of flying.

> *Oh! I have slipped the surly bonds of earth*
> *and danced the skies on laughter-silvered wings.*
> *Sunward I've climbed, and joined the tumbling mirth of*
> *sun-split clouds—*
> *and done a hundred things you have not dreamed of—*
> *wheeled and soared and swung high in the sunlit silence.*
> *Hov'ring there I've chased the shouting wind along*
> *and flung my eager craft through footless halls of air.*
> *Up, up the long, delirious, burning blue*
> *I've topped the wind-swept heights with easy grace,*
> *where never lark or even eagle flew.*
> *And, while with silent lifting mind I've trod*
> *the high untrespassed sanctity of space,*
> *put out my hand and touched the face of God.*

Daddy never spoke to me about the poem, but somewhere along the way he obtained a copy, had it framed, and kept it for the rest of his life.

The second clue was something I observed while Daddy was living with Carrie and me his last two years. So that he would get some exercise, we would take him outside on nice days and stroll slowly around the small circle in our neighborhood. He used his walker, and one of us walked on either side. Every minute or two, he would stop to rest and look up to the sky, searching for jet contrails. When he spotted one, he would point it out and smile, as if it were a miracle. For someone born in 1921, I guess it was.

The same month Daddy started classes at Ole Miss, Germany invaded Poland. Britain and France responded by declaring war on Germany, and World War II began. The next two years, as the fighting escalated and America's involvement became more likely, were anxious times for young men of Daddy's generation. Then came December 7, 1941, the date of the Japanese attack on Pearl Harbor that would live in infamy. The United States declared war on Japan the next day, then Germany and the United States declared war on each other. A month later, when the spring semester began, Daddy signed up for extra classes so he could graduate early and enlist in the military.

When it came time to choose a branch, Daddy picked the Navy over the Army. His great-niece Elizabeth Leake interviewed him more than sixty years later for a school project and asked him why. Daddy said he chose the Navy because you could sleep in a berth on a ship, but in the Army you had to sleep on the ground. That may have been his thinking in 1942, but it seemed preposterous for him to say so when Elizabeth interviewed him in 2003. By then he'd been camping with Troop 12 for more than fifty years and had spent far more nights sleeping on the ground than any infantryman spent in World War II.

Because he already knew how to fly, Daddy entered flight school when he joined the Navy. He looked forward to fighting in the Pacific when he earned his wings, but the officers in charge of training had other plans. Undoubtedly because of the same qualities that made Daddy a great Boy Scout leader—patience, discipline, attention to detail—they made him a flight instructor and ordered him to remain in the States. Daddy appealed the decision; he had joined the Navy to fight for his country, not to stay home and teach others. In the same 2003 interview, he told Elizabeth he was crazy but lucky—crazy because he appealed, lucky because they turned him down. He trained at Auburn and the Universities of South Carolina and Georgia, where the exercise regimen included playing football between the hedges at Sanford Stadium, then spent the rest of the war helping other young pilots earn their wings.

In August 1945, while Daddy was on a training flight over Atlanta in a large, amphibious, patrol bomber called a PBY, the radio transmission was interrupted for a special report. A new secret weapon, something called an atomic bomb, had been dropped on the Japanese city of Hiroshima. When the pilot at the controls heard the news, he banked into a turn and headed back to the base. When asked why, he said the war was over.

And soon enough, it was. Nine days after the bombing of Hiroshima and six after a second bomb was dropped on Nagasaki, Emperor Hirohito announced Japan's unconditional surrender. Daddy was discharged from active duty in June of the following year but continued to serve in the Naval Reserve.

Though Daddy didn't see combat, many of his friends did, and some were killed in action. One was Louis Benoist from Natchez. He and Daddy had both entered Ole Miss in the fall of 1939 and joined Phi Delta Theta together. They became very close, and Louis traveled to Tupelo with Daddy and spent time with the Easons. Long after Daddy died, while going through family papers we'd brought home from Tupelo, I found three letters from Louis and one about him.

In the first, written while he was in basic training in Camp Shelby in south Mississippi, Louis wrote that he'd learned to fall asleep wherever he hit the ground. In the second, from Fort George Meade in Maryland, Louis had two pieces of news: He had just been ordered to go overseas, and his wife Anne was expecting their first child. In the third, written from the Battle of the Bulge in Belgium, Louis said he'd been trapped in his foxhole by eight inches of snow the night before and was rescued by his men. He wrote that he would love to be home with his wife, Anne, and their newborn son. The final letter, from Anne, reported that Louis had died a hero, killed by machine gun fire leading his men into battle while taking a town in Germany so small it wasn't even on the map. She closed the letter by telling Daddy that Louis had loved him deeply. Carrie suggested that I send the letters to Louis's family. I tracked down his son, also named Louis, a retired physician who never knew his father, and mailed the letters to him.

To the best of my recollection, I had never heard of Louis Benoist before I read the four letters. It would have been a simple matter to ask Daddy if he lost any close friends in the war, but World War II was ancient history by the time I came along, and it never occurred to me. And Daddy would not have brought it up on his own. It wasn't his nature to talk about either himself or the past.

I also never asked Daddy his feelings about his role in the war, how he felt about staying behind when so many of his contemporaries were sent into combat and paid the last full measure of devotion. He should have had no feelings of guilt—after all, he appealed the decision—but because of his sense of duty, he might have. But even if he didn't feel guilty, being spared from combat and possible death may have given him a stronger commitment to serve others after the war ended. Whatever his thoughts may have been, he took the role he was given in stride, as he took all things.

After his discharge from the Navy but before coming home to Tupelo and getting a job, Daddy took advantage of the GI Bill and returned to Ole Miss in the fall of 1946 to make up for the semester he'd missed by graduating early. Because he already had his degree, he audited classes rather than taking them for credit. How hard he studied, I don't know, though I can't picture Daddy as a slacker who slept late and skipped classes. But maybe he did. Maybe he viewed the semester as a break between the end of his time in the Navy and the start of his life in the civilian world.

Because the semester he missed was in the spring and he returned in the fall, Daddy was on campus for five football seasons. Before the last game of the 1946 season, the Egg Bowl against arch-rival Mississippi State, he and some other veterans who'd returned to Ole Miss hatched a plan. Three days before the game, they drove fifty miles east to Tupelo, rented planes, and flew south to Starkville, the site of the enemy campus. Each plane was manned by a pilot to fly it and a passenger to drop leaflets on the campus. What the leaflets said is unknown and at this point is unknowable.

It was a windy day, and the leaflets dropped on the first pass scattered widely. The formation, led by a decorated fighter pilot who'd fought in the skies over Europe, swooped low for a second run, disregarding the risk of crashing into the ground. As Daddy followed the leader through the campus quadrangle, he said he looked up and saw the top of the university's flagpole. The leaflets hit the target with a thud. Mission accomplished, the squadron returned to Tupelo, then drove back to Oxford.

The mission was successful, but the game was not. Ole Miss lost 20-0 and finished the season with two wins and seven losses. Daddy was at Ole Miss for five games against Mississippi State, and the Rebels lost all five, scoring a total of only eighteen points. The following year, 1947, Ole Miss reversed its fortunes. Led by new coach Johnny Vaught and future New York Giants star Charley Conerly, the Rebels beat the Bulldogs by three touchdowns and went 9–2 on the season. Ole Miss didn't lose the Egg Bowl again until 1964.

Chapter Three

1946-1957

When Daddy's bonus semester ended, he returned to Tupelo, where he lived the next sixty-five years. He had just turned twenty-five and been away from home for more than seven years, first in college, then in the Navy, then in college again. He was no longer the shy, skinny seventeen-year-old who left for Oxford in the fall of 1939. He was now a strong, confident Naval officer who could do one-armed push-ups, a feat that amazed the boys in his early years as the Scoutmaster of Troop 12.

Shortly after Daddy moved back home, he treated himself to a Christmas present. For the first time since the leaflet bombing raid, he returned to the Tupelo airport on Christmas Day to go flying. When the official on duty saw him, he demanded to know where Daddy and his friends had gone in November and what they had done. Daddy told him, and the man said he had something to show him. There were bullet holes in one of the planes. Someone at Mississippi State, almost certainly another veteran taking advantage of the GI Bill, had spotted the enemy planes flying through the quadrangle and opened fire.

When I was growing up, Daddy told me about getting shot at on the flight to Starkville and learning about it the next time he went to the airport. Many years later, while cleaning out the house on Rogers Drive where I grew up, I found a flight log with entries in Daddy's meticulous handwriting. It listed two flights from Tupelo in the last two months of 1946, the first on November 20, three days before the Mississippi State game, the second on Christmas Day.

Daddy's first job after moving back to Tupelo was checking customers' credit for L. P. McCarty & Son, a wholesale grocery founded by Buddy McCarty's great-grandfather. Daddy worked six days a week, ten hours a day, and lived at home with his parents and sister Doris, who was still in high school. He'd sold or given away the old Model T Ford by then, had not yet bought a car to replace it, and walked to and from his job in downtown Tupelo.

One evening when Daddy was on his way home, a car pulled over in front of the Lee County Library at the corner of Madison and Jefferson Streets, and the driver got out to speak. A. P. Bennett, who was both the principal of Tupelo High School and the Scoutmaster of Troop 12, said he was busy with school and needed help with the troop. He promised Daddy that the need was temporary; it would last for only a few months. When Daddy was interviewed by Elizabeth Leake more than half a century later, he told her of Bennett's assurance, laughed, and said, "But you know how that goes."

Bennett's request changed Daddy's life forever. Despite his sixty-hour work week, Daddy agreed to help because he always agreed to help. And his new role suited him to a tee. He was young and energetic, and he loved the outdoors. Because he was only a decade or so older than the boys in the troop, they could relate to him, but because he'd served in the Navy during the war, they also looked up to him. Bennett soon decided the troop was in good hands and bowed out, leaving Daddy in charge. He said he didn't give any thought at the time to how long he would keep the job. If he had, he could not have imagined he would keep it as long as he did.

From Daddy's earliest days as the Scoutmaster, Troop 12 grew and prospered. After Bob Weaver became his first Eagle Scout in 1948, eight more boys became Eagles in 1949. Daddy had found his life's calling.

13

Another significant event took place in Daddy's life in 1949. He asked Mama to marry him, and she said yes. At least that's how I assume it happened. I know nothing about their courtship or how Daddy proposed because I never asked either of them. If I had asked Mama, she would have spent an hour telling me. Daddy would have taken five minutes. I wasn't around then, but I would wager a fair sum that Daddy was much more comfortable leading the Scouts than courting Mama. It wouldn't even surprise me if Mama did most of the courting. But whoever took the lead, it worked, and they married on January the 21st of the following year. The wedding was held in the sanctuary of the First Methodist Church, where Daddy had been a member all his life and Mama's father had served as the preacher during the Depression.

Many a new bride would object if her husband chose to spend his spare time with a bunch of adolescent boys, camping and attending meetings, teaching knots and merit badges, and spending hours each week planning it all. But not Mama. Daddy was the Scoutmaster of Troop 12 before he was her husband, and she understood and approved of his devotion to the boys in the troop.

And she played a key role too. She bought groceries for campouts and washed Daddy's dirty clothes when he came home. When Daddy earned a patch for hiking one of the trails at the Shiloh Civil War battlefield or brought one home from one of the troop's many other destinations, she sewed it onto his red Boy Scout jacket. At the beginning and end of their marriage, before my sister Margie and I were born and after we were grown and gone, Mama stayed home alone while Daddy went camping. In the years in between, she kept Margie and me by herself.

At a Troop 12 reunion in 2001, two years after Mama died, a former Scout called me aside and said he wanted to thank me and the rest of our family for letting the boys in the troop borrow Daddy. I had never thought of it that way because his being gone was never a hardship for me. Before I was old enough to join the troop, I had plenty to keep me busy while Daddy was camping. I had my friends, the vacant lot beside our house, and the creek beside the vacant lot. And I'm sure I got away with more than I would have if Daddy had been at home. But his being away must have been hard for Mama, especially when Margie and I were little. But if she ever complained, I never heard it. She was proud to be married to the Scoutmaster.

It has often been said that behind every great man is a great woman. Mama walked beside Daddy, not behind him, but otherwise the saying holds true. Her unselfishness allowed him to pursue his calling, and the lives of thousands of boys were enriched as a result. And who knows how many more lives have been enriched by those boys since they became men? After Daddy died, one of his former Scouts wrote that "the inspiration to do good that Paul Eason instilled in so many people will ripple through the world forever."

Mama learned quickly how much time Daddy's commitment to Troop 12 would consume. Less than six months after their wedding, he and a group of Scouts from troops in different towns in the Yocona Area Council boarded a train for the thousand-mile ride to Valley Forge, Pennsylvania, to attend the 1950 National Boy Scout Jamboree. But their journey was delayed when they reached Baltimore. The Korean War had begun while they were en route, and the Army commandeered their train.

There was another leader on the trip. He was from a troop in New Albany, a small town twenty-five miles northwest of Tupelo. While they waited for another train, he called home and learned that his Army reserve unit had been called up. He had to return home immediately. Daddy saw the man for the last time when they parted ways in Baltimore. He was killed in action in Korea.

After spending a night in the station, Daddy and the boys were able to catch another train to Valley Forge. While they were there, one of the Scouts on the trip, Neal Biggers of Corinth, displaying the judgment that later earned him a lifetime appointment as a federal judge, caught a skunk with his bare hands. He was quite pleased with his prize until the skunk did what skunks do. Neal had to bury his clothes. The jamboree lasted ten days. Including the train trips going and coming, Daddy was away from Tupelo for two weeks. When he returned home, Mama sewed the official jamboree patch onto his jacket. I still have the jacket with the patch.

The following year, a suggestion made during a campfire conversation led Troop 12 to begin an extraordinary tradition, one that is almost certainly unmatched by any other Boy Scout troop in America, or anywhere else for that matter. Troop 12's senior patrol leader was a young man named Ken Kirk, who later became an Eagle Scout, co-captained the Ole Miss national championship football team in 1959, and played in the NFL. Before he did any of that, while Ken and Daddy were sitting by a campfire enjoying one of the great joys of camping in the spring of 1951, Ken had an inspiration. Camping was the very best thing about Scouting, he told Daddy. The troop should go every month.

Daddy wasn't one to make rash decisions, and I'm sure he didn't make one then. He no doubt wanted to think about it, and he probably talked it over with Mama and others. But before long, he decided Ken was right. Camping really was the very best thing about Scouting. It was certainly the most fun. Going every month would keep boys who grew bored with meetings and merit badges interested. More would remain in the troop and benefit from Scouting. More would become Eagle Scouts.

Daddy soon announced the plan to the boys, who went home and told their parents. Camping every month would mean camping not only in the dead of winter, when the temperature in north Mississippi is often below freezing, but also in the heat of summer, when it's miserable if you sleep in a tent and mosquitoes attack you if you sleep under the stars. But so be it; every month meant every month. The troop didn't go camping in July 1951, but they went in August, and a tradition began that continues today.

To appreciate the extraordinary duration of Troop 12's tradition of monthly campouts, consider the state of America in August 1951.

Harry Truman was in his second term as president, having upset Republican Thomas Dewey in 1948. World War II had ended six years earlier, but the Korean War that had begun the year before would last for two more. There were just over 150 million people living in the forty-eight United States of America. Alaska would not come into the country until 1958, Hawaii not until the following year. Interracial marriage was still illegal in the South, and schools throughout the country remained racially segregated. *Brown v. Board of Education* would not be decided for three more years. There was not only no internet, but there was no color television. And no cars had air conditioning. Even the richest man in America couldn't buy one. Computers were in their infancy. They were enormous, expensive, and computed very little.

Much has changed in America in the years since then. The population has more than doubled to 330 million. More wars have begun and ended, some badly. Public schools were desegregated long ago, and interracial marriage is both legal and accepted by most Americans. Gay marriage is as well. We've had thirteen more presidents, one a black man who was elected twice. We take for granted many conveniences that were unimaginable in 1951. Cars without air conditioning and black-and-white televisions can no longer be found. Most Americans, even children, carry advanced computers in their pockets. They're no larger than a wallet, but they can do far more than the largest computers of 1951. With only his thumbs, a person can take photos, send messages, make phone calls, and balance his checkbook. In a matter of seconds, he can determine the population of America in 1951 and the years when Alaska and Hawaii were admitted to the Union.

Though many things have changed in America since 1951, one thing has not. Every month, rain or shine, Troop 12 still goes camping. Ken Kirk died in 2009, and Daddy died four years later, but the monthly campouts continue. From Truman to Biden, from the Korean War to the COVID pandemic, the troop has never missed a month. In July 2023, the month this book is scheduled for release, the consecutive monthly campout streak will reach 864.

That's seventy-two years without a miss. By the time you read this, the streak will be even longer.

The new troop members who were eleven in August 1951 and went on the first campout are now in their eighties. Before long, the streak will have outlived every Scout who was there at the start. The tradition began six years before I was born, and I've known about it all my life, but it still amazes me. I hope I'll be able to attend the troop's campout in November 2034. I'll be seventy-seven then, and Troop 12 will go camping for the thousandth month in a row.

Daddy missed very few campouts during his more than sixty years of service to the troop. Mama had a severe stroke in her mid-seventies and was diagnosed with terminal cancer three years later. Daddy missed campouts to take care of her, but he almost never missed one because of his own health. He was rarely sick and was a young man physically until he was very old. He continued camping with the troop until well into his eighties. The last campout I know he attended was at Camp Yocona, the Boy Scout camp west of Tupelo. It was in January 2008, two months after his eighty-sixth birthday. Nearly sixty-one years had passed since Daddy took Troop 12 to Camp Yocona after he became the Scoutmaster in the spring of 1947.

On their wedding day, Mama and Daddy were almost thirty, older than the norm for marrying in the post-war years. They probably tried to start a family right away, but they were unsuccessful. After several years, a doctor determined that Daddy was unable to father a child. The news must have been devastating. They both wanted children, and Daddy was his father's only son. He no doubt wanted a son to carry on the family name. Two of his younger sisters already had sons of their own, but their last names were Leake and Ruff, not Eason.

But as with all setbacks he faced in life, Daddy took the news in stride. He and Mama explored alternatives and contacted Methodist Home Hospital in New Orleans, a home for unwed mothers from which many couples in Tupelo adopted children. Mama and Daddy applied, were approved, and adopted Margie in 1955. They soon asked to be put on a waiting list for a baby boy. I was born on July 3, 1957, and Mama and Daddy were soon chosen to be my parents.

When I was nearly fifty, through an extraordinary sequence of events that I wrote about in *Fortunate Son,* the Louisiana Supreme Court granted a lawyer's request for access to my confidential adoption file. The court's rationale was language in my biological great-grandfather's will that made me a potential heir to his substantial fortune. The lawyer, who had been appointed to represent my interests before anyone knew who I was, found the file with my two birth certificates in it—the original and a replacement identifying Paul and Margaret Eason as my parents—and sent it to me.

The file was filled with fascinating news, including that my birth mother's name was Julie Francis and that my name, at least until my adoption was finalized when I was thirteen months old, was Scott Francis. I knew I was adopted but not that I started life with a different name. I read that the staff at Methodist Home Hospital chose Mama and Daddy to be my parents because they thought I would look like Daddy. They were wrong, but I'm grateful that they thought so. I also learned that a social worker described me after a visit to our home on Rogers Drive as a husky child who jabbered constantly. Some might say that not much has changed.

When Mama and Daddy drove three hours south to Jackson to see my children for the first time, I noticed something odd about his behavior. As a rule, grandparents want to hold their new grandchildren the instant they see them. But not Daddy. He didn't seem comfortable and declined our offers to let him hold our newborn babies.

In my adoption file, I learned what may have been the reason. It revealed that Mama and Daddy did not pick me up from Methodist Home Hospital to take me home to Tupelo until I was eleven weeks old. I weighed half again as much as when I was born. Presumably

they took custody of Margie when she was a similar age. I concluded that Daddy was reluctant to hold a newborn baby because
he never had.

Chapter Four

1957-1968

I had an idyllic childhood. I grew up in a wonderful place at a wonderful time—at least for me and my friends. Tupelo was full of good families, and helicopter parents were not yet a thing. My friends and I were free to roam and explore, catching all sorts of creatures in the creek beside our vacant lot during the day and playing kick the can in the neighborhood at night.

And I had the greatest gift a child can be given: wonderful, devoted parents. We didn't have much money, but when you've never taken a fancy trip or eaten a fancy meal, you don't miss either one. Mama and Daddy never had a garbage disposal. I guess they didn't miss that either.

But though we were far from rich, we weren't poor, and I never wanted for anything that really mattered. And what Mama and Daddy gave me was far more valuable than anything money can buy. They were my parents, but they were my role models too. I learned the value of hard work and honoring commitments from them. I learned to treat people with respect. I never saw either of them do otherwise. They also gave Margie and me unconditional love, discipline, and a sense of security. Children need stability, and we had it in spades in the house on Rogers Drive. From the time I outgrew my crib until I left for college, I slept in the same bed in the same room in the same house. There was little for me to worry about other than my next tennis match or whether girls would ever pay attention to me. And there was no drama. I never once heard Mama and Daddy raise their voices to each other. If they ever argued, they did it outside of my presence. They were totally devoted to each other, to Margie, and to me.

And, because Mama was devoted to Daddy, he was able to continue his devotion to Troop 12, meeting with the Scouts every Monday night and camping with them every month even when Margie and I were young. My earliest memory of Daddy is one of my favorite memories of all. He had just come home from a campout. He put down his gear, picked me up, spun me around, and tickled the back of my neck with his unshaven chin. I smelled the wonderful, mysterious smoke of the campfire he'd sat beside the night before. I knew the smell of a campfire long before I first saw one.

When Troop 12's monthly campout weekend came, Daddy would climb into the attic, bring down his camping gear, and pack his Boy Scout duffel bag, which has now been passed down to his grandson, Paul Eason the younger. I would watch him drive away, then wait for him to come home a day or two later. I couldn't wait until my eleventh birthday, the day I would become a Boy Scout, put on a uniform, and start camping with Daddy and the troop.

But Daddy took me camping without the troop before then. One weekend at the end of every summer, he and Mama would take Margie and me to Camp Yocona. They let each of us invite a friend. I'm sure Mama wasn't thrilled about sleeping outside in August, but she did it without complaint. It was at Camp Yocona that Daddy taught me to split firewood, build a campfire, and cook on a fire. We hiked the trails through the woods, and he identified trees and birds for us. I learned to recognize the calls of the kingfishers that patrolled the lake and the barred owls that called to each other at dusk. Daddy taught us to canoe, and Mama took us fishing. One summer my friend Dan Purnell and I caught a catfish so big it took both of us to pull it in. The fish wasn't all that big, but we weren't either.

Daddy was conservative by nature. He was never flashy, flamboyant, or controversial. He never danced, sang only in church, and then barely loud enough to be heard. He was resistant to change and was never tempted to believe the grass was greener on the other side. He and Mama owned only one home. They bought the small house on Rogers Drive in 1956, the year after they adopted Margie and the year before they adopted me. They lived in it together until Mama died in September 1999, then Daddy lived there alone until he moved south to live with Carrie and me twelve years later.

The house was built by Daddy's brother-in-law Bob Leake. The market was slow in 1956, and the finished house remained unsold until the day Bob told Daddy he would make him a great deal on it. Daddy asked how much, Bob said $12,000, and Daddy said it's a deal. He had saved $4,500 in the Navy, when his only expenses were food and uniforms, and he used the money for a down payment. The mortgage payments were $45 a month. Daddy wondered if he would be able to make them.

When Margie and I were little, Daddy built a small playhouse for us in the backyard. The ceilings were only four feet high, which struck me when I was older as poor planning. But he probably figured we would lose interest before we outgrew it. He was right, though he didn't consider what it would be used for after that. After we stopped playing in the playhouse, he turned it into a cramped tool shed, but then a big oak blew down in a storm and smashed it flat. Daddy fixed the problem by building a real workshop that was tall enough for him. I learned basic carpentry from Daddy, who didn't hire contractors to do anything he could do himself. I'm no craftsman, but I've enjoyed building things all my life, from decks to pergolas to a treehouse for my grandsons.

Not long after Daddy became Troop 12's Scoutmaster in 1947, he left his six-day-a-week job at McCarty Holman for a position at Milam Manufacturing, which owned a facility in downtown Tupelo that made children's clothes. He rose through the ranks and was ultimately promoted to the position of plant manager. He treated his employees, mostly women, the same way he treated his Scouts, and they felt the same way about him the Scouts did. Daddy's salary was modest, but it was a good, stable job with two weeks of vacation a year, one at Christmas and one over the

Fourth of July. He would have been content to spend the rest of his career there.

But when Daddy was forty-three, his life plan was derailed. In the summer of 1965, the Milam family sold the business, and the purchaser moved the equipment and operations to Georgia. Daddy could have moved to Georgia, and he was also recruited by other garment manufacturers to manage facilities in other states. I recall that one was in North Carolina. Moving would have meant a pay increase, but it also would have meant leaving Tupelo, Daddy's parents and sisters, the First Methodist Church, and Troop 12. I don't know how seriously Mama and Daddy entertained the prospect of moving, but neither of them was primarily motivated by money—they were too wise for that—and they believed there was no better place to live than Tupelo. From then until his retirement more than twenty years later, Daddy was underemployed.

After the sale, Daddy and several Milam employees went to Georgia for two or three months to set up equipment and train employees. By the time he returned, he had found a new job. He would become the purchasing agent for another garment manufacturer, this one in Mantachie, a small town fifteen miles east of Tupelo. Before his first day, he took off some extra time to give himself two straight weeks of vacation for the first time in many years. During those two weeks, he turned the lemon of losing his job into the lemonade of our best-ever family vacation, and I got to go camping in the West for the first time.

We put nearly 4,000 miles on our Ford station wagon on the trip, driving to and from Bozeman, Montana, where Mama's twin sister Marjory was the Dean of Home Economics at Montana State. On the way west, we attended my first major-league baseball game in Kansas City; visited Dodge City, Kansas, the setting of *Gunsmoke*, Daddy's favorite TV show; toured the Air Force Academy in Colorado Springs; and drove to the top of Pikes Peak. We camped in Yellowstone National Park with snow on the ground on July 3, 1965, my eighth birthday. If Mama didn't like camping at Camp Yocona, she really didn't like camping in Yellowstone. Not only was it cold, but there were bears. We saw more than twenty during our two days in the park. But once again, she did it without complaint. The following night, we shivered through a fireworks display in Bozeman. It was the only time I've ever been cold on the Fourth of July. On the way home, we stopped at the Little Bighorn and Mount Rushmore and saw the Black Hills and Badlands of South Dakota.

Two weeks after we backed out of our driveway, we drove back in. Daddy had a new job, but otherwise life was unchanged. Two years later, CBS moved *Gunsmoke* from Saturday night to Monday night. Monday was Scout meeting night, there was no way to record shows then, and Daddy was never able to watch his favorite show again. He and I did not go to the West together again until we rafted the Grand Canyon in 1991.

In one of his jobs, maybe at Milam but probably in Mantachie, Daddy had a company pickup truck. On summer weekends, he would ask Margie and me to round up the other kids in the neighborhood, and we would climb into the back. Nobody thought riding in the back of a pickup was dangerous then. Daddy would head west on Highway 78 and treat us all to ice cream cones at a gas station owned by a man named Bill Bates. It seems like it was a dime for one dip and fifteen cents for two, but I'm not sure.

What I am sure of is how Bill Bates served the ice cream. His was a full-service station, as they all were then, and his hands were always dark from oil and grease. But he paid no mind to that when it came to serving ice cream. He would pull down a cone with a grimy hand and add a scoop or two of ice cream. Then, before handing it to the customer, he would wrap the cone with a paper napkin.

Daddy was a generous man and enjoyed treating us to ice cream, but I think he enjoyed Bill's method of serving it even more. He would stand behind us, grinning, the only one getting the joke. When his turn came, he didn't ask for special treatment. He knew a little crud never hurt anybody.

Mama and Daddy loved Christmas and loved making it special for Margie and me. We weren't spoiled the rest of the year, but we were spoiled on Christmas. When Mama and Daddy bought the home on Rogers Drive the year before I was born, Daddy planted a pine tree outside the window of what became my bedroom. The tree grew much faster than I did, and it soon became our outdoor Christmas tree. Daddy would drape it from top to bottom with strings of large lights in a rainbow of colors. White Christmas lights, like helicopter parents, didn't exist back then.

As the tree grew taller, stringing the lights became harder and more dangerous. Daddy would climb up the tree holding a long board with a notch in the end to hang the lights from the highest limbs. My job was to stay on the ground, circling the tree from below and unrolling the strings of lights as he needed more. After years of this annual ritual, Daddy decided that climbing thirty feet up a tree to string it with lights was not very wise. But we couldn't just leave the lights in the attic, unused and gathering dust. That would have been wasteful, and Daddy wasted nothing. He was thrifty.

For the next several years, two weeks or so before Christmas, we would drive to the property on the outskirts of town where Daddy's sister and brother-in-law Puddie and Guy Ruff lived with their four children. Daddy and I, and sometimes Margie, would hike past the Ruffs' lake and into the woods. We took an axe and a handsaw, never a chainsaw, and searched for just the right tree. Our goal was a perfectly shaped cedar between fifteen and twenty feet tall. After it fell, we would drag it back to the Ruffs' house and bring it home in Troop 12's van known as the White Elephant. Daddy would then stand the tree up in our front yard, using stakes and guy wires to keep it from falling over. Once it was steady, he would retrieve his stepladder and the notched board and, with my help, string the tree with lights.

One of those years, it was cold and gray when we set out to find a tree. A red-tailed hawk flew over and screeched as we hiked into the woods. Soon snow began to fall. Big, soft flakes slowly drifted down. By the time we found the right tree, the ground was white. After Daddy cut it down, he grabbed a limb on one side of the trunk, I grabbed a limb on the other, and we dragged it back to the White Elephant, leaving a trail behind us in the snow.

Daddy didn't attempt to recruit young black men to join Troop 12, though if one had wanted to join, I'm sure Daddy would have welcomed him. But to my knowledge, that never happened. Even after the schools were fully desegregated, nearly all Boy Scout troops in the area remained either all white or all black, likely because they were sponsored by churches that voluntarily remained all white or all black. Troop 12 helped start a black troop in the 1940s, but no thought was given to including both races in a single troop. Segregated troops were the way it was and always had been, and Daddy didn't try to change it. But he was not a racist by any means. He treated all people, both black and white, with respect. He didn't have it in him to do otherwise. And he also taught us to be generous to those who were less fortunate, no matter their race. As usual, he did it by showing, not telling.

Mama worked on and off when Margie and I were growing up, more on than off because Daddy's modest income just wasn't enough. When Mama worked, we had housekeepers. They were called maids then, and they were all black. Our favorite was a sweet woman with a beautiful smile named Zeola. We called her Oley, and she lived in a tiny duplex on the north end of town.

After years with us, Oley developed some debilitating condition—diabetes or arthritis perhaps—and could no longer work. I suppose she got by on disability benefits. Every now and then, Mama would cook some food for Oley, and Daddy would ask me to go with him to deliver it. While we were there, Daddy did any odd jobs she needed doing. I helped if I could but mostly watched. Daddy would also give Oley a little spending money. He didn't tell me why we were there, but he didn't need to.

We were fixtures at the First Methodist Church on Sunday. On rare occasions, Mama might let us play hooky if Daddy was camping with the troop on Saturday night, but otherwise we attended Sunday School and the 10:50 a.m. church service every week. Nobody ever told me why our service started before eleven o'clock, but I suspect it was so the Methodists could beat the members of the other churches to restaurants for Sunday dinner.

When we arrived at church on Sunday morning, we would park in the lot behind the sanctuary and go our separate ways for Sunday School. Daddy was in the all-male Chapman Men's Bible Class. Just as churches were segregated by race in the 1960s, Sunday School classes were often segregated by sex. After Sunday School, the four of us would gather in the fellowship hall, then sit together in church except during the years when Mama sang alto in the choir. Then Margie and I would sit on either side of Daddy. For a year or two, we attended Sunday night services too. The Gothic Revival sanctuary was built before 1900, and from the outside at night, with the lights on inside, the stained-glass windows were beautiful.

Until he was in his late eighties, Daddy attended a church service nearly every Sunday of his life, including on campouts. Yet I never heard him talk about his religious beliefs, with one exception. After I had children, he and I took them to Camp Yocona for a weekend in the woods. The kids were off somewhere playing, and our talk turned to religion for the first and only time. Daddy said he couldn't bring himself to believe that children who died without ever knowing about God or Jesus didn't go to heaven. That's all he said, and I don't remember his ever mentioning his beliefs again. Nor did he tell me about his deepest thoughts or his hopes and dreams. I would be surprised if he talked to Mama about them either. He was too busy doing to spend time thinking about what he could be doing. And he was a private man. It wasn't his way to talk about such things.

Because Mama worked full time most of the time, she had neither the energy nor the time to be a gourmet cook. She made simple meals—pork chops, meatloaf, fried chicken, and such—and kept us well fed. Daddy loved to eat. He could put away impressive quantities without gaining weight, a trait I wish I shared. He wasn't picky and was always appreciative. He would compliment Mama by describing her cooking as "larrapin," and after finishing second helpings would rub his belly and say, "I believe I've had a sufficiency." But there was always room for ice cream.

We had a regular rotation of meals, with Daddy cooking on weekends when he wasn't camping. He would make waffles or pancakes for breakfast and grill something outside on Saturday night, either burgers or a thin sirloin steak we split four ways. Once a week, on Sunday night, we were permitted to eat dinner on TV trays in the den. We watched *60 Minutes* or *Mutual of Omaha's Wild Kingdom* and ate grilled-cheese sandwiches.

Because Monday night was Scout-meeting night, Mama had to make something that was fast and easy. Our standard Monday night meal for years was scrambled eggs and bacon with canned spaghetti. I realize now that it was a weird combination, but nothing seems weird when you're a child. We rarely went out to eat, but sometimes we made the trek to Johnnie's Drive-In in east Tupelo, where they brought the food to your car on a tray that hooked onto the driver's window. More than half a century later, Johnnie's is still in business and still serving dough burgers, part meat and part mystery ingredient.

I vaguely remember the vacant lot beside our house when it was still overgrown with weeds and underbrush. When I was very young, Mama and Daddy bought it, and Daddy set out to clear it. It was a long, hard job, but when he finished, we had a three-quarter-acre grass field that became the neighborhood playground. My friends and I played every game imaginable: baseball, football, whiffle ball, kick ball, and others we invented.

When Daddy came home from work, I would grab our baseball gloves and a ball, and he and I would play catch. He threw ground balls for me to learn to field them and towering pop flies for me to learn to catch them. One day Daddy threw one as high as he could. I squatted down to catch it but lost it in the sun. It landed so hard on my thigh we could see the imprint of the baseball's stitches on my skin. He rubbed it, said it would be only a bruise, and we resumed our game of catch. Daddy never turned a small injury into a big one or a molehill into a mountain. He was never dramatic.

When Daddy wasn't camping with the Scouts or working in the yard or around the house, he came up with fun things for us to do on weekends. One spring he made us a box kite. On a windy Saturday, we launched it from the vacant lot. It was a spectacular success and was soon flying high. Other neighborhood kids joined us.

To add to the entertainment, Daddy created a tiny parachute by putting an open safety pin through the center of one of his handkerchiefs and tying a short string from each corner to something to give the parachute some weight. He then put the open safety pin over the kite string, gave the parachute a push, and the wind blew it up the string. When it was fifty feet or so off the ground, Daddy gave the string a jerk, the safety pin popped off the string, and the parachute came floating down. Then we did it again.

The kite kept rising and eventually was out of sight. We couldn't see it, but we could feel it. Wherever it was, the wind was blowing hard. Just holding onto the roll of string became a challenge. Then we heard a pop, hundreds of feet of string drifted down to the ground, and we never saw the kite again. All we knew was that it was headed east. I hope some other kids found it and had as much fun as we did.

Daddy mowed the vacant lot with his Toro twenty-inch push mower until I was old enough to mow it. Then it became my job, and he paid me ten dollars to do it. I learned more valuable lessons: that mowing three-quarters of an acre with a push mower is hard and boring, that the end result is satisfying, and that something earned is far more valuable than something free. As Thomas Paine wrote, "What we obtain too cheap, we esteem too lightly."

Daddy resumed mowing the lot after I left for college and continued for decades. Two years after Mama died, the year he turned eighty, his neighbors tried to give him a riding mower. He appreciated the offer but turned it down. He wanted to keep using a push mower as long as he could. He told one of the neighbors that quitting would be a sign of giving up. Daddy also hung a swing from a high limb in a hickory tree on the edge of the lot. He pushed his grandchildren in the swing and, in the years before he came to live with Carrie and me, he pushed his great-grandchildren too.

After twenty years as the Scoutmaster of Troop 12, Daddy was well known as an outstanding leader, and his opinions were highly respected. In 1967 he was one of twenty-four Scout leaders from across the country chosen to attend a conference in Chicago on how the Boy Scouts needed to change to keep up with the times. I never discussed the conference with Daddy, but he was a traditionalist and would have opposed radical change. Years later, he was disappointed when the requirements for Cooking merit badge were modified to allow some meals to be cooked on a stove at home instead of a campfire in the woods. I doubt he would be unenthusiastic about having girls in the Scouts.

Chapter Five

1968-1975

For many years, Troop 12 held a father-son campout on the lawn of the First Methodist Church in downtown Tupelo every February. Daddy invited the fathers of all the Scouts and encouraged them to attend. His motive was probably to get more fathers interested in helping with the troop. Many did so when their sons were in the troop but stopped helping when their sons stopped camping and going to meetings.

But there were others—among them W. E. Plunkett, James Byrd, Paul Fairley, and Buddy Miller—who continued for years after their sons became Eagle Scouts and left the troop. Like Daddy, they were committed to serving the boys. They also enjoyed camping, and they loved and admired Daddy. When Daddy received one of his many awards, Paul Fairley said, "If a boy wants to work on a merit badge, all he has to do is let Paul Eason know, and he'll be down to open the Scout Hut on Saturday morning. He is very patient and a tremendous leader. I've always wanted to acquire some of his attributes." After Daddy had been the Scoutmaster for thirty years, assistant Jim High said that he "does the same things now, with the same enthusiasm. He has been totally dedicated to the position during the time he has been the leader. Not a day goes by that he does not think about Scouting."

Five months before I turned eleven and joined the troop, I attended my first Troop 12 campout. In February 1968, when fathers were guests at the father-son campout, I was allowed to attend as a guest because I was the son of the Scoutmaster. Near the Sunday School building was a low circular brick wall around the base of a tree. One of the older boys picked me up. It wasn't hard; I weighed less than eighty pounds. I tried to pull free, succeeded, and fell face down on the brick wall. My only injury was a chipped front tooth. My mouth must have been open because I was still jabbering on my descent. I've never gotten the tooth capped. Few people notice it, perhaps because I jabber less now than I did then.

You might wonder how I know I weighed less than eighty pounds in February 1968. One of my prized possessions is the closet door from my bedroom on Rogers Drive. When Margie and I were growing up, Mama and Daddy would stand us up against the door every six months or so, mark our heights, then send us to the bathroom scale so they could record our weights. A generation later, on family trips home to Tupelo, Mama and Daddy marked the heights of their six grandchildren, my three children and Margie's three. A generation after that, when Daddy moved in with Carrie and me and sold the house, I claimed the closet door and bought a replacement. The door that's older than I am now hangs on an upstairs wall in our house, and a third generation of heights is making its way up.

The markings on the door now span sixty-six years, from July 1956, when the house and door were new and Margie was thirteen months old, until June 2022, when I marked the heights of my grandchildren. My grandson Eason Forster is now taller than I am. While writing this chapter, I walked up the stairs to see if there was a record on the door showing what I weighed in February 1968. Not exactly, but I weighed seventy-five in November 1967 and eighty-two in July 1968. I must have weighed less than eighty in February.

In July 1968, I turned eleven and was finally able to join the troop. I no longer had to watch as Daddy packed and left for campouts, and I could smell like campfire smoke too. Troop 12 had spent its annual week of summer camp at Camp Yocona in June, and my classmates whose birthdays were before mine had joined the troop and gone to Yocona. But Daddy wouldn't let me jump the gun by three weeks. You had to be eleven. That was the rule, and he wasn't going to bend it for me.

He also didn't make advancement easier for me than for the other boys. He recused himself from signing off on anything I did. I had to satisfy one of the assistants. Maybe he told them not to go easy on me, but I doubt he needed to. They would have known he wanted no favoritism for his son.

Some Scouts raced through the ranks to become Eagle Scouts as fast as they could. Steve Mills, a gifted athlete and now a successful physician, was a grade behind me but earned his Eagle a year before I did. I was not as motivated as he was, though I was perceptive enough to realize it would be a scandal if Paul Eason's son did not become an Eagle Scout. But I was in no hurry, and I took my time. I was much more interested in campouts than merit badges, and campouts are what I remember.

I spent far more time with Daddy at home than I did on campouts when I was in the troop. I wanted to hang out with my buddies, and I'm sure he wanted me to be thought of by the other Scouts as just another boy in the troop, not as the Scoutmaster's son. Daddy and I went on more than forty Troop 12 campouts together during my years as a Scout, but we never slept in the same tent or paddled in the same canoe.

Campouts with bad weather or some other unpleasantness are more memorable than those that come off without a hitch. The first campout I remember from my time in the troop included a rainstorm, the second one bitter cold. I camped at Tishomingo State Park with the troop for the first of four consecutive Octobers in 1968. The older Scouts got dibs on tents, and another new Scout and I were stuck in one without a floor. Rain came in the night, we had not dug trenches around the tent, and our sleeping bags got soaked. I'm sure Daddy would have told us to dig trenches if we had asked. We learned to ask.

A few months later, the troop camped on one of the coldest nights of the winter. There was ice in our canteens the next morning. There weren't as many boys on the campout as there had been at

Tishomingo, so three of us were able to get a canvas tent with a floor called a Voyager. But we still couldn't get warm. We solved the problem by inviting three more first-year Scouts to leave their tent and join us in ours. The six of us crowded into it like a litter of puppies and used our combined body heat to make it through the night.

Daddy was a devoted Ole Miss football fan, so naturally I became one too. Though Oxford was only fifty miles from Tupelo, season tickets weren't in the family budget, so we rarely attended games. But on Saturdays during the fall, we would listen on the console stereo in the living room as Ole Miss announcers Stan Torgerson and Lyman Hellums called the games. We rarely spoke but smiled at each other when something good happened and shook our heads when something bad did. Unless Ole Miss was way ahead, we were too nervous to enjoy ourselves.

The two most memorable campouts of my second year in Troop 12 happened to coincide with two games in the fall of 1969 that remain among the most famous in Ole Miss football history. The first was at Tishomingo on the first weekend of October. We drove to the park on Saturday, set up camp, and built a rope monkey bridge spanning Bear Creek. After cooking dinner, we sat around the campfire waiting for the game, which started late to keep from conflicting with *The Lawrence Welk Show*, then the top-rated show in America.

The opponent was Bear Bryant's Alabama Crimson Tide. It was the first-ever nationally televised college football game that was played at night. We couldn't watch it but instead listened on a transistor radio as the teams traded touchdowns. When Ole Miss scored, Daddy and I smiled at each other from opposite sides of the fire, but in the end we shook our heads. Though Rebel quarterback Archie Manning broke the NCAA record for total offense by a player in a single game and secured his place as a college football legend, Ole Miss lost the game 33–32.

The second of the two games was six weeks later against

undefeated, third-ranked Tennessee. We were camping at the Shiloh National Military Park on the Tennessee River. Our Saturday-afternoon hike through the battlefield began just minutes before the kickoff. I was a Civil War buff and was interested in the battle, but I learned nothing about it that day. I had a radio glued to my ear from the beginning of our hike to the end.

This time it was nothing but smiles. Ole Miss had lost to Tennessee 31–0 the year before. When asked about the Rebel quarterback after the game, Volunteer linebacker Steve Kiner responded with a question of his own: "Archie who?" A year later, Ole Miss was out for revenge. I recently happened to meet Hap Farber, who was the All-SEC defensive end on the Rebels '69 team. Hap told me he was one of the team captains for the Tennessee game, and when he went out for the coin toss, Kiner wouldn't look him in the eye. He knew what was coming. Ole Miss crushed the Vols 38–0. Daddy would have loved to listen to the game, but he was too busy being the Scoutmaster. As always, duty came first. I told him all about it after we finished the hike and returned to camp.

Ole Miss won its last regular-season game against Mississippi State and beat Arkansas in a thrilling Sugar Bowl. After the season ended, a country group calling itself the Rebel Rousers recorded "The Ballad of Archie Who" to the tune of Johnny Cash's "Folsom Prison Blues." The record was a huge hit among Ole Miss fans. Daddy bought it for us, and I played it often. A decade later, when I was in law school and had no money for Christmas presents, I wrote a short story about the two campouts and two games in the fall of 1969 and gave it to Daddy.

Most of our monthly campouts were for just one night, either Friday or Saturday. Exceptions were the annual canoe trips during spring break in March, a big trip at the end of school in May, and summer camp at Yocona. I remember three of the trips in May. A dad served as a poor role model on the first, I wound up in an emergency room twice on the second, and Daddy and I discovered what we thought was a culinary delight on the third.

The first May I was in the troop, we drove to Atlanta and visited Six Flags, Stone Mountain, and the Cyclorama, an enormous painting depicting the Civil War battle of Atlanta. We also attended a Braves game. I don't remember the team they played or who won, but I recall that Hank Aaron didn't start because he was attending a graduation ceremony for one of his children. He arrived when the game was nearly over and pinch hit. He hit a long drive, but the left fielder made a great catch to rob him of a home run. But for the catch, Aaron would have ended his career with 756 home runs instead of 755.

I didn't ride in the car with Daddy to or from Atlanta. On the way home, somewhere in Alabama, the dad I was with decided to see how fast his station wagon would go. It was exciting to go more than a hundred miles an hour for the first time in my life—he made it to nearly 115—but it occurred to me that Daddy would not have approved. I didn't rat the dad out. I don't think Daddy would have approved of that either. He didn't care for tattletales and wanted Scouts to learn to resolve their problems without coming to him.

Another May we camped on the beach at the Pensacola Naval Air Station, where Daddy was stationed during the war. The first afternoon, I was running barefoot in the shallow water and gashed my right foot on a rock. Daddy studied my foot and took me to the ER at the Navy hospital. The doctor stitched me up, gave me a pain shot, wrapped my foot in an Ace bandage, and told me to stay off of it.

Emboldened by the pain shot, I ignored the doctor's orders. When I woke up the next morning, the shot had worn off, I was hurting, and the Ace bandage was soaked with blood. Daddy took me back to the ER, but they were having an emergency drill, and we had to wait forever to see a doctor. When we finally did, he checked the stitches, wrapped my foot in a fresh Ace bandage, and repeated the advice to stay off of it. I did better the second time.

A third May we drove up to southeast Missouri to canoe the Current River. The weather was rainy and cold, and the first day on the river was miserable. We were soaked to the bone, but we had covered some wood with tarps and were able to start campfires when we made it back to our campsite. Our dinner entrée was Beefaroni, which we'd never had on a campout and I had never tasted. The preparation was simple. We opened the cans, sliced onions, dropped them in, then put the cans in the campfire and waited. When steam rose and the Beefaroni started bubbling, it was ready. The hot, filling pasta was sublime. It was comfort food for the uncomfortable and transformed us from miserable to content.

On the drive home, Daddy and I agreed that Mama should add Beefaroni to the family dinner lineup. She was game—it was fast, easy, and cheap—and a week or so later Beefaroni made its debut at our house. When we took our first bites, Daddy and I looked at each other. It wasn't the same; it wasn't even close. The difference was the setting, not the food. At the dining table in our den, we weren't wet or cold, and we weren't eating dinner by a campfire in the woods beside a river, where everything tastes better. We never ate Beefaroni again.

By January 1972, I had completed all the requirements to become an Eagle Scout. At a Sunday-morning church service, Daddy stood beside me in his Scout uniform while Mama pinned the badge on the front of mine.

The head of a large company once told me the most important accomplishment he could see on a man's resumé was Eagle Scout. But becoming an Eagle was not a great accomplishment in my case. For most boys, proceeding through the ranks, earning at least twenty-one merit badges, and completing all the other requirements take perseverance and determination, but for me all it took was a sense of shame. The prospect of my shame and Daddy's disappointment if I had not become an Eagle Scout was more than enough to see me through.

I became an Eagle Scout more than half a century ago. It's impossible to look back across such a span of time and recall all that I learned from my four years as a member of Troop 12 and all that's still a part of me. But I can say to a certainty that one thing is: a deep and abiding love for the outdoors. I still love hiking and canoeing, camping and campfires, birds and trees. I thank Daddy for that. Whenever the weather permits, I want to be outside. That's where the birds are, and I want to be out there with them. The screened porch on the front of our house is my favorite room. I tell people it's my office. It's where I've written most of my last three books.

Like most Scouts, I stopped going to meetings after I became an Eagle Scout. Most of my friends were finished with their time in the troop, so I was finished too. We now had other interests—cars and girls for all of us and the high-school tennis team for me. Daddy probably could have used my help with the troop, but he didn't ask, and I didn't offer. It now seems odd that he continued to put on his Scout uniform and go to the Scout Hut every Monday night while I stayed home, but like spaghetti with bacon and eggs, it didn't seem odd at the time. Daddy thought about stepping down after I became an Eagle—he had just turned fifty and had been the Scoutmaster for twenty-five years—but he decided to press on. Serving the boys of Troop 12 was his calling, and he chose to keep doing it as long as he could. That turned out to be thirty-five more years.

Though I was no longer a member of the troop, I still went on the monthly campout once or twice a year. I didn't need to be just one of the Scouts in the troop anymore, so Daddy and I spent more time together. We sat by the same campfire and stayed in the same tent. I was older and a tad wiser, and I watched Daddy with a new appreciation for the many qualities that made him a great leader. His calm leadership could tame the wildest boys.

At least half a dozen times, when I was in high school and college and when I returned to Mississippi after law school, I went on the troop's annual canoe trip on Bear Creek. We began paddling a different section of the river and camping the first night at the head of a waterfall where a rock ledge forces the entire river over a ten-foot drop that's no more than ten feet wide. The next morning, we would portage the canoes around the waterfall. It was a beautiful place to camp and filled with opportunities for adventure and danger for boys.

And not just for boys. One year a poor deer trying to swim across the river panicked at the sight of the approaching canoes, tried to make it back to the opposite shore, and was swept over the waterfall to her death. Screaming like Banshees, boys landed their canoes on the rock ledge, raced down below the fall, and found the deer. They brought it back to camp, four of them holding one leg apiece, and grilled the backstraps. Daddy couldn't think of a reason to intervene, so he didn't.

When we were at the same place a year or two later, a Scout lost his grip on a rope tied to the shore and was carried by the current over the same waterfall that killed the deer. The boy was more fortunate; he suffered only a minor ankle injury. Daddy climbed up to the ridgeline and found a farmhouse, just as he had years earlier when we had to cut the trip short because of high water. He summoned the boy's parents, came back down to the campsite, and we carried the boy on a stretcher up to the house. He had fully recovered by the time we returned to Tupelo two days later.

Daddy and I also canoed Bear Creek by ourselves two or three times. Mama would drive us up to the river and come back and pick us up at the take-out point two days later. I had never gone camping before with just Daddy, and it was a treat to share a campfire with just him and without the constant roar created by forty boys. One night a great horned owl glided into our campsite, landed on a limb ten feet above us, and stayed there for fifteen minutes. That would never happen on a Troop 12 campout. The noise from the boys turned our campsites into wildlife-free zones.

In 1973 Daddy changed jobs for the last time. He left Mantachie and became the human resources manager for FMC Technologies, a new industrial plant north of Tupelo. The position was still called personnel manager then. I was a self-absorbed teenager and didn't ask Daddy why he decided to leave his old job for a new one. Years later he said he could see the handwriting on the wall for the garment business, which was abandoning Mississippi for cheaper labor overseas.

Daddy was the first Mississippian hired by FMC, and his first task was to hire others to staff the new plant. He had no experience in HR, but he was a quick study and knew how to evaluate and treat people. He was successful in staffing the facility with excellent workers and held the job until he retired in 1986.

I recall two instances not long before I left for college that reinforced one of the fundamental principles that Daddy lived by and I learned from him. If you say you're going to do something, Daddy believed that you do it, every time, with no exceptions and no excuses.

During a summer when I was in high school, I volunteered to lead a group of Troop 12 Scouts on a series of bike rides to help them earn Cycling merit badge. I liked riding bikes, but I'd recently discovered beer and learned that I liked it even more. One weekend I learned something else—that cycling after drinking beer, at least in large quantities, is not prudent.

At the end of a long Friday night of way too much beer with my buddies, we decided it would not be prudent to go home to our parents and face the consequences. One of my friends had a cabin. We decided to stay there, sleep late, and head home around noon on Saturday. I called home to say where I planned to spend the night and get approval. Daddy answered, said it was fine for me to stay at the cabin, but reminded me that I'd promised to meet a group of boys at the Scout Hut at eight o'clock the next morning to lead them on a twenty-five-mile bike ride.

I had forgotten, but I had promised to do it, so I did it. I showed up at the appointed time, but I was suffering. We rode south on the Natchez Trace for twelve and a half miles, then turned around. About halfway back, I could tell that I was about to be sick. I told the boys to keep going, that I would catch up. As I was on my hands and knees retching in the grass, I was wishing I had thought about Saturday morning on Friday night.

The other occasion was during my senior year. Scouting has a program called Explorers for teenagers from fourteen to eighteen, and I joined Explorer Post 12 a year or two after I earned my Eagle. We had only a few members, but our leader, a National Park Service Ranger named Mac Heebner, loved the outdoors and took us on some fun camping trips. Before Christmas 1974, he planned a trip to the Sipsey Wilderness in northwest Alabama. My best friend Paul Coggins and I agreed to go with him. It would be just the three of us.

But when the time for the campout came, I decided not to go. That fall I had fallen in love for the first time. The forecast called for temperatures below freezing. I decided I would rather stay home and snuggle with Susan than sleep on the cold ground in a tent with Mac and Paul. I told Daddy I was going to skip the campout.

He didn't receive the news well. I was almost grown. Daddy wouldn't be able to tell me what to do for much longer, but he could still tell me then. I had said I was going, they were counting on me to go, and I was going. It was a miserable weekend, but I'm grateful to Daddy for making me go.

I graduated from high school in May 1975 and, after a summer working on a loading dock, left home for college at Ole Miss in August. I had few belongings and no car, so Daddy drove me to Oxford. Fraternity rush was scheduled to begin a few days before classes started.

Daddy had not given me advice about where I should go to college or what I should study. For the most part, he let me make my own decisions and offered his thoughts only if I asked or if I said I was skipping a campout I'd promised to attend. But shortly before we got to Oxford, Daddy said something that surprised me. He wanted me to join the fraternity that was best for me, of course. But if it was a close call, he said it would mean a great deal to him if I joined Phi Delta Theta so we could be fraternity brothers. It was a close call before then, but not after.

Margie had left for college two years earlier, and my departure made Mama and Daddy empty nesters. They had no children at home for the first time in two decades. At Mama's funeral nearly twenty-five years later, a friend of hers told me about a talk they had shortly after I left for Ole Miss. Mama seemed lonely, and the friend tried to cheer her up by talking about all the free time she was going to have with both of us gone. Mama was unconvinced but said there was one benefit of our being away at school. If she heard a siren at night, she knew it couldn't be for one of us.

Chapter Six

1975-1999

For most men, donating thousands of hours to the Boy Scouts would have been a sufficient contribution, but it wasn't enough for Daddy. He viewed having both of his children away in college not as a time to slow down or find a hobby but as an opportunity to serve the people of Tupelo in even more ways than he had in the past.

Daddy was nearly fifty-four when I left for Ole Miss in 1975. He had a sterling reputation in Tupelo. Civic leaders knew that if they asked Daddy to serve on a committee or work on a project, he would do it and do it well. As a result, he was asked over and over, always said yes, and always did the job well.

The decades after I left home were the busiest time of my life. Five days after taking my last exam at Ole Miss in May 1979, I married Betsy Ann Simpson, whom I'd met on a blind date when I was a freshman and she was a senior in high school. To save money, we lived with Mama and Daddy the summer we married, then moved to North Carolina, where I spent the next three years in law school at Duke. When I graduated in 1982, we returned to Mississippi. I clerked for a federal judge for a year, then joined a firm in Jackson. Betsy Ann and I had three children born in 1984, 1987, and 1990. Margie's three children were born the same three years.

As the years rolled by, my commitments as a lawyer, husband, and father left me with little time for being a son, and I didn't get home to Tupelo or talk to Mama and Daddy as often as I should have. I wish I had done more. It pains me when I listen to the verse about the son who couldn't find time to see his father in Harry Chapin's "Cat's in the Cradle."

Because I was busy and Daddy never talked about himself, I can't begin to compile a complete list of all of his volunteer work. But he was busy too, and I know about some of it. Daddy served on the Tupelo Parks and Recreation Commission for twenty-five years and was the chairman for eight. During his tenure, the city's park system grew from one park to eight. Unlike other towns in the South, Tupelo's parks and swimming pools were desegregated without incident and without closing.

Daddy served the First Methodist Church in many capacities. He taught Sunday School and served on the church's administrative board as well as its board of trustees. He chaired the church's Bus/Van Committee and spent countless hours taking elderly residents of Traceway Manor retirement home shopping and to and from church services. He was still driving the van in his eighties, when some of those he chauffeured were younger than he was. When Ann Lowrey told him he was probably older than some of his passengers, he said he hadn't thought about it, but he guessed she was right.

Daddy also served on the Board of Directors of Habitat for Humanity and used his self-taught construction skills to help build affordable homes for the needy. When he received an award for his community service, he was characteristically modest. "I'm not a carpenter. I'm not an electrician. I'm not a plumber. I'm just a gopher. I paint walls or do whatever they need me for." Habitat's Executive Director said, "Paul has been a steady force for us, dependable and trustworthy. It's a pleasure working with him because you know if he says he will get something done, it will be done. I wish I had a lot more volunteers like him."

Daddy was also a member of the Education Committee of the Community Development Foundation and volunteered his services to United Way of Greater Lee County. In addition, he worked with Meals on Wheels, delivering food to the homebound. This is only a partial list of Daddy's volunteer work. A complete list would be impressive even if Troop 12 were not on it.

In November 1984, like most Novembers, Troop 12 camped at the Shiloh National Military Park. It was the troop's 400th consecutive monthly campout. Jan Dale, a young reporter at the *Tupelo Daily Journal* who graduated from high school with me, took an interesting approach to her article about the campout. She interviewed several men who'd been members of the troop when the campout streak began thirty-three years before. Lindsey Clark told her the equipment was primitive then, that the troop slept in used war surplus tents that were made of two pieces that buttoned together. Jim Strain said some older boys took him snipe hunting on one of his first campouts. They left him in the woods with a paper bag and told him to be still and wait. He stayed until he realized no snipe were coming. "When I got back to camp, we all got a good laugh out of it. It was wonderful. I can't think of anything but pleasant thoughts about the campouts."

The Scouts played practical jokes on each other but also on Daddy. At Yocona one year, one of them said he wanted to dive off the pier one last time. He dove in but didn't come up. Daddy came running, but just before he leaped into the murky water, he heard laughter from underneath the pier. The boy had doubled back underwater, come up for air out of sight under the pier, and provoked the exact reaction from Daddy he wanted.

Daddy turned sixty-five in November 1986 and retired from FMC. His co-workers marked the occasion by hosting a party in his honor and presenting him with a scrapbook. But unlike most men, Daddy didn't ease into a quiet retirement. Not only was he still the Scoutmaster and still involved in many other civic activities, but former Tupelo Mayor Clyde Whitaker soon came calling and asked him to consider a run for the at-large seat on the Tupelo Board of Aldermen.

Daddy was not a backslapper or a glad-hander, and he told Mayor Whitaker he knew nothing about politics and had no money for a campaign. But he saw a seat on the board as another opportunity to serve the people of Tupelo, so he agreed to run. Campaign contributions came pouring in, supporters did most of the campaigning, and he won in a landslide. When he joined the board, he followed in his father's footsteps. Cliff had served on the board for six terms spanning nearly a quarter of a century.

Daddy became a leader on the board immediately. He was not outspoken, but when he spoke, the other members listened. They also chose him to serve as vice mayor. As a result of a city-wide referendum, Tupelo changed to the mayor-council form of government in 1993. Daddy was reelected, but now as a city councilman. He was reelected to a third term in 1997 and served as the acting mayor for six weeks when incumbent Mayor Glenn McCullough stepped down to accept a position on the Board of Directors of the Tennessee Valley Authority. Daddy declined to seek a fourth term in 2001, the year he turned eighty. He told me it was time, that he needed to make way for someone younger. Daddy never stayed with anything too long, be it Scoutmaster, the city council, or driving his minivan and the church van.

In 1991, the year he turned seventy, Daddy went to the Grand Canyon twice, once with the troop, once with me. The troop's trip in mid-summer was much harder than ours in September. Daddy and the troop drove to and from Arizona; he and I flew. Daddy and the troop hiked across the canyon; he and I rafted the length of it.

From rim to rim, the Grand Canyon averages ten miles wide as the crow flies. The hike from one rim down to the Colorado River and up the other side is twenty-four miles. The drive from one rim to the other is more than 200. After Daddy and the troop reached Arizona, they split up, with half driving to the North Rim and half to the South. The two groups began their descent at the same time, met at the river, and swapped car keys. After climbing a vertical mile up to the opposite rim from where they started, they rendezvoused east of the canyon for the 1,500-mile drive back to Tupelo. Daddy said he used muscles on the hike he didn't know he had. His difficulty on the trip made him start thinking it would soon be time for Troop 12 to have a new Scoutmaster.

Our trip in September rafting the entire length of the Grand Canyon was Daddy's idea and a rare extravagance. I was a partner in my law firm by then and earning more than Daddy ever earned, but I also had three young children, and he insisted on paying both his own way and half of mine. Though nine days alone with three children seven and under would be exhausting, Betsy Ann encouraged me to go.

The trip began with two stark contrasts. Daddy and I flew to Las Vegas, checked into our hotel, then walked through the loud casino and down the Strip. A hawker handed us a flyer advertising exotic "dancers" who would come to our room and perform for a price. Before dawn the next morning, we boarded a bus, left the loud, neon Gomorrah behind, and headed for the secluded, spectacular Grand Canyon, where the only sound was the river. Vegas and the canyon are worlds apart to be so close together.

The second contrast was along the ride. We stopped for last-minute provisions at Jacob Lake above the North Rim, more than a mile higher than the river. I was dressed in shorts and a tee shirt for the river, but it was still early morning, cold with a brisk wind. I raced from the bus into the store, bought a few things, then raced back to the bus. We then wound down to the launch area on the river below Glen Canyon Dam. In an hour and a half, we descended from an evergreen forest at fifty degrees to the floor of the desert at ninety.

The trip, which lasted eight days and seven nights, was magnificent. We rode the rapids on the wild river, marveled at the rock walls stretching a mile high on either side, hiked to Anasazi ruins, and played horseshoes on the sandbars when we stopped to camp. Daddy had been responsible for planning Troop 12's campouts for more than forty years, but on the Grand Canyon trip he was responsible for nothing. The guides picked all our campsites and prepared all our meals. Daddy called it a sissy trip.

There was no need for tents. We slept under the stars every night., and there were far too many to count. Far from city lights, with no humidity, the night sky was spectacular. Before going to sleep, Daddy and I would have a contest to see who could spot the most shooting stars. He kept a journal while we were on the river. The canyon is one of the most amazing places on Earth, but Daddy stuck to the dry facts: the names of the rapids we ran and the food we ate at each meal. Flowery prose was not his style.

Two months after the trip, Daddy turned seventy, and the following year he decided to step down as Scoutmaster. The Scout Oath requires a Scout to keep himself physically strong, mentally awake, and morally straight. Daddy would always be morally straight, and he was still physically strong and mentally awake. But he wanted what was best for the troop, and he believed he should give up the position before he was too old to help the new leader. Daddy ended his long tenure on a high note. In his last five years as the Scoutmaster, fifty young men became Eagle Scouts in Troop 12.

One of Daddy's assistants, Sam Agnew, agreed to become the new Scoutmaster. Taking over from Daddy must have been daunting, but the transition was smooth. Daddy still attended every meeting and every campout, but he was comfortable letting Sam run things. If going from being the Scoutmaster to an assistant was hard for him, he never let on.

The first weekend of March 1993 was one of the most enjoyable and emotional times of my life. It must have been for Daddy too. The occasion was Troop 12's 500th consecutive monthly campout. When Ken Kirk suggested in 1951 that the boys in the troop should go camping every month, Daddy could not have imagined that they would still be camping every month more than forty years later, much less that he would still be camping with them.

Betsy Ann and I drove up to north Mississippi on Friday with our three children. She dropped me off at Camp Yocona with the two oldest, Ann Lowrey and Cliff, who were eight and five. We would spend the next two nights camping with Daddy, the troop, and the scores of Troop 12 alums who returned for the weekend. Betsy Ann drove on to Tupelo with Paul, who was not yet three.

They would spend the weekend with Mama but return to Yocona with her for the banquet on Saturday night.

The gathering included more than a hundred Troop 12 Eagle Scouts, some who had come from as far away as California. Those in attendance included men who had become Eagle Scouts in every decade from the 1930s—Daddy in 1939—to the 1990s—the newest Eagles who were still in the troop. There were multiple father-son Eagles and four sets of three Eagle-Scout brothers—Eugene, James Hubert, and Stuart Worley; George, Dan, and Kirk Purnell; Jim, Jeff, and Jay Williams; and Lynn, Hamp, and Locke Bryan.

It was a grand weekend, the weather perfect. Daddy had a smile on his face the whole time. We had a bonfire Friday night and multiple activities Saturday, including canoeing, riflery, sailing, and the camp's outdoor course. The weekend was capped off with the banquet in the dining hall Saturday night. Jim Beane, a Tupelo restaurateur and Troop 12's 102nd Eagle Scout, fed more than 300 people who made the trip to Camp Yocona. Jack Reed Sr., a Troop 12 alum and former Mississippi gubernatorial candidate, emceed the program with assistance from his son Jack Jr., the troop's seventy-sixth Eagle Scout. After Mayor Jack Marshall of Tupelo spoke, former Scouts told stories, and Assistant Scoutmaster Jim High presented a slide show. Music was performed by Eagle Scouts Scott Reed, Jim Leake, and Jim Williams, who dubbed themselves the Moose Patrol. Daddy spoke briefly and, as expected, took no credit for the troop's success or the campout record. Assistant Scoutmaster Reed Hillen closed the evening by presenting an award to Mama as the Queen Mother of Troop 12.

We were fortunate the planners of the campout chose the first weekend of March rather than the second. On the Friday after the campout, Daddy wrote a letter to everyone who had come for the grand weekend and noted that he was watching the snow fall and listening to predictions of mid-teen temperatures by Sunday morning. He thanked everyone whose work had made the 500th campout the biggest and best campout Troop 12 had ever experienced and said it was wonderful to see so many who came from far and near to be reunited in Troop 12 fellowship. He believed he could have told a story of a Scouting experience about every Scout who was there. Daddy closed the letter by hoping everyone had half as much fun as he did.

I wrote a letter after the campout too. Mine was just to Daddy, though I asked him to show it to Mama. I started by saying he and I weren't much for baring our souls to each other, but I could write some things I could never say. After thanking him for teaching me to love time in the woods and around a campfire, I turned to the campout.

I looked forward to the weekend as much as anything I can remember. I have bragged on you to everyone within earshot. Lawyers and clients all over the country know about Paul Eason, the 500th campout, and all the Eagle Scouts. To say that I am proud of you does not approach describing how I feel.

The weekend itself was an extraordinary tribute to you. You should know that, but because of your humility I suspect you have thought of other reasons why former Scouts came from all across the country. But Dave Burnett and Stuart Worley didn't come from California just to see their brothers and relive old times. They came to honor you. That's why we all came—to honor you.

You will reject the label, but I will give it to you anyway. By any measure, you are a great man. And you are my hero.

I love you.

Reed Hillen chaired the committee that planned the campout. To mark the occasion, the committee sought donations from all the troop's Eagle Scouts to do something special to honor Daddy. Reed called me before the campout to ask my thoughts on what it should be. He told me the committee was considering retaining an artist to sculpt a bronze bust of Daddy to be placed outside the Scout Hut. I didn't have veto rights, but I did my best to veto the bust. As I told Reed, Daddy was not a bust kind of guy.

While Reed and I were talking, a thought occurred to me. After Daddy and I came home from the Grand Canyon, one of my law partners who had rafted both the canyon and the Middle Fork of the Salmon River in Idaho told me he preferred the latter. I suggested to Reed that Daddy's Eagle Scouts give him a raft trip on the Middle Fork. Others could go on their own nickel. I planned to be one of the others.

My suggestion was adopted enthusiastically by the committee, and planning for the trip the following summer began. But far too much money was contributed for just one trip. With the surplus, Mama and Daddy were given a ten-day tour of California, where they experienced the wonders of Yosemite National Park for the first and only time.

Like my law partner, I preferred the Middle Fork to the Grand Canyon, but not because of the rafting or the scenery, which were magnificent on both. The difference was the company. By the time we headed west in July 1994, thirty-five Scouts and friends of Troop 12 had signed up to join Daddy on the river. They were all men and boys with one exception. Ann Lowrey, who had just turned ten, was the youngest person on the trip and the only girl. Next to Daddy, she was the most popular member of the Middle Fork expedition.

The six days we spent on the river were unforgettable. The trip was better than any bust. We ran the rapids and saw wildlife every day and told stories around the campfire every night. I caught cutthroat trout on dry flies in the crystal-clear water. After we made camp one afternoon, several of us hiked up a creek to a hot spring that Chinese miners had dammed with huge timbers a century earlier to create a giant hot tub. As on the Grand Canyon, the guests had no responsibility for anything. The guides set up camp and prepared all our meals. This time we slept in tents, and the guides pitched them too. They grilled filets on our last night on the river, and we offered toasts to Daddy, our friends, and a wonderful trip. After the Middle Fork, it was hard to persuade Ann Lowrey to camp in Mississippi.

When our children were young, they spent more time in Tupelo with Mama and Daddy than Betsy Ann and I did. Raising any three children is a challenge, but our son Cliff had behavioral issues that made our lives especially difficult. Mama and Daddy realized how hard it was, and every month or two they offered to keep the children for a weekend to give us a break. It was another way they put others ahead of themselves.

On Friday afternoon or Saturday morning, Betsy Ann or I or both of us would head north on the Natchez Trace in her Suburban with the children. The designated meeting place was the McDonald's in Kosciusko, a small town seventy miles north of Jackson. The drive south from Tupelo was longer than ours, but that's the way Daddy wanted it. They would take the children back to Tupelo, feed and entertain them until Sunday afternoon, then we would meet at McDonald's again. We did it so many times that the kids thought the name of the McDonald's was Kosciusko's. They loved spending time with their grandparents, whom they called Margaret and Big Paul, and they played in the creek and vacant lot just as I had. Mama and Daddy enjoyed spending time with them too, but they were in their seventies. It had to be tiring, but they were always willing.

One Saturday morning, I planned an early start on the drive to Kosciusko so we could stop at Cypress Swamp, an oxbow lake alongside the Natchez Trace. The swamp, which was formed long ago when the Pearl River rerouted itself, is filled with bald cypresses and water tupelo trees and has a walking trail around it. Ann Lowrey stayed home, so I just had Cliff and Paul. On our walk around the swamp, Cliff spotted a small alligator in the water that was maybe four or five feet long. It was the first one he'd ever seen, and he was thrilled. Even Paul, my taciturn son, was excited.

When we reached Kosciusko, the boys climbed out of the Suburban and into Daddy's minivan, and I headed back to Jackson. When I returned to pick them up on Sunday afternoon, the minivan was already in the McDonald's parking lot. Daddy was usually early and almost never late. When Cliff spotted me, he came bounding out of the passenger side and marched toward me. Daddy followed close behind, a big smile on his face. Cliff was indignant. He said Big Paul didn't believe him when he told him about the alligator. He demanded that I corroborate his story. I confirmed that Cliff was telling the truth; we really did see an alligator at Cypress Swamp. But though the story was true, Cliff had embellished it. Daddy exposed him with a question: "Was it as big as the Suburban?" Chastened, Cliff climbed into the back seat of the Suburban—which was bigger than the alligator.

I had a sexual harassment trial in federal court in Biloxi the second week of August in 1995. The defendant was Ingalls Shipbuilding, the owner of the Naval shipyard in Pascagoula and my biggest, best, and most loyal client. I started representing Ingalls in 1991, and I still represent the company today.

On the last day of the trial, I spotted a lawyer friend of mine, Bob Smith, seated in the gallery. Bob and I litigated several of my first Ingalls cases against each other in the early nineties, learned that we both enjoyed camping and canoeing, and took several great trips together. When the judge took a recess, Bob told me he had bad news. My mother had suffered a severe stroke. Daddy had called Betsy Ann to tell her. She had no way to reach me while I was in trial, so she called Bob, who came to the courthouse to tell me.

I drove home after the trial ended that afternoon, then we headed up to Tupelo the next morning. Mama's life wasn't in danger, but she had lost the use of her right arm and her ability to speak. After months of physical therapy, she could shower, dress, and feed herself, but she was never able to talk again. Mama was right-handed and could communicate only by nodding and shaking her head and writing in chicken scratch with her left hand. Watching her struggle was painful.

Daddy took over nearly all the household duties, including the grocery shopping and most of the cooking and cleaning. But after it became clear that Mama could stay home by herself, he resumed camping with the troop, and our children began going to Tupelo again. They were now solely Daddy's responsibility, but he was still willing to take them to give us a break. I tried to go to Tupelo more often, but it was a very busy time in my law practice. I didn't go as often as I should have, but Daddy never suggested I should go more.

Mama was a lifelong smoker. She even sneaked cigarettes when she was in the hospital with breast cancer. In early 1999, she was again diagnosed with cancer, this time in her throat. When the oncologist explained the treatment options, Mama made it clear by shaking her head that she wanted nothing radical that would just prolong the inevitable.

She was soon placed on hospice care, though she was able to stay at home. In late August, her cousin Charles Harvey came to see her for the last time. The nurse had said Mama probably had at least a month to live, but Charles, a retired physician, told Daddy he believed it was only a matter of days. Daddy called me, and Betsy Ann and the children and I drove up to Tupelo the next morning. Mama was in good spirits, but she was ready to go. Daddy must have been in pain—his wife of nearly fifty years was dying in the bedroom they'd shared for more than forty—but he didn't show it. He spent his life taking care of others, and he never seemed to need anyone to take care of him. Taking care of others was probably the way he took care of himself.

Charles was right. Mama died on September 8, only a few days after we returned to Jackson. Marjory, her twin sister, had died just over two months earlier. After retiring from her career as an educator, Marjory had returned to Tupelo and bought a house on Rogers Drive down the street from Mama and Daddy. Daddy took care of her home just as he took care of his own. I learned from interviewing a former Eagle Scout, Lindsey Leake, that Daddy painted both of them. Lindsey sold him the paint and remembered the colors.

Chapter Seven

1999-2011

I went back to Tupelo more often to check on Daddy in the months after Mama died. He must have been grieving, though you couldn't tell it. He seemed fine but, then again, he always seemed fine. And he kept busy with the city council, Troop 12, and all his other volunteer activities.

Before one of my trips to Tupelo, I proposed that he and I undertake a construction project. In the mid-1960s, Mama and Daddy added a den onto the back of our house. Daddy later built a brick patio beside it with a large sweetgum tree in the middle. Over the years, the sweetgum's roots caused the bricks to buckle. There was no easy fix, so I suggested we cover up the patio by building a deck three feet above it.

When I arrived, the lumber had been delivered, along with bags of concrete to anchor the posts. The plan was for a deck of 500 square feet, plus benches, a rail, and two sets of steps. Building it took us three full days. Daddy had just turned seventy-eight, but he worked every bit as hard as I did. He showed no sign of growing old.

The first year of the new millennium was an eventful one for Daddy. He stepped down from his position on the city council in June, Troop 12 camped for the 600th month in a row in July, and he celebrated his eightieth birthday in Scotland in November.

Sensible people don't camp in Mississippi in July, but Troop 12 did it for the fiftieth year in a row in 2001. The temperature and humidity rose to customary levels in early July, and the weekend of the 600th campout was the hottest of the year. The plan was to camp Saturday night on the church lawn. The boys in the troop would be joined by former Scouts foolish enough to sleep outside in the torrid heat.

We drove up on Friday and went to dinner with Daddy and his childhood friends Harwell and Bill Dabbs. They had come to Tupelo for the weekend but wisely chose not to camp. Harwell had brought an old newspaper, an issue of the *Tupelo Daily Journal* from 1939. On the front page was a photo of Harwell and an article announcing that he had attained the highest rank in Scouting, the Eagle. When I said I was surprised that becoming an Eagle Scout was front-page news even then, Harwell said he had an after-school job at the paper and received special treatment. I looked at the old newspaper and the prices in the ads and thought about all that had changed in the six decades since Daddy and Harwell had become Eagle Scouts. When Bill Harwell became the troop's seventh Eagle Scout at the end of 1941, he didn't get the same treatment from the *Daily Journal*. Pearl Harbor had just been bombed, and there was no room on the front page for a new Eagle Scout.

Daddy headed downtown right after breakfast the next morning to help put up tents and supervise the Scouts. The plan was for the boys to erect a monkey bridge on the church lawn to entertain themselves and the people passing by. As the temperature rose to ninety, I stalled inside in the air conditioning. But guilt got the better of me. If Daddy was out in the heat, I should be too, and at 10:30 I drove downtown to join him. Half a dozen men and boys huddled in a small square of shade under a tarp on the church lawn. The looked like cattle in the shade of an oak tree.

I found Daddy in the un-air-conditioned Scout Hut organizing the monkey-bridge project. I told him the oppressive heat came with a silver lining. It underscored the magnitude of the troop's achievement. Going camping every single month for fifty years, no matter the weather, was an extraordinary feat. Daddy was not impressed because he was not impressed with himself. I was soon rescued from the heat by Dan Purnell, who had paddled me down

Bear Creek thirty years earlier while I sat in the middle of the canoe with a broken arm. We went to lunch and talked about old times.

The highlight of the weekend was the banquet Saturday night, just as it had been at the 500th campout more than eight years earlier. Ann Lowrey spotted a boy she'd become friends with on the Middle Fork in 1994. They were ten and eleven then, seventeen and eighteen now. The dynamic between them had changed. Many former Scouts lined up to have their pictures taken with Daddy. I took one of him with three of his very first Scouts: Rob Leake, Richard Condrey, and Charles Johnston. Rob and Richard were already members of the troop when Daddy became the Scoutmaster in 1947, and all three became Eagle Scouts before the monthly campout streak began in August 1951. Daddy was a dozen years older than they were, but you couldn't tell it from the picture. One of the former Scouts at the banquet said he wanted to thank me and the rest of our family for sharing Daddy with them. I wish Mama could have been there to hear him.

Jack Reed Sr. again served as the master of ceremonies, Jim Beane again prepared the meal, and Daddy again gave a talk about the troop that was long on facts and figures and short on sentimentality. And he again took no credit for the troop's remarkable achievement, though we all realized that it was first and foremost his achievement.

Daddy was raised too well to toot his own horn about the campout streak or anything else, but I don't think it was just that. I believe he never truly recognized the extraordinary value of his gift to the boys of Tupelo. Some of the boys at the banquet who benefited from that gift were eleven years old and had just joined the troop. Others—Rob Leake, Richard Condrey, and Charles Johnston among them—were almost seventy.

Former members of the troop gave speeches that were much longer on sentimentality than Daddy's. Ken Kirk, the former football star who had proposed fifty years earlier that Troop 12 go camping every month, gave an emotional speech thanking Daddy for everything he'd done for three generations of boys in Tupelo. Lewis Whitfield spoke about his time as a Scout in the early 1950s, when Mama and Daddy were newlyweds living in a tiny apartment and he lived near them. Lewis said he would wait for Daddy to come home from work, greet him before he could make it inside, and ask for help on merit badges. Daddy always had time for him. In 1957, the year I was born, Lewis became Troop 12's forty-third Eagle Scout. He earned his Eagle just before Buddy McCarty, who was delayed by the training at Robins Field. Twelve years after speaking at the banquet, almost to the day, Lewis gave the eulogy at Daddy's funeral.

I had considered asking to speak at the banquet. I would have talked about what it meant to have a man like Daddy as both my Scoutmaster and my father and about the years before I joined the troop when he would come home smelling of campfire smoke. But I also would have spoken about my hiking trips in the mountains of the West with my best friend and reminded everyone, young and old, that an outdoor life doesn't have to end when childhood does. I decided not to ask to speak because I was afraid I would become too emotional. After listening to Ken and Lewis, I knew I'd made the right call.

When the festivities ended at 9:30, it was still almost ninety degrees. The children wisely decided to go back to Daddy's house with Betsy Ann and spend the night there. I tried to convince Daddy we should go too. The facts were on my side. He would be eighty in less than four months. He didn't need to be sleeping outside in the stifling heat. He shook his head. I tried to make it easy. We could wait until all the boys were in their tents, drive home, rise early, and come back to the church at dawn. No one would ever know we left. He said I could leave, but he was staying. I stayed too.

Daddy retired to our tent at eleven. He fell asleep immediately, as always. I stayed up talking to old friends for an hour or so, then climbed into the tent. The temperature was still in the eighties. I lay on top of my sleeping bag, sweating. Cars drove by, the windows rolled down and the volume turned up. I thought back to the silver lining I'd suggested to Daddy earlier in the day. If the weather had always been perfect, camping for 600 months in a row wouldn't be such a big deal. As Daddy once said, anybody can camp in pretty weather. But the weather was rarely perfect, and it was a big deal.

Four months later, Daddy's friend and neighbor Mike Armour, whose son Mikey would become Troop 12's 386th Eagle Scout in 2009, talked Daddy into going to Scotland with a group from the First Methodist Church. While they were there, the group scheduled a program and a traditional Scottish dinner at a restaurant adjacent to Edinburgh Castle. It happened to be on Daddy's eightieth birthday. Mike pulled the emcee aside and asked him to announce that one of the guests, former Tupelo vice mayor and legendary Boy Scout leader Paul Eason, was celebrating his eightieth birthday. When young Scottish women heard the announcement, they swarmed around Daddy, wanting to have their picture taken with the handsome vice mayor. Mike said Daddy had a bounce in his step on the walk back to the hotel.

Daddy had the first serious health issue of his life the following year. There was a problem with one of the valves in his heart, and he came to Jackson for surgery to replace it. The one night he spent in the hospital was the very first one in his more than eighty years. Like many children in the early 1900s, he was born at home. He came home the day after the surgery, and he and I took a walk in the neighborhood that afternoon. At his follow-up appointment two days later, the surgeon was amazed by Daddy's recovery. I asked if he needed to change his diet, and the doctor said he could eat anything. I told Daddy we would take him to dinner that night and asked what he wanted. He thought a minute and said barbecue. We went to a place called Red Hot & Blue and discovered a local family band, the Pates, who became our favorites and played at Ann Lowrey's wedding reception four years later. Two days after our barbecue dinner, Daddy drove himself home to Tupelo.

Daddy fully recovered from the surgery and was soon back to his old self. He had stepped down as the Scoutmaster more than a decade earlier, but he still went on every campout and never missed a Scout meeting. He spent his time at meetings working with the newest Scouts and teaching them everything they were required to learn. He taught them the Scout Oath: "On my honor, I will do my best to do my duty to God and my country and to obey the Scout Law; to help other people at all times; to keep myself physically strong, mentally awake and morally straight;" the Scout Law: "A Scout is trustworthy, loyal, helpful, friendly, courteous, kind, obedient, cheerful, thrifty, brave, clean, and reverent;" the Scout Motto: "Be Prepared;" and the Scout Slogan: "Do a good turn daily." He also taught the boys how to tie knots and worked with them to meet the other requirements to become a Tenderfoot, the first rank on the road to Eagle.

In December 2003, a month after his eighty-second birthday, Daddy served as the grand marshal of the Tupelo Christmas parade. He could have ridden in a convertible like a Homecoming queen, but he chose to march at the head of the parade with the Scouts of Troop 12. I drove up from Jackson and marched with them. The photo of Daddy on the cover of the book was taken by Buddy McCarty at the parade.

Ann Lowrey was a sophomore at Ole Miss in the fall of 2003. The week before Halloween, she came home with some startling news: She was pregnant, and her longtime boyfriend had abandoned her. Near the end of the year, it was time for me to share the news with Daddy. Because he lived such an upstanding life, it would have been easy for him to be judgmental about others, but he wasn't built that way. When I told him Ann Lowrey was expecting and her boyfriend had left her, he said nothing critical of either of them. His concern was for his granddaughter and the baby. After asking how Ann Lowrey was handling the situation, he said the child will need a father.

My beautiful, precocious granddaughter Ada Brooks was born in June of 2004. She was Daddy's first great-grandchild. He had said she would need a father, and she soon had one. Ann Lowrey had a friend in the Honors College, Paul Forster, who took her to doctor's appointments while she was pregnant and helped take care of Ada after she was born. A romance between Ann Lowrey and Paul developed, and they decided to get married at the end of their senior year. Daddy came to Oxford for the wedding, and Ada served as the flower girl, making it a four-generation affair.

On most Sundays when Ann Lowrey was at Ole Miss, she drove the fifty miles to Tupelo to spend the afternoon with Daddy. He would take her to lunch, she would do laundry at his house, and they would do the crossword puzzle in the Sunday paper. With his knowledge of history and hers of current pop culture, they were a formidable pair.

During Ann Lowrey's last two years in Oxford, Daddy had three visitors on Sundays. She and Paul would come to Tupelo for the day and bring Ada Brooks. The two Pauls were far apart in age but similar in nature. Both had modest needs, were never idle, and always wanted to be of use. After Daddy treated them to lunch, they would spend the afternoon at his house. While Ann Lowrey washed clothes and Ada napped, Paul offered to help around the house. Because Daddy liked doing things himself, they had some disagreements. One Sunday Daddy retrieved the extension ladder from his workshop to clean out the gutters on the roof. Paul said he should do it instead. Daddy said he would climb the ladder and Paul could stay on the ground and hold it. Paul persisted and said they should swap roles. Daddy didn't like it, but he relented. He was eighty-four, Paul twenty-one.

Mama and Daddy told me I was adopted when I was still too young to understand what it meant. I thought of it as an interesting but insignificant detail, like being left-handed. Daddy told me once that he couldn't imagine loving a biological child any more than he loved Margie and me. It was a rare moment of revealing his feelings. Mama wrote me a letter saying it's well known that parents who adopt their children love them more than biological parents do. Whether that's true or not, I never felt a moment of insecurity about being adopted. And I never searched for my birth parents and never would have. But in June 2004, a week before Ada Brooks was born, I learned my birth mother's identity.

The discovery began with a voicemail left on Daddy's home phone. The caller said she worked for a lawyer in New Orleans who had been ordered to conduct a nationwide search for Paul Eason, age forty-six. My name is Paul Brooks Eason, and I was less than a month away from my forty-seventh birthday. The woman asked Daddy to call her back, but instead he called me, and I returned the woman's call. Her first words were, "I can't believe we found you." I was easy to find because Daddy still lived at the address on the replacement birth certificate that was found in my adoption file. When I asked what the call was about, she said an inheritance. That got my attention.

Over the next several weeks, I learned the stories of both my origin and the search that led to my discovery. My birth mother Julie Francis was from a wealthy, prominent family in Tulsa. She learned she was pregnant during the fall of her freshman year in college and was sent to the home for unwed mothers in New Orleans where I was born. After naming me Scott, she signed the papers giving me up for adoption and never saw me again. Lawyers searched for me because Julie's son, his identity and location unknown, was a potential heir to her grandfather's fortune.

As I learned new details about the story, I would call Daddy to tell him. He was interested to hear it all and never showed any concern that I was learning about my biological family and what I might think about that. I believe he knew where he stood with me and that nothing could change the way I felt about him. He should have.

As the years rolled by and I met people who knew Julie, two of them gave me the name of the man they suspected was my biological father. He was still alive, and I tried to contact him. He didn't respond, so I let it go. I wrote in *Fortunate Son* that he might be a very good man, but he couldn't be as good as the man who raised me.

Buying gifts for Daddy was always a challenge. He was the least materialistic person I've ever known. He didn't have much, but he didn't want more. When asked what he wanted, he would say not to get him anything. For many years, I have given everyone in the family a book for Christmas, but I didn't give Daddy books because he would fall asleep on the second page. And I could only give him so many cardigan sweaters.

But then Hurricane Katrina came and solved the challenge of what to give him, or at least I thought it did. My best friend Bobby Ariatti, the subject of my first book, lived in Long Beach on the Mississippi Gulf Coast. When it appeared that Katrina would make landfall near his home, I invited him and his family to come stay in our lake cabin north of Jackson. They packed up and headed north.

Bobby served in Vietnam in the 1970s and in Iraq thirty years later. A woman who was with him in Iraq tried to get in touch with him after Katrina. She failed to reach him, called me, and I told her where he was. A week later, a package arrived at our house. It was a gift to Bobby from the woman, eight pints of Graeter's ice cream packed on dry ice. But as fate would have it, Bobby and his family had returned to Long Beach the day before. The ice cream couldn't be shipped again, so we had no choice. It was delicious.

Not only that, but it solved my gift-giving problem. Two months later, when Daddy turned eighty-four, I sent him eight pints of Graeter's ice cream shipped on dry ice from the company's facility in Cincinnati. It was expensive—seems like it was a hundred dollars or so—but Daddy was worth it, he loved ice cream, and I was set. I bought him more Graeter's ice cream for Christmas, then Father's Day, then his eighty-fifth birthday.

A month or two after the fourth Graeter's gift, Betsy Ann and I went to Tupelo one weekend. While we were there, she took Daddy grocery shopping. When they reached the ice cream aisle, he told her the ice cream we gave him sure was good, but he thought the Kroger Private Selection brand was just as good. I had to find something else to give him. I couldn't bring myself to keep sending him Graeter's ice cream when the ice cream he liked just as much cost a fifth as much.

In his mid-eighties, Daddy began to decline physically, though he remained determined to do as much as he could for as long as he could. He continued to camp with the troop and mow the yard, though he surrendered to the use of a riding mower and gave up driving residents of Traceway Manor in the church van. He also began having memory problems, for which his doctor suggested he take an herb called ginkgo biloba. When I asked if it helped, Daddy joked that he didn't know because he couldn't remember to take it. He still did the best he could on the crossword puzzle in the *Daily Journal* to keep his mind as sharp as possible.

If Daddy was ever lonely during the dozen years he lived alone, he didn't mention it, though he never would have. His memory may have been fading, but when I went to Tupelo to see him, he was always prepared. A six-pack of Sam Adams Boston Lager was always waiting for me in the refrigerator along with burgers to grill on Saturday night. Daddy would sometimes drink a beer with me, two once or twice, never three. I began taking Ada Brooks with me and, when they were old enough, her brothers Eason and Collins. They played in the creek I had played in, and Daddy and I took turns pushing them in the swing my children had swung in. It is a rare privilege for an old man to be fit enough to swing his great-grandchildren.

As I've noted, the last time Daddy camped with the troop, or at least the last time I've been able to confirm, was at Camp Yocona in January 2008. Sam Agnew had stepped down as the Scoutmaster three years earlier, and Ty Robinson was the troop leader. Ty told me Daddy went on the campout but was cold and came home early.

When I was in Tupelo six months later, I reminded Daddy that he went camping nearly every month for more than sixty years. I asked if he missed it. He thought about it for a few seconds, then smiled and said, "I think I camped enough."

In November 2009, the month Daddy turned eighty-eight, I drove up to Tupelo on the weekend of Troop 12's 700th consecutive monthly campout. The temperature was fifty degrees colder than it had been for the 600th, but neither of us camped with the troop. Daddy now walked with a cane, his memory had become worse, and he had been diagnosed with dementia. He had stopped driving and given his old minivan to my son Cliff. He now depended on his nephew Phil Ruff to take him to the Kiwanis Club, the grocery store, and doctors' appointments.

But Daddy's decline did not keep him from touring the site of the 700th campsite. We walked among the tents and greeted the Scouts and leaders. The younger boys in the troop didn't recognize Daddy, but they'd been told about him. We also attended the banquet that night, where Daddy was honored by state representative Alan Nunnelee, who was later elected to Congress but died of brain cancer when he was only fifty-six.

In addition to the Scout Law, Oath, Motto, and Slogan, new Scouts are required to learn about the history of Scouting and Lord Robert Baden-Powell, who founded the Scouting movement with the publication of the first installment of *Scouting for Boys* in 1908. A century later, and more than half a century after Troop 12 began camping every month, one of the troop's newest members was tested about the history of Scouting on the 700th campout. When asked to identify the Father of the Boy Scouts, the new Scout did not say Lord Baden-Powell. His answer was "Paul Eason."

In late 2007, after twenty-eight years of marriage, Betsy Ann and I separated. She stayed in our home in Jackson, and I moved to our lake cabin twenty-five miles north of the city. Betsy Ann insisted that we not tell Daddy. She didn't want to upset him and was afraid he wouldn't be able to deal with it. I disagreed—by then he had lived through a depression, a world war, and the deaths of his parents, his wife, and two sisters—but I dreaded having the conversation with him. I also had an excuse for procrastinating: Betsy Ann and I had not yet made a final decision, Daddy was in his late eighties, and there was a possibility I would never have to tell him. So I agreed to keep quiet. Over the course of the next year, Betsy Ann and I traveled together to Tupelo several times to see Daddy and pretended nothing had changed.

But we were unable to work things out, and our divorce was finalized in December 2008. A month later, we took one last trip together to see Daddy, but we still didn't tell him. For the next two years, my trips to Tupelo were either alone or with one or more of my children or grandchildren. But I still didn't break the news. Even after Carrie and I married on New Year's Day in 2011, I kept the secret.

In the summer of 2011, I decided I would keep it no longer. Carrie and I had been married more than six months, and she'd never met Daddy. As things stood, I couldn't take her to see him, and I couldn't bring him to our house to see her. Both limitations were no longer acceptable to me. Daddy's declining health was also an issue. He was nearing his ninetieth birthday, and it was clear he would be unable to live alone much longer. I knew he wouldn't want to leave the house where he'd lived for fifty-five years, I needed to begin talking to him about it, and he and I would need to decide where he would go. Betsy Ann had also remarried. I told her my plan, she did not object, and I drove alone to Tupelo to have the conversation I had long dreaded.

Along the way, I rehearsed what I planned to say a dozen times. Daddy and I followed the standard Saturday night routine, grilling burgers and watching TV, a ritual that had begun with burgers and *Gunsmoke* fifty years earlier. At nine o'clock, after one show ended but before another could begin, I pushed the power button on the remote and pulled up a stool in front of Daddy's chair. He looked at me and waited. He was good at waiting.

I began by saying I was sure he wondered why Betsy Ann had stopped coming with me to Tupelo. That seemed like a good way to start, but I could see from the look on his face that he hadn't wondered at all. Or maybe he'd forgotten. I took a deep breath and continued. I told him the divorce was amicable, that Betsy Ann and I were both happy, and I explained why we hadn't told him. I said Carrie was wonderful, the grandchildren loved her, and his nephew Eason Leake, Elizabeth's father, was the chairman of the board of the bank where she worked. I told him Betsy Ann's new husband was a fraternity brother of ours and had roomed at Ole Miss with Phil Ruff.

I spoke for ten minutes; he neither interrupted nor changed expression. When I reached the end, he still said nothing. I asked what he thought. He said he was shocked, but I sure couldn't tell it from his tone or his look. I asked if I could bring Carrie to Tupelo to meet him, and he said that would be fine. A few seconds passed in silence, then he reached for the remote and turned the TV back on. He never once asked me why my marriage of nearly three decades had ended. Not then, not ever.

Two weeks later, in early September, Carrie and I took Ada Brooks, Eason, and Collins to Tupelo. Daddy was glad to meet Carrie, and she was thrilled to meet him after all I'd told her. I kicked myself for not telling him sooner. He could have come to our wedding. We had a nice weekend, but it had become obvious that Daddy could no longer live alone.

Carrie and I went for a walk and talked about what to do. When we returned, the grandchildren were in the den watching television and Daddy was lying on the kitchen floor. He wasn't hurt, but he couldn't get up. We needed to decide on a plan right away. I would need to have another conversation with him that I dreaded. I wanted to bring him home with us, but I knew he would resist and, with the back seat full of grandchildren, there was no place to put him.

Chapter Eight

2011-2013

But on the way home, something happened that spared me from the second painful conversation. While we were at Ann Lowrey and Paul's dropping off the grandchildren, my cell phone rang. Daddy had fallen on his front porch while taking down the American flag, which he put up every morning and took down every evening. It was fortuitous that he was outside. A neighbor saw him, helped him inside, and called Phil Ruff, who called me. The doctor, Troop 12 Eagle Scout Bill Rice, found that Daddy had broken a bone in his foot.

We decided to move Daddy to our house, at least temporarily. I had to be in federal court on the Gulf Coast the next day, so Carrie made a second trip to Tupelo and brought him home with her. She said she talked the entire three hours of the drive and wondered if Daddy thought a crazy woman had kidnapped him.

We initially thought we would find an assisted living facility for Daddy, and we visited a very nice one that was less than ten minutes from our house. He was worried that he couldn't afford it, but he didn't need to be. Though Daddy said he never made any money anywhere he worked, he always saved part of what he made. Thus, despite his modest income and the fact that he always gave generously to the Methodist Church and other charities, he managed to accumulate significant savings by the time he retired. And his savings continued to grow during the next quarter century because he spent almost nothing on himself. The mortgage had been paid off long ago, and all the furniture was more than twenty years old, as were most of his clothes. When he asked if he could afford the assisted living facility, I told him I'd done the math. He could cover the cost until he turned 126.

But he didn't need to cover it for even a single day. The facility's staff evaluated him and concluded that he would need to be admitted to the Alzheimer's wing. Some Alzheimer's patients exhibit strange behaviors, but Daddy's only noticeable symptom was his profound memory loss. Carrie and I toured the Alzheimer's wing and decided it wasn't for him. We were back to square one.

After Daddy had been with us for two weeks, Carrie told me we should stop looking. She said Daddy needed to live with us, that no one would love him as much or take care of him as well as we would. I was thinking the same thing but was reluctant to suggest it. We were newlyweds and had never discussed bringing an elderly parent into our home, though ours was perfect for it. There was a guest bedroom downstairs with a full bath beside it. Daddy spent nearly two years with us and never saw the second floor.

Though Daddy lived almost ninety-two years, he and I lived together for only twenty, my first eighteen and his last two. I will always be grateful to Carrie for those two years, for welcoming Daddy into our home, feeding him, loving him, and helping me take care of him. After all he did for me and thousands of others, it was an honor to be able to help him when he needed me. Not long after Daddy came to live with us, he told me we had saved his life.

Carrie and I took Daddy back to Tupelo for a special occasion on November 4, 2011, two months after he moved in with us. It was his ninetieth birthday and ranks among the best days of my life.

Carrie, the thoughtful one in our marriage, suggested that we have a birthday party for Daddy in the fellowship hall at the First Methodist Church. Members of the church staff were delighted to help. Before the party, we went to the lunch meeting of the Kiwanis Club, which Daddy had attended for more than half his life. Jack Reed Jr., the Mayor of Tupelo, gave a short speech honoring Daddy and presented him with the key to the city. It had been more than forty years since Jack became an Eagle Scout in Troop 12.

The birthday party at the church that afternoon was wonderful. The fellowship hall was filled with old friends and former Scouts, including a handful of men who were in the troop with me. I don't know how many of the guests Daddy remembered, but he acted like he remembered them all.

After the party, we gathered around a computer screen and watched a video that had been made that morning. The video featured Alan Nunnelee, now a member of Congress. He was presenting a resolution on the floor of the House of Representatives honoring Daddy for his lifetime of service to Tupelo and the young men of Troop 12. The resolution stated that "America needs more young men who understand the meaning of duty, excellence, and honor." Because of Daddy, thousands of men understood the meaning, though most of them were no longer young.

Margie and her husband, Brendan, had flown up from their home outside Ft. Lauderdale to be with us, and we took Daddy to an Italian restaurant in Tupelo for dinner. He'd been smiling all day, just as he had at the 500th campout. When I asked if he'd enjoyed his birthday, he said he couldn't wait till next year.

The honors Daddy received on his ninetieth birthday were the last ones, but they were far from the first. He never sought recognition, but his contributions in the close-knit community of Tupelo were impossible to ignore. Because I didn't live in Tupelo after the summer of 1979 and he didn't tell me, I don't know all the honors he received, just as I don't know all the volunteer work he did. But I know many of his honors from newspaper clippings, plaques, and certificates that Mama saved. She was far prouder of Daddy than he was of himself.

In 1959, more than fifty years before he was honored on the floor of the House of Representatives, the Yocona Area Council chose Daddy for the Silver Beaver Award, which recognizes Boy Scout leaders of exceptional character who have provided distinguished service to the Scouts. Fifteen years later, Daddy was presented with a statuette entitled "The Scoutmaster," and an article in the

Daily Journal declared that "the names of Paul Eason-led Eagles read like a roll call of Tupelo's community leadership." Two years after that, Daddy was named the city's outstanding citizen by the Junior Auxiliary. His father had been selected for the same honor a decade earlier. Nearly twenty years after Daddy was honored as the outstanding citizen in the city, the readers of the *Lee County Courier* chose him as the best man in the county.

In 1987 Daddy was invited to the Mississippi Capitol, where he was honored by the state legislature for his forty years of service as the Scoutmaster of Troop 12. Daddy was the first Tupelo citizen chosen for the Liberty Bell Award, which was presented by the Mississippi Junior Bar Association and Lee County Bar Association for outstanding community service. He also received the Julius G. Berry Award for his work on behalf of United Way as well as the Jefferson Award, which recognizes unsung heroes who make the world a better place through volunteering and community service.

Two of Daddy's honors included in the papers Mama saved were amusing. In recognition of his twenty-five years as a member of the Tupelo Parks and Recreation Commission, the city christened the first soccer field at Ballard Park on the west side of town Paul Eason Field. It was amusing because Daddy never watched a soccer game in his life and knew nothing about the sport. I also came across an article from 1997 that included a photo with Daddy in the middle wearing a purple crown and matching cape flanked by the members of his court. A purple crown was not his style, but he had been crowned King Eel in the annual Oleput Festival. Oleput is Tupelo spelled backward; I suppose King Eel is for Lee County.

When Daddy received honors and awards, he made light of his efforts and achievements. He was interviewed shortly before his fortieth anniversary as the Scoutmaster and said, "There's no noble reason for what I do. I simply do it because I enjoy it." When asked why none of his predecessors in the position had served more than a few years, he blamed himself and his buddies. "We were so mean and bad back then that we used to run off a new Scoutmaster every year or so." Years later, he reacted to learning that the readers of the

Lee County Courier had chosen him as the best man in the county by asking, "What happened, did I get one vote and nobody else voted?" I don't know if he was embarrassed by the attention or too humble to see what everyone else saw.

Carrie and I treasured the time we spent with Daddy after he moved in with us, but meals were a challenge. Carrie's a fabulous cook, but she doesn't eat beef, pork, or chicken. Daddy was accustomed to eating beef, pork, or chicken at nearly every meal. In his first week with us, she made an arugula salad with a homemade balsamic vinaigrette to accompany our shrimp pasta dinner. Daddy, who was an iceberg-and-thousand-island man and not accustomed to fine dining, stared at the strange salad suspiciously and poked it with his fork. Before risking a bite, he asked Carrie if she'd picked it out of the yard. Though she had a demanding job as senior vice-president of a community bank, she started making two meals every night, one for him and one for us. Their diets overlapped each other's hardly at all, but they both overlapped mine. I sat at the end of the table with Carrie to my left and Daddy to my right. I was the omnivore in the middle.

When Daddy came to live with us, we were temporarily without a dog. We decided to adopt one so Daddy would have a companion during the day while we were at work. I had served on the board of directors of an animal shelter in Jackson called CARA. Carrie and I went there in search of a gentle dog that would be good with Daddy and the grandchildren. We came home with a sweet cocker spaniel named Mollie.

Daddy loved dogs and took to Mollie right away. He spent his days in our red recliner and, when not watching television, would throw a tennis ball for her to retrieve. She would chase it, drop into a slide on our slick hardwood floors to keep from slamming into the wall, and bring the ball back to him. Then he would throw it again. They kept at it until she grew tired and refused to bring it back. I don't know who enjoyed their game more—Daddy, Mollie, or Carrie and me.

Mollie took to Daddy because of the tennis ball but also because of food. He shared all his meals with her, eating most of what was on his plate, then holding it a few inches above the floor for her to eat the rest. He even shared his ice cream, which he ate after dinner every night. It wasn't good for her, but how do you tell your ninety-year-old father to stop feeding the dog? We chose to let Mollie get fat.

Because of his poor memory, Daddy couldn't remember that Mollie was a girl and repeatedly insisted she was the opposite. We would remind him, but he would forget. To prove him wrong, Carrie would hold her belly up to show him. But it didn't stick. In a day or two, he was back to telling Mollie what a good boy she was.

Not long after Daddy's ninetieth birthday, we took him back to Tupelo to clean out the house to prepare to sell it. I found many treasures: his log recording the flight on which he was shot at in November 1946; a list of donors and amounts for the construction of Troop 12's first Scout Hut in 1953; and the notes Mama's father used to preach sermons, some of which were a century old. I also found an issue of Sports Illustrated from 1954 that included paintings of two ducks that Mama used as models to paint the same two ducks. Her paintings hung on the wall of their bedroom for as long as I can remember.

While we were packing, the doorbell rang. It was a man who looked to be in his forties. I didn't know him, and I don't remember his name. He'd seen the U-Haul parked out front and stopped to see if Daddy was there. I don't know if Daddy remembered him, but he was glad to see him.

The man spoke about his wonderful memories from his years as a Scout in Troop 12 and how much Daddy meant to him. He said his parents were divorced, and he walked to and from the Scout Hut on Monday nights. When Daddy saw him en route one night, he began picking him up in the White Elephant and taking him home when the meetings ended.

I had found three or four of Daddy's old Boy Scout Handbooks he'd used through the years, and I asked the man if he wanted one. He was thrilled. When I pulled one out of a box and handed it to him, you would have thought I'd given him the Holy Grail.

Carrie and I initially planned to have our wedding just before Christmas in 2010. But, being thrifty, I asked the accountant who prepared my tax returns if it mattered whether the wedding was before or after the end of the year. She said it would be better to wait. Putting off the wedding until New Year's Day wasn't my most romantic decision, but we saved enough to pay for our honeymoon on a live music cruise.

I realized before our wedding that one benefit of marrying on 1/1/11 was that I would never forget our anniversary, but I didn't consider the downside. Most restaurants are closed on New Year's Day, and we couldn't find a nice one that was open on our first anniversary. We decided to take Daddy with us and do the best we could. We wound up at Applebee's, which wasn't very romantic either. Carrie has reminded me about our first anniversary on every anniversary since then.

Daddy continued to deteriorate as the months went by. He was never a big talker and now talked very little, though he was still rational and could still carry on a normal conversation. He still had impeccable manners as well and thanked us for everything we did for him. But his memory was all but gone.

My son Cliff had spent many weekends in Tupelo with Daddy, but when Cliff came to stay with us for several weeks, Daddy asked me, "Who is that young man living upstairs?" When I said it was Cliff, his grandson and my son, Daddy was astonished. Daddy loved it when his great-grandchildren came for a visit and climbed onto his lap, but he didn't remember who they were either. More than once, he asked after they left, "Those children sure are smart; now, whose are they?" It didn't matter. He loved them, and they loved him.

For Daddy's first Christmas with us, I made him a scrapbook

of the story of his life, filled with newspaper clippings Mama had saved and five generations of family photos, from his parents at the beginning to his great-grandchildren at the end. I went through it with him and explained who everyone was. I don't think he remembered many of them, but he always knew who I was. When Carrie came home from work first, he always asked when I would arrive.

Daddy also became weaker and feebler as the months passed. We had traded in his cane for a walker after he injured his foot, and his pace on the walker slowed as time went by. We still took him outside for walks around the circle in our neighborhood, but they took longer than they had when he first moved in. He hadn't flown a plane in more than sixty years, but he still stopped and looked up, searching the sky for jet contrails.

After Daddy had been with us more than a year, we decided a dog to keep him company while we were gone during the day was insufficient. We hired a lovely retiree named Chris to stay with him. She sat on the couch and read her worn Bible while Daddy sat in the recliner, watched television, and threw the tennis ball for Mollie. Chris made him a sandwich every day for lunch and brought it to him on a TV tray. He rarely rose from the recliner from morning to evening.

Daddy turned ninety-one in November 2012, and his health deteriorated rapidly the following spring. His left foot turned dark red, almost purple, and he and I sat for hours in waiting rooms trying to find out what it was and what to do. The problem was a blocked artery, and the surgery to correct it was unsuccessful. Daddy again spent only one night in the hospital, his last one, which gave him a lifetime total of two. The surgeon told me he could try again, but he always reminded himself that his goal was to prolong life, not prolong death. We agreed not to put Daddy through it.

After the surgery, Daddy stopped eating almost altogether. He didn't even want ice cream, which meant poor Mollie didn't get any either. Chris was worried that Daddy wasn't eating. I asked his primary physician, Lee Sams, an old friend of mine who grew up in Tupelo, what we should do. He suggested that we offer him food but not force him to eat, that if we did, he might live just long enough for his foot to have to be amputated.

Daddy ate little of what we offered, but with my help he was still able to get out of bed and make it to the recliner. And he could still throw the tennis ball for Mollie to fetch. Wonderful caregivers from hospice came and told us what to expect. I drafted his obituary, which was my honor to write, and asked Lewis Whitfield if he would give the eulogy at Daddy's funeral. He said it would be his honor to give it.

Daddy was easy to care for, never seemed depressed, and never complained about his failing health. But near the end, he became very stubborn about one thing: having to bathe. We would beg and plead, and Carrie would stress the need for him to be fresh when his great-grandchildren came to visit. I was more direct. He would finally relent, and I would put on a swimsuit, help him onto a chair in the shower, then get in and bathe him. He would complain that the water was too cold or too hot, and I would remind him of all the nights he spent sleeping outside in all kinds of weather, both colder and hotter than the shower.

The first day the hospice workers came, we left them there with Daddy and Chris. That afternoon the nurse called. She said the elderly often don't want to bathe, and hospice workers are trained to deal with their objections and persuade them. They had tried everything with Daddy, but he was unpersuadable. I told her I would stay home the next morning and try to convince him.

After the orderly arrived, I stood at the foot of Daddy's bed and explained his options. The orderly could give him a sponge bath. He was trained to do it, he would use warm water, Daddy could stay in bed, and it would take only a few minutes. Or, if he didn't want that, the orderly and I would get him out of bed and onto his wheelchair and roll him to the bathroom. We would lift him up, take off his pajamas, and put him on his chair in the shower. I would get in the shower and bathe him. The orderly and I would then lift him back up, dry him off, dress him, and bring him back to bed. Daddy was shaking his head the whole time I was talking.

If it were up to me, I said, I would choose the sponge bath. I asked Daddy if he would cooperate with the orderly. With a look of disgust, he said one word: "somewhat." Before he could change his mind, I walked out the door and headed to the office.

Daddy slept almost all the last weekend of June. He died at noon on Monday, July 1, four months before his ninety-second birthday and two days before my fifty-sixth. My phone rang twice while I was at the office giving a presentation to the young lawyers in our firm. I saw from Caller ID that the first call was from Chris, the second from Carrie. I didn't answer either one, but I knew what they meant. When I made it home, Chris told me she had been sitting beside Daddy when he stopped breathing. She said being with him when he passed was a blessing on her soul.

Her mission complete, Chris was now out of a job. After the coroner left and the undertaker took Daddy's body, I told her I was going to the bank to get some cash for a severance payment. She asked if I would do her a favor and get her something else too. To my astonishment, that sweet, Bible-reading woman wanted a pack of Marlboro Lights. Daddy had died, and she wanted a smoke.

Two days later, on my birthday, the *Daily Journal* published a wonderful tribute to Daddy. Former Mayor Glenn McCullough was quoted as saying that Daddy "loved Tupelo. He worked hard for many years to make Tupelo a better place to live, work, worship, and play. He was successful. Mr. Eason was a mentor to me. He personified servant leadership and showed what it means to be a good Boy Scout." Longtime Assistant Scoutmaster Jim High said Daddy "positively affected the lives of more young boys than anyone else in Tupelo ever has. There has not been and likely will never be another man as truly good as was my friend Paul Eason. All of us who came in contact with him in any way are better off for the experience."

After Daddy's death, I sent his obituary and a note about his last two years with Carrie and me to many friends and colleagues, who forwarded them to many more. I received numerous beautiful messages in response, mostly from Daddy's former Scouts. Some said Daddy had been the most influential man in their lives, others that he was one of the two most influential and their own father was the other one. Bill Rice, who treated Daddy when he broke his foot, wrote that Daddy "undoubtedly had a greater impact for good on more lives than anyone in our community—past, present, or future." Richard Condrey sent me a letter saying he was a better man for having known Daddy, that Daddy was his hero and role model. Former governor William Winter wrote of Daddy that he did not know of anyone who so unselfishly gave of himself and his talents for the betterment of others.

My favorite messages were from Tupelo lawyer Mike Bush, who was not in Troop 12 but camped often with the troop when his son was a member. He wrote me the first one on the day he learned of Daddy's death.

My nephew Jason Bush told me today about your father's death. I send my condolences to you and your family. Reading the obituary brought back many memories of your father and your splendid family.

Mr. C. C., Cliff, was a strong leader for so many years, and on the Board of Aldermen. In the early '70s I remember an acquaintance telling me that an issue important to him was coming up on the board's agenda. He, then a customer at Bank of Tupelo, went to Mr. Eason, suggested he was considering moving his business to People's Bank, and mentioned the upcoming vote. Mr. Eason stiffened. 'Sir, what goes on here in this bank has no bearing on my participation in city government.' The meeting was over.

It was always a pleasure to be with Bob Leake, jovial and upbeat as he was, but his best asset was Myra. A splendid person. When did they quit making them? Puddie and I taught swimming for many years at that terrible circular pool on Madison Street. When I listed her as a reference on a college application, I had to call around to find out her real name.

I could go on about your family but will not. It is no disparagement to the rest of your family to say that your father was a standout. He knew what was important in life. One just felt better in his presence, always. You mentioned Carrie taking him in. I do not know her but would place a healthy wager that she was well rewarded by the relationship. I certainly was.

When my son Marshall was in Troop 12, I did my share of camping. Your father prepared a peach cobbler toward the end of every evening, cooking it under the coals of the fire as I recall. He cooked by smell; when it smelled done, it was. I do not think I ever camped with your father when he did not eat a red apple before turning in at night.

We should all be more like Paul Eason. We just do not know how.

I emailed Mike in response. "Thank you for your wonderful email, Mike. I just read it to Carrie. It made both of us cry. I'm glad you got to eat the cobbler. A year or so ago, someone with the troop emailed to ask me to ask Daddy if he remembered the recipe. I responded that it was a long shot, but I would ask. I did, and he just grinned and shook his head."

I also told Mike a story Paul Fairley had told me. Whoever was in the tent with Daddy could never get to sleep until he had chomped his nightly apple. On one campout, to avoid the chomping, the assistant leaders took the apple and replaced it with a quarter. They never confessed, and Daddy never confronted them.

Mike responded the next day. "Brooks, your father was like a horse with his apples. I am not surprised that others remember the cobblers. Somewhere around ten p.m., all these spoons would gather around his campfire, drawn by the smell, no faces mind you, just outreached spoons in the dark of the night, reflecting the campfire light. Magical."

Mike would have won his wager about Carrie. She will tell anyone who asks that she was very well rewarded by her relationship with Daddy. She only wishes she could have known him sooner. He lived with us less than two years and has been gone far longer than that, but every now and then, out of the blue, she will turn to me and say, "I miss your daddy."

Daddy's funeral was a testament to a life well lived in service to others. Dozens and dozens of Daddy's former Scouts were there. Some came from far away. At the beginning of the eulogy, Lewis Whitfield asked all the Eagles in the sanctuary to stand. I stood in the front row, turned around, and looked at all of Daddy's Eagle Scouts standing with me.

Lewis said Daddy was like a second father to him during his adolescent years. He believed that hundreds of other men would say the very same thing. He spoke of Daddy's quiet leadership, impeccable character, basic goodness, and said he was one of the best of the Greatest Generation, a true gentleman, a committed Christian, and a model of leadership.

Lewis told of Daddy's unsuccessful effort to join the war in the Pacific and his combat over the campus at Mississippi State, which proved he had a genuine sense of adventure. Lewis also talked about all the Eagle Scouts and all the campouts. And he talked about Mama and the 2,500 Monday nights and 575 campout weekends she spent alone or taking care of Margie and me.

Lewis said he believed being a Scoutmaster was truly Daddy's calling, and he listed the qualities that made Daddy a great leader. He was totally committed and devoted thousands of hours to the boys in the troop. He was humble, unselfish, and asked nothing for himself. He was unflappable and had infinite patience. He was a great listener and tremendous teacher and always put the responsibility back on the boys. He was a model of planning and organization. He cut the boys no slack and expected them to do their best at all times. He provided the boys with leadership opportunities and let them make mistakes and learn from them. He expected the Scouts to do the right thing, and he always did the right thing himself. Lewis said he'd known Daddy almost sixty years and had never seen him do anything remotely wrong. He lived the twelve points of the Scout Law.

Lewis closed the eulogy by quoting from General Douglas MacArthur's speech entitled "Duty, Honor, Country" that he delivered to the Corps of Cadets at West Point in 1962. The general closed his famous speech with these words: "Today marks my last roll call with you. But I want you to know that when I cross the river, my last conscious thoughts will be of the Corps, and the Corps, and the Corps." Lewis said he hoped and believed that Daddy's last conscious thoughts were of God, his family, and Troop 12, and Troop 12, and Troop 12.

When I was a member of the troop, a bugler played Taps every night during the week we spent at Camp Yocona in June. I kept my composure through the eulogy and almost to the end of the service. But when we closed Daddy's funeral by singing Taps, it was too much for me.

Chapter Nine

2013-2018

Less than a week after Daddy's funeral, Troop 12 headed west to Yellowstone National Park. It was the troop's 744th consecutive monthly campout and one of its grandest. Ten days later, Scott Reed, my former doubles partner and Troop 12 Eagle Scout number 138, wrote a column about Daddy in the *Daily Journal*. He began with these words:

Paul Eason was a man of few words but many actions. When he talked, it was worth your time to listen. His words ended earlier this month, but the results of his actions will continue to live on through the countless young men who have become leaders in their adult lives because of Paul.

For Christmas 2012, Daddy's last one, Carrie gave me a portrait of him surrounded by Ada Brooks, Eason, and Collins. When Daddy died, Ann Lowrey was expecting her fourth and final child. Elsa Gray was born four months later. We were hoping she would come into the world on Daddy's birthday—I instructed Ann Lowrey to jump on their trampoline on the morning of the fourth so she would go into labor—but Elsa Gray came two days late. I wish she and Daddy could have known each other, but at least I can tell her stories about him.

Six months after Daddy's death, in January 2014, Troop 12 went camping for the 750th month in a row. To celebrate the milestone, the troop's leaders commissioned tee shirts with a likeness of Daddy on the front and back. When I found out, I went on a buying spree, ordering shirts for Margie, her husband Brendan, and their three children and for Carrie and my children and grandchildren. For me, I bought three. Carrie later bought me four more. I wear them to walk the dogs and work in the yard—neighbors probably think I have only one shirt—and I'm gradually wearing them out. Carrie says I should save them, but I don't think Daddy would approve. He was a practical man, and what good is a shirt if you don't wear it?

After Daddy died, Eason and Ellen Leake, Elizabeth's parents, gave me her file from her interview of Daddy in Tupelo in 2003. When I finally got around to opening it, I discovered four cassette tapes inside. I didn't know Elizabeth had recorded the interview. Cassette players were hard to find by the time I discovered the tapes, but I borrowed an old one from a friend at work and brought it home one weekend in the summer of 2018 to listen to the tapes. Hearing Daddy's voice for the first time since his death was bittersweet. He had a good voice—deep, calm, confident—and an easy laugh, especially when he was laughing at himself. I smiled and cried as I listened.

Daddy told Elizabeth a story about Eugene Worley, who became Troop 12 Eagle Scout number thirty-eight in 1956. Eugene was a brilliant student, studied engineering, and joined NASA in the space program in Huntsville after graduating from Mississippi State. In the mid-1960s, he came home to Tupelo one weekend to go camping with the troop. While sitting by a campfire with Daddy, he declared that NASA was going to put a man on the moon. Daddy said he was crazy, that nobody was going to the moon. Daddy enjoyed telling stories on himself.

I learned from the tapes about the Model T Daddy bought for twenty-five dollars so he could take flying lessons to prepare for the coming war and about the day A. P. Bennett asked if he would help with Troop 12 for a few months. During the interview, Daddy remarked that his orange tabby cat named Pip had strolled into the room. Pip had belonged to Mike and Janet Armour when they lived across the street. They moved two miles away and took Pip with them, but he liked Daddy and his old neighborhood more than he liked them. He repeatedly disappeared from his new home and showed up on Rogers Drive. Daddy would return him, or Mike and Janet would come get him, but he kept coming back. The Armours finally gave up, and Pip became Daddy's cat.

While he was talking to Elizabeth, Daddy related something odd about Pip that I'd forgotten. The cat refused to drink water from a bowl and demanded running water. When he was thirsty, he would jump onto the kitchen counter, sit by the sink, and wait for Daddy to turn on the faucet. When he had drunk his fill, he would jump down, and Daddy would turn it off.

In Elizabeth's file was a draft of the letter she sent Daddy thanking him for his time and telling him how much the experience meant to her. Elizabeth suffered from juvenile diabetes in her teens, and she also thanked Daddy for making a gift in her honor to the Juvenile Diabetes Research Foundation. Fifteen years later, shortly before I read Elizabeth's letter, her mother Ellen was selected to serve as the chair of the international board of directors of the foundation.

Four months after listening to the tapes, on what would have been Daddy's ninety-seventh birthday, I wrote a Facebook post about him and added a photo in his Navy uniform that was taken three quarters of a century earlier. I ended my message with a question: How many lives did he touch? Some whose lives he touched wrote comments in response. They included:

He touched too many lives to count!

No way to tell but in the many thousands!! He was a quiet, hardworking hero.

He touched my life in many positive ways. After my dad, he was the second most influential man in my life.

He is still touching lives every day. I am a Scoutmaster because of him. He can take credit for another Eagle Scout this week, a young man in our troop.

He was a major influence in my life. My four sons also became Eagle Scouts.

I have been involved with Scouting for the last ten years. My son earned his Eagle this summer. I can still remember listening to Mr. Eason as he helped me during many a campout.

Because of Mr. Eason, I am still involved in Scouting. All that I am is because of him and my father, who was also one of his Eagles.

He was an incredible man and a huge influence in my life. He told me the only way out of Scouts was to attain your Eagle. He expected great things from young men and got great things from them.

Paul was a wonderful man. He was the best Scoutmaster in the world and the finest man I've ever known.

He helped me raise two sons.

The inspiration to do good that Paul Eason instilled in so many will ripple throughout the world forever.

I have a friend in Atlanta who is a lawyer inexplicably named Doc. Doc Schneider is not only a fine lawyer, he's also a gifted songwriter. While Daddy was still alive, I shared with Doc the story of my adoption, the wonderful parents who raised me, and how I learned that Julie Francis was my birth mother. He liked the story and promised to write a song about it. When Daddy died, Doc was one of the friends to whom I sent his obituary and the note about Daddy's last two years living with Carrie and me. He responded immediately.

"In your Dickensian tale, your wonderful tribute to your daddy takes the cake—and well it should. The man had a heart as big as the Milky Way. I love your story and how you found Carrie and how you and Carrie took care of your daddy. And how he lasted as long as he did on this Earth, like a river of love. I have not forgotten your story or your song, and your daddy's goodbye is the light I need to finish it right."

Doc completed his song several months later. He called it "Baby Boy Francis" because that's what I was called in the litigation when the lawyers were trying to find out who and where I was. After

the song was finished, Doc had it professionally recorded. I cried
the first time I heard it.

The song is a tribute to Mama and Daddy for making me their
son and for loving me as if I were their own flesh and blood. But
more than that, it is about my gratitude to Julie for the great gift
she gave me by giving me away. The lyrics include these lines:

Margaret and Paul loved that baby so much,
More than found fortune or fame.
They loved every bit of the way that he was,
And all that they changed was his name.
All that he knew was the grace of this world
That had carried him on his way.
And he wrapped his arms round the heart of his family
That came from the giving away.
Julie, you did not forsake that boy,
Though you never saw it that way.
When you surrendered your Baby Boy Francis,
You gave him the whole world that day.

The Scoutmaster

With the first of his many dogs (top) and with his sisters Myra and
Puddie (bottom).

As a young teenager (top) and as a Naval officer (bottom).

On their wedding day in January 1950 (top) and forty-five years later (bottom).

The top photo, taken in 1950, is eight of Daddy's first Scouts, seven of whom became Eagle Scouts. In the front row are Frank Lyle, Glenn Stevenson, Richard Condrey, O'Neil Tate, and Ed Furr. In the back are Charles Johnston, Rob Leake, and Roger Friou. The bottom photo, taken at the banquet for the 600th consecutive campout in July 2001, is with three of those Scouts, Charles Johnston, Rob Leake, and Richard Condrey.

At Pensacola Naval Air Station in April 1956.

In the center is Ken Kirk, co-captain of the 1959 national championship Ole Miss football team, at Troop 12's annual Father-Son banquet in February 1960. With Ken and Daddy in the photo are fellow Troop 12 alum and Rebel teammate Jimmy Hall and Troop 12 Eagle Scouts Andy Lawhon and Dave Shands. Three months before the banquet, Troop 12 camped for the hundredth month in a row.

Daddy is standing behind his parents on Mother's Day 1964 at the Hotel Tupelo. The older woman to the right is Mama's mother, Ethel Brooks. The photo includes two Troop 12 Eagle Scouts—Eason Leake and Daddy— and three future Troop 12 Eagles—Phil Ruff, David Ruff, and me.

With Mama, Margie, and me in 1958.

With Marshal Adams on a canoe trip in May 1965 (top) and surrounded by Scouts at Camp Yocona six months later (bottom). Kneeling and sitting are Phil Ruff and David Franks. Standing are Stan Byrd, Hank Barger, Rodney Rogers, Jim Beane, Stuart Worley, George Ruff, Steve Mattox, Assistant Scoutmaster James Byrd, Jim Bauman, Dave Langston, Rick McCarty, Will Lott, and Bill Carroll. None of the boys were Eagle Scouts when the photo was taken. Four years later, ten of them were.

Beside a campfire in April 1977 (top) and receiving a plaque commemorating the 400th consecutive monthly campout in November 1984 (bottom).

The 500th consecutive campout at Camp Yocona in March 1993
(top) and alongside the Middle Fork of the Salmon River in Idaho
in July 1994 (bottom).

With granddaughter Ann Lowrey (top)
and with grandson Paul Eason the younger (bottom).

At the Christmas parade in December 2003 (top) and napping in his
camp chair at Davis Lake in 2007 on one of his last campouts (bottom).

Receiving the key to the City of Tupelo from Mayor Jack Reed on his
ninetieth birthday (top) and at his party that afternoon (bottom).

With five Troop 12 Eagle Scouts on his 90th birthday — Lewis Whitfield in one photo (top) and Jim Leake, Scott Reed, Clay Stewart, and Presly Wallace in the other (bottom).

Daddy with Carrie, Mollie, and me on his last Christmas and in a portrait with great-grandchildren Eason, Ada Brooks, and Collins.

"Well done, good and faithful servant."

PART TWO

What They Say About You When You're Not Around

Over the span of more than a year in 2022 and 2023, I interviewed forty-two men and women who knew and loved Daddy. They included men who served as Assistant Scoutmasters in Troop 12, the head Scoutmasters after Daddy stepped down, his friends and neighbors, two of his nephews, two of his grandchildren, and men who became Eagle Scouts under his leadership in the 1940s, '50s, '60s, '70s, '80s, and '90s.

I talked to men who were lawyers and government officials, a Marine colonel and a Navy fighter pilot, a preacher and a math professor, an architect and a nuclear engineer; men who've started and run successful businesses and a woman (my daughter) who started and leads a successful school; a former Scout who is a member of a FEMA team with trained search-and-rescue dogs and another who trained sled dogs that raced in the Iditarod. At the time of the interviews, those I spoke to ranged in age from thirty-two to eighty-eight. They live all over the country, from sea to shining sea.

Yet despite the differences in age, occupation, and location, these men and women have fundamental qualities in common. They are all good people who are devoted to their families. They are all responsible and successful. And, without exception, they are grateful to Daddy for what he did for them and still means to them.

Thirty-five of those I interviewed were former members of Troop 12, nearly all of them Eagle Scouts. All thirty-five attested to the lasting value of their experience as Boy Scouts under Daddy's leadership. Their lives serve as compelling evidence that Scouting

builds character and creates respected leaders and responsible citizens. The Boy Scouts of America has had hard times of late, but
the fine men who spoke to me about Daddy are a useful reminder
that Scouting is an invaluable institution and a powerful force for
good in the country.

Patterson Hood of the Drive By Truckers wrote a song with
an odd title, "Dead Drunk and Naked." His lyrics include a pearl
of wisdom:

"Daddy used to tell me, everything comes down
To what they say about you when you're not around."

If the daddy in the song was right—if the best measure of a
man is what people say about him when he's not around—then
my daddy is in rare company indeed. Read on and you will see.

RICHARD CONDREY, CHARLES JOHNSTON, AND GREG JOHNSTON

My first interview was with Richard Condrey and Charles and
Greg Johnston. Richard and Charles have been close friends for
nearly eighty years. They were two of Daddy's first Eagle Scouts.
Richard became an Eagle in 1949, Charles two years later. They
were in the same class, but Charles started out in a troop that fizzled
and disbanded. After his first troop failed and he joined Troop 12,
he was behind Richard and his other classmates in rank, but he
didn't give up. Like Daddy, he became an Eagle Scout the year he
graduated from high school.

Charles and his wife Joyce's only son Greg was two classes behind
me and earned his Eagle in late 1973. His sister Lynn, a member
of my class and a dear friend, was killed by a drunk driver on
Christmas Eve in 1999. At the man's trial, he mouthed the words
"I'm sorry," and Charles and Joyce forgave him. In the years that
followed, they helped Lynn's husband raise his three young sons
who had lost their mother.

Charles and Joyce have lived in the same house in Tupelo since
1966, the year Lynn and I started the fourth grade at Joyner Elementary School. When Carrie and I walked into the Johnstons'
home for the interview, it had been forty-five years since I was

there. Richard lives in Birmingham, Greg in Austin. Charles and Joyce escorted us to the living room, where Richard and Greg were on the phone waiting to talk about Daddy.

That Richard and Charles were two of Daddy's first Eagle Scouts is not all they have in common. They both graduated from Tupelo High School in June 1951, two months before Troop 12 began its consecutive monthly campout streak. They both went to Vanderbilt, and both studied Mechanical Engineering. Both joined ROTC and later served in the armed forces, Charles in the Army, Richard in the Marines. They both graduated in 1955 and married their college sweethearts that year. At the time of our interview, both were eighty-eight years old and had been married for sixty-six years.

But despite all they have in common, Charles and Richard are very different. Like Daddy, Charles is soft-spoken and understated. Richard is neither. In the military, Charles would be in charge of developing a meticulous battle plan and considering every contingency. Richard, who retired from the Marines as a full-bird colonel after thirty years, would lead the cavalry charge. On the day of our interview, when one of us said something Richard approved of, he punctuated it with an amen. His first amen was when I said Daddy was still camping with Troop 12 after his eighty-sixth birthday.

Richard was already a member of the troop when Daddy became the Scoutmaster in early 1947. He said that's when the troop really took off. One of Troop 12's first campouts that spring was to Camp Yocona, which was still under construction and preparing to open for summer camp that year. The land for the camp had been purchased more than a decade earlier for a dollar an acre.

The boys went fishing in the camp's new lake, and one of them hooked Richard in the chest while casting sidearm. The incident occurred seventy-five years earlier, but Richard recalled the name of the lure. It was a Lucky 13. Daddy followed standard protocol and tried to push the hook the rest of the way through, but he succeeded only in getting it stuck in one of Richard's ribs. Daddy loaded up the boys and drove the fifteen miles to Pontotoc, where Richard and the lure were separated from each other in the emergency room. They returned to Yocona, but after they broke camp the next day, Daddy's car got stuck, and they had to rig a makeshift Spanish winch to pull it out. It was not an auspicious beginning for Daddy's tenure as the Scoutmaster of Troop 12.

Richard became an Eagle Scout and was elected to serve as the troop's senior patrol leader in 1949. Daddy proposed to Mama later that year, and she accepted. When Richard heard the news, he took it upon himself to speak to Mama on behalf of the boys in the troop and scheduled a meeting at her apartment in Tambour Court on Church Street. Daddy was not invited.

Richard's mission was to explain to Mama how things were going to be and secure her assent. He told her Daddy was already married to the Scouts, and she needed to understand that he would be meeting with them every Monday night and camping with them nearly every month. She and Daddy had no doubt already discussed his commitment to the Scouts, and she agreed to Richard's terms. Mama kept her side of the bargain, though she never could have dreamed that the meetings and campouts would last for the rest of her life.

Charles recalled that the boys in the troop asked Daddy how he decided which of the Brooks twins to marry. At the time, manufacturers of soft drinks—Coke, Pepsi, and others—often touted the results of comparative taste tests to market their products. Daddy laughed and said he'd kissed both twins and picked Mama based on the taste test.

Five months after Daddy and Mama married in January 1950, Daddy, Richard, and Charles went camping, though they didn't all go together. Charles returned to summer camp at Yocona to earn the remaining merit badges he needed to become an Eagle Scout. He failed Rowing merit badge because he couldn't row in a straight line, but he passed enough other ones to earn his Eagle the following year. Richard had already earned his Eagle and skipped Yocona in favor of taking the train with Daddy to the national jamboree in Valley Forge.

Daddy was still flying then and rented a Piper Cub during the jamboree to take Richard and another boy up on the first flight for both of them. They had an aerial view of the site where nearly

50,000 Scouts were camping and where George Washington crossed the Delaware to launch his surprise attack on Christmas night in 1776. Richard said the flight was marvelous and the campground the biggest thing he'd ever seen. Daddy later took Charles and fellow Troop 12 Eagle Scout Rob Leake on a flying tour of the Tupelo area. Charles said it was a highlight of his time in the troop.

Charles, Richard, and Greg all credit Daddy for their commitment to serve others, and all three have done so throughout their adult lives. After moving to Birmingham, Richard started Boy Scout Troop 320 from scratch in the 1960s and became its first Scoutmaster. He did everything Daddy did, camping every month and even going to a national jamboree, though he didn't rent a plane. He served as the new troop's Scoutmaster until his sons became Eagle Scouts. I told him Daddy talked about stepping down as the Scoutmaster of Troop 12 when I earned my Eagle in 1972, but for some reason he changed his mind. Whatever the reason, he continued to serve the boys in the troop for another thirty-five years. That prompted another amen.

After the interview, I googled Troop 320 to see how it was doing. When I saw that it was still going strong and had produced more than 300 Eagle Scouts since Richard founded it, I said amen too. Troop 320 is one of many examples of how the ripples from Daddy's life continue to spread.

Charles served as the president of the Tupelo Kiwanis Club and the Community Development Foundation and contributed his time to many other civic organizations, including the Tupelo Concert Association, Tupelo Symphony Orchestra, Helping Hands, and the Family Resource Center. He was the Finance Chairman of the First Methodist Church for many years and chaired the church's administrative board. In 2007, three decades after Daddy received the annual award honoring Tupelo's outstanding citizen, Charles and Joyce shared the award. They were recognized for "doing the right things for the right reasons with a natural gift for helping others in need" and received a standing ovation.

When I asked Charles about his volunteer work, he said very little and changed the subject. Daddy would have done the same thing. But a week after the interview, Greg sent me a newspaper article about his parents, the outstanding citizen award, and the details of his father's community service. Greg and I were raised at the same time in the same way and learned the same rules about bragging. Bragging on yourself is impermissible, but bragging on others, including your parents, is not.

Greg said little during the first hour of our talk, deferring to his dad and the man he refers to as Uncle Richard. When it was Greg's turn, he said he moved to Austin in 1984 and joined the Young Men's Business League. Inspired by the love for camping he learned in Troop 12, he and other young men in the league established two summer camps for underprivileged children, one in Zilker Park near downtown Austin, the other at Lake Travis. The camps, like Troop 320, are still going strong. More recently, Greg applied to become a volunteer fireman. He had no relevant experience, but the head of the department saw from his application that he was an Eagle Scout and accepted him on the spot.

Greg has also served on the Board of Directors of the Capital Area Council of the Boy Scouts for many years. After Hurricane Katrina, he was asked to start and chair the council's Disaster Preparedness Committee, only the second of its kind in the country. The committee's mission is to take being prepared to the next level. Greg said he learned the importance of being prepared during his years in Troop 12, often by being unprepared. He told me he learned more in his four years in the troop than in his four years of college.

When I asked what Daddy meant to the three of them, Richard said, "In all my years, including the thirty I spent in the Marines, my grandest experience was with Paul Eason in Troop 12. It was the finest time of my life." Charles felt the same way and was glad I was writing about Daddy. He said, "The story of his life should be documented and shared far and wide."

Richard said Daddy never acted like a drill sergeant or a commanding officer. He led the troop as a gentleman. Greg agreed and said Daddy was calm and quiet but gave great advice. He always trusted the boys to do what was right and help everyone

who needed it. Greg never wanted to disappoint him. He said his
father was the most important man in his life, but mine was second.

That prompted another amen from Richard, who said the three
outstanding events in his eighty-eight years were having Daddy
as his Scoutmaster in the 1940s, marrying his wife Jean in 1955,
and coming to know Jesus Christ in 1981. When I pointed out
that Daddy had him first and prepared him for Jean and Jesus,
Richard said amen again.

Richard and his son Mike went with Daddy, Ann Lowrey, and
me on the wonderful raft trip on the Middle Fork of the Salmon
in 1994. Mike and I are the same age, and we had a grand time
together in Idaho. I'm reluctant to ask about people I haven't seen
or heard from in decades, but near the end of our talk I took
a chance and asked about Mike. I was glad I did. Richard said
Mike was currently on a round-the-world sailing trip and had just
passed through the Panama Canal. The grand journey was scheduled to last eighteen months. Along the way, if all went according
to plan, Mike's wife was planning to meet him in South Africa
for Christmas.

The number of people who knew Daddy and benefited from
his lifetime of service is enormous, certainly in the thousands. But
the lives Daddy touched are not limited to those who had the
good fortune to know him. The good he did benefited thousands
more who never met him and never knew his name. They include
those who've become Eagle Scouts in Troop 320 in Birmingham,
who've attended Young Men's Business League camps in Austin,
and who've benefited from the many civic organizations in Tupelo
that Charles Johnston has served. Richard, Charles, and Greg have
given of their time to others because they were inspired by Daddy
and the gift of his time to them.

Daddy not only inspired others to serve, but he also instilled in
them a love for adventure and the outdoors. Many of his Scouts,
including me, have gone on far grander adventures than Daddy
ever did. Several years ago, I was flipping through a book and
came across a familiar name, Stuart Worley, the youngest of three
brothers who were all Eagle Scouts in Troop 12. Eugene, the NASA

engineer, is the oldest of the three. The book was about hiking trips taken by Stuart and the author, including one to Patagonia on the southern tip of South America.

Stuart Worley's hiking trip to Patagonia made me wonder about Mike Condrey's sailing trip around the world. Mike's father was inspired to start Troop 320 because of his experience with Daddy in Troop 12. But was Mike's love for adventure sparked by his experience in Troop 320? Can his decision to sail around the world be traced to another decision that was made seventy-five years earlier? To Daddy's decision to become the Scoutmaster of Troop 12? I don't know, but I like to think so.

WILL AND JIM MURPHREE

I interviewed Will and Jim Murphree at Will's home in Tupelo. All three of us attended the 500th campout, but they didn't remember me, and I didn't remember them. But Jim knew not to take me too seriously. His mother had given him *Bedtime with Buster* for Christmas, and he and his son Boone were reading it aloud to each other, with Jim playing me and Boone playing Buster. I arranged the interview through the Murphrees' dad, Bill, who was also one of Daddy's Scouts. I wanted to talk to Bill too, but he was in California.

Will and Jim became Eagle Scouts in Troop 12 in the early 1990s. As they reminisced and talked about their time in the troop, I was struck by how little Daddy changed over the years. More than four decades passed from the time Richard Condrey and Charles Johnston were members of Troop 12 until Will and Jim were, but Jim described Daddy using almost exactly the same words Richard used. Jim said Daddy was even-keeled and constant. He was always a gentleman, which made Jim want to be a gentleman too. Daddy wasn't heavy-handed. He let the boys police themselves and intervened only when necessary. He didn't ask you to do anything he didn't do himself. Because of how much the Scouts respected him, it was impossible to tell him no. The Murphrees thought of Daddy the way they thought of their grandfather—Daddy turned seventy when they were in the troop—and they didn't want to disappoint him.

Jim was the last senior patrol leader elected before Daddy stepped down as Scoutmaster. He was in the position at the time of the 500th campout in March 1993. After he was elected, he wasn't sure he was up to the task and shared his reservations with Daddy. If he couldn't do it, Daddy said, the other Scouts wouldn't have voted for him. Jim couldn't argue with that. He said his year as senior patrol leader was special because he was able to spend extra time with Daddy planning campouts and meetings.

Will remembered Daddy's lessons in knot tying and a story Daddy told to illustrate the importance of the bowline knot. I said I bet I knew the story but asked Will to tell it anyway. Daddy said some airmen were holding ropes to keep a blimp from taking flight, the wind picked up, and the blimp lifted the men off the ground. As it rose higher, some of the men lost their grip and fell to their deaths. But two had been Boy Scouts, and they held on to the rope with one hand and used the other to tie a bowline. They sat in the loops they created until the blimp came down again. Daddy had told the same story to me twenty years before he told it to Will and fifty years before Will repeated it to me. It made an impression on both of us.

Both Murphrees spoke fondly of riding to campouts in the White Elephant. Daddy also drove the Elephant to Monday night meetings, picking up boys along the way and dropping them off on the way home. The van had no air-conditioning. For circulation, the front and back doors were left open, and a grill was used to block the opening in back. The gas gauge didn't work, so Daddy stuck an oil dipstick into the gas tank to check the level. Daddy let Scouts take turns shifting gears with the long stick shift that rose from the floor between the two front seats. Somehow the Elephant never ran out of gas, the gears never got stripped, and no boys fell out.

Daddy became disenchanted at times with the teenage counselors at summer camp at Yocona. Some Scouts came home with merit badges only half complete, others with tasks signed off they hadn't performed. When Daddy was unable to get the council solve the problem, he decided that Troop 12 would hold its own summer camp.

For a handful of summers, the troop spent a week camping at J. P. Coleman State Park on Pickwick Lake in the northeast corner of Mississippi. There was no kitchen or dining hall and no paid staff, but Daddy and the others made it work. He recruited assistant leaders, dads, and recent Eagle Scouts to teach merit badges and other skills. Scouts took turns cooking and cleaning up. Will and Jim said they had a great time during the weeks they spent at J. P. Coleman. Daddy had been the Scoutmaster for more than forty years when he undertook the task of planning and running a separate summer camp for Troop 12. He was just as committed to the job as when he started.

Long after Will's years in the troop, he was on his way to go fishing one day and came upon Daddy mowing the steep slope along the road that led down the hill to his neighborhood. Will stopped and asked Daddy why he was doing it. It wasn't his property or his responsibility. Daddy said he figured the city crews must be busy, the grass was high, so he was mowing it himself. Daddy was in his mid-eighties at the time.

Jim said Daddy served others not because he wanted a pat on the back but because it was the right thing to do. He didn't want recognition; he wanted to help. I asked Jim if he'd been inspired by Daddy to serve others. He said he led a group of boys in his church from the seventh grade through the twelfth, but after six years he was tired and needed a break. I wonder how many times Daddy was tired and needed a break during the sixty years before he took one.

Because their dad was an Eagle Scout, I asked Will and Jim if he'd pushed them to become Eagles. Like many boys before and since, including my grandsons, they'd been offered the carrot of a driver's license. It was a simple proposition: no Eagle, no license. But Will said he didn't need the extra incentive. He'd decided he would be an Eagle Scout when he was only five or six, and he remembered exactly when. He was in the sanctuary of the First Methodist Church when a young man in Troop 12 was awarded his Eagle. As part of the ceremony, all the Eagle Scouts in the congregation were asked to stand. Will remembered looking up at his father and all the other men and vowing that someday he would stand up with them.

Will's story made me think of Daddy's funeral, when Lewis Whitfield asked all the Eagle Scouts in the congregation to stand and be recognized. There were old men and young, some separated in age by more than half a century, all there to honor their Scoutmaster.

SAM AGNEW AND TY ROBINSON

Sam Agnew and his identical twin Walker are a year older than I am and became Eagle Scouts in Troop 12 on the same day in 1971. Fourteen years and nearly eighty Eagle Scouts later, Ty Robinson earned his Eagle in the troop. Sam and Ty said there was no way they could repay Daddy for everything he did for them. Instead, they have paid it forward by giving of their time to the boys in the troop just as Daddy gave of his time to them. They finished college more than a decade apart, but both became Assistant Scoutmasters in Troop 12 when they returned to Tupelo. In 1992, when Daddy stepped down as Scoutmaster, Sam was chosen to succeed him. I asked Sam if following in Daddy's footsteps was wise. He said it was like succeeding Bear Bryant as Alabama's football coach, but he did it anyway. Sam's thirteen years as Troop 12's Scoutmaster are second only to Daddy's forty-five. In 2005, when Sam decided it was time for someone new to take the reins, Ty volunteered.

During all of Sam's tenure as Scoutmaster and part of Ty's, Daddy served as an assistant. Sam and Ty thus spent time in the troop with Daddy in three different roles. Daddy was the Scoutmaster when they were Scouts, they served as assistants when he was still in charge, and they had the benefit of his help and advice when they were in charge. When I met with them in Tupelo, they had a lot to say. I asked very few questions, but the interview lasted for two and a half hours.

Not surprisingly, Sam and Ty believe very strongly in the Boy

Scouts' mission to turn immature young boys into responsible young men and upstanding citizens. Both recalled mothers thanking them for what Troop 12 did for their sons. The mothers saw the difference even if their sons didn't.

Ty described Scouting as the minor leagues of life, a time when a boy finds interests and learns skills he will carry with him for the rest of his life. Sam said he had no athletic ability, but joining Troop 12 and putting in the work to become an Eagle Scout gave him an opportunity to excel. He also said that making mistakes is essential to growth, and a Scout troop is a safe place to make them.

Sam's mention of safety led to a discussion of Troop 12's extraordinary safety record. In the troop's long history, there have been many scrapes and bruises, at least one broken bone, and an occasional cut that required stitches such as the one I suffered running in shallow water on Pensacola Beach. But to the best of Sam and Ty's knowledge, no member of the troop has ever been hospitalized because of an injury suffered on a campout. Using a conservative estimate of twenty-five boys per campout and twenty nights of camping a year, the total number of boy-nights spent in the woods since Troop 12's monthly streak began exceeds 35,000. The safety record is in part the result of learning first aid, being prepared, and relying on the buddy system, in which each Scout is responsible for the safety of another, but it is also the product of pure, dumb luck.

Since Sam became a Scout in 1967, either he or Ty or both have gone on hundreds of the troop's campouts. Sam was also on the ill-fated canoe trip on Bear Creek that we had to abort because of high water. Assistant Paul Fairley was assigned to be in the lead canoe, Daddy and assistant Jim High would bring up the rear, and all the Scouts were to stay in the middle. Some of the boys capsized not long after we started. In the back of the pack, unbeknownst to the rest of us, so did Daddy and Jim. As Paul Fairley was struggling to empty the water from a canoe that had turned over, Sam said he saw Daddy's cap floating down the river. I asked Sam if he checked to see if Daddy's head was still under it.

Sam recalled another Bear Creek trip years later that he and I both attended. I was practicing law in Jackson and had three young children, but I managed to get away for a long weekend to go canoeing with Daddy and the troop. On the drive back to Tupelo on Sunday in the White Elephant, Sam recalled that I asked Daddy how he got away with it. When Margie and I were little, how did he manage to go camping every month? Sam said Daddy just shrugged.

Sam and Ty were both at the 500th campout at Camp Yocona in March 1993. When Reed Hillen presented the Queen Mother award to Mama and thanked her for staying at home all those weekends so Daddy could go camping, Ty recalled her response. Mama declared that she never said she stayed at home.

Surprisingly for someone who later became a Scoutmaster, Ty didn't like camping when he was in the troop. Camping was the last merit badge he earned to become an Eagle, and Daddy scheduled a special campout so he could get it. But Ty had fond memories too. One summer at Camp Yocona, the kitchen staff had the night off, and Daddy loaded up the boys in the back of the Elephant, drove into Pontotoc, and bought them all ice cream cones. Daddy no doubt bought one for himself too. Sam noted that Daddy was an expert at cooking on a campfire. He taught the boys but was far more efficient than they were. He often cooked, ate, cleaned up, and put away his mess kit before they took their first bite.

Ty told a story from summer camp at Yocona when he was the Scoutmaster. One of future Congressman Alan Nunnelee's sons was in the troop, and at the end of the week he brought home a bag full of filthy clothes. Like most Scouts, he ignored the directive in the Scout Law to be clean, and his mother had to run the washer three times before the water ran clear. When she was finally satisfied and pulled them out, she let out a blood-curdling scream. She had washed both the clothes and a snake. The snake was dead but clean as a whistle.

Ty grew to love camping as a leader and said he and Daddy had great times together, though not all campouts went according to plan. At Space Camp in Huntsville, Daddy suggested the two of them pitch their tents away from the boys so they would get a good night's sleep. A hard rain came in the night, Daddy heard a noise, and Ty put on his rain gear and went to investigate. He pulled back the flap on one of the boys' tents. It was empty. He checked the others. They were empty too. When he returned to tell Daddy, a security officer appeared, instructed Ty to identify himself, then ordered both of them to come with him. They walked to his van, which was filled with scared Scouts. A tornado had been spotted. The officer took them to a building and made them sleep inside.

I knew Sam's family had given the White Elephant to the troop when I was a Scout, but I didn't know its history. Sam said the Elephant was a 1956 Chevrolet Step-Van that began its long life as a bread delivery truck. Someone later turned it into a makeshift motor home to use at hunting camp, adding bunks, a stove, and an exhaust pipe. Sam's grandfather Walker Spicer then bought it for Sam's mother to use at Pickwick Lake. She loved having a motor home but soon decided she wanted a real one. The Agnews bought a new one and gave their old one to Troop 12. Daddy removed the bunks and stove, and the Elephant became the troop's all-purpose vehicle. For the next quarter century, every member of Troop 12 went on camping trips in the White Elephant, some to destinations as far away as Philmont Scout Ranch in the Sangre de Cristo Mountains in northern New Mexico. The Elephant finally gave up the ghost in the mid-nineties when replacement parts for ones that broke could no longer be found.

When I asked Sam and Ty about Daddy's leadership qualities, they emphasized that he was patient and almost never got upset, though Ty remembered one occasion when Daddy's effort to get the boys' attention was interrupted by a bird that flew over and pooped on his uniform. The Scouts thought it was hilarious; Daddy did not. To Daddy, Sam said there was no requirement that couldn't be met and no obstacle that couldn't be overcome. It just took will and work.

Daddy kept meticulous records of the troop's activities. He recorded the weather and made a list of all the boys and leaders who attended every campout. He was also very pragmatic. The year he turned seventy, when he struggled to complete the hike across the Grand Canyon, Daddy decided it was time to consider stepping down as Scoutmaster. More than fifteen years later, when he was in his late eighties, one of his neighbors told Ty that Daddy's minivan had not been seen at his house for several days. When Ty called to check on him, Daddy explained matter-of-factly that he had decided it was time to stop driving and had given the van to one of his grandsons.

When Ty became the Scoutmaster, he was in his thirties and Daddy was in his eighties. He spoke fondly of Daddy's transition from being the mentor he called Mr. Eason to the friend he called Paul. He said Daddy offered him many opportunities, he always took them, and it was always the right decision.

Ty recalled the first offer. He had come home from college and was moving into an apartment behind the Methodist Church. As was often the case, Daddy was at the Scout Hut working. The battery in Ty's car died, Daddy produced a set of jumper cables, and they were able to start the car. He then asked if Ty would agree to teach Citizenship in the Community merit badge on Monday nights. The car was running; what could he say?

Both Sam and Ty stepped down as Scoutmaster more than a decade ago, but they are still active in Scouting. Ty currently serves as Committee Chairman for Troop 85, another troop that needs help, and is Advancement Chairman and Commissioner for the Yocona Area Council, which recently merged with another council to form the Natchez Trace Council. Ty has also been the Order of the Arrow Promotions Advisor, and he serves on a marketing subcommittee of the Boy Scouts of America's National Commissioner Service Team. He has been recognized for his many years of service both here and in the United Kingdom, and this year's class of Yocona Area Council Eagle Scouts was named in his honor. The 1986 class, the first to honor anyone, was named for Daddy.

Sam did not have a son during his years as the Scoutmaster. Once a new Scout's mother called Sam's wife to find out what their son was taking on a campout. When she responded that they didn't have a son, the woman was speechless. But to his surprise and joy, Sam had a son late in life. Andrew Agnew is younger than both of my grandsons and is now a member of Troop 12. Sam served as

Den Leader and Cubmaster when Andrew was a Cub Scout, and he returned to camping after a hiatus of fifteen years when Andrew joined the troop. Sam was helping plan an upcoming trip to the Mississippi Gulf Coast on the day we met and looking forward to the day his son becomes an Eagle Scout. It has been more than half a century since Sam did. Almost a year after our interview, I learned that Sam had agreed to serve a second stint as the Scoutmaster.

Near the end of our talk, Ty told me Daddy had a nickname I'd never heard. Adrian Thompson was Daddy's friend and contemporary, a longtime member of the First Methodist Church, and president of the Chapman Men's Bible Class, which sponsored Troop 12 for ninety-five years. When Adrian would ask Ty how Daddy was doing, he didn't call him Paul. He asked instead, "How's the Apostle?"

BUDDY MCCARTY, ROBIN FAUCETTE, AND BRITT ROGERS

Buddy McCarty, Robin Faucette, and Britt Rogers are all the same age, all became Eagle Scouts in Troop 12 more than sixty years ago, and all have sons who are Eagle Scouts. As I wrote at the outset, Buddy was awarded his Eagle badge in September 1957, four days after Mama and Daddy took custody of me from the maternity home in New Orleans. Britt also became an Eagle in 1957 and was my leader a decade later when I was in Webelos, the Scouting organization that bridges the gap between Cub Scouts and Boy Scouts. I remember playing hide and seek among the azaleas in Britt's yard. Robin did not join the troop until he was thirteen and earned his Eagle in 1960. Carrie and I met with Buddy and Britt over lunch in Buddy's office in Tupelo. Robin was at home recovering from COVID and joined us by phone.

When Robin was in the troop, his family lived on Rogers Drive across the street from our house. He usually rode with Daddy to the Monday night meetings and always rode home with him. They often talked for a few minutes in the Faucettes' driveway before parting ways, and Daddy would ask him how the troop could be improved. Robin said being asked his opinion by an adult who really wanted to know made a great impression on him. He also had a clear memory of something else Daddy said. Daddy's habit was to address the boys in the troop by their last names, a practice he must have picked up in the fraternity or the Navy or both. "Faucette," he said, "there is going to come a time when you have to give back."

Robin said he's tried in the decades since then to heed Daddy's advice. When Robin's sons were young, he became a Cub Scout Den Leader and Packmaster, and he later served as an Assistant Scoutmaster, though not in Troop 12. Because he's a Presbyterian, Robin became an assistant in Troop 3, which the First Presbyterian Church sponsored. He worked with Miles Garber, the fine gentleman who led that troop for many years.

Because of Robin's devotion to Scouting as an adult, he was chosen to become a member of the Order of the Arrow when he was fifty. To be inducted, all the candidates, including current Scouts and Robin, had to spend a night alone in the woods with neither a tent nor a sleeping bag. Robin said he was too old to do it, but he did it. He still serves on the board of review that evaluates Scouts who have completed the requirements and are eligible to become Eagle Scouts. He makes a point to tell them the same thing Daddy told him in the 1950s: "There will come a time when you have to give back."

Robin began taking mission trips years ago with a group from the Presbyterian church, first to Mexico, then to Guatemala and Cuba. On the group's early trips, the mission was to build homes, but then they became more ambitious. For more than two decades, they have built and installed water systems for churches. To help him communicate with the locals, Robin hired a tutor to teach him Spanish. He's far from fluent, he said, but he gets by.

Though they all became Eagle Scouts more than six decades earlier, the three friends had clear memories of Daddy and their time in Troop 12. Their fondest memories were of campouts. Britt remembered hiking north on Madison Street with Daddy in the lead, heading to the campout at Livingston Lake. When the troop camped at Ruff's Farm one January, Britt tiptoed out onto the frozen surface of the pond. They also recalled campouts at Tishomingo State Park and on the lawn of the First Methodist Church. Britt said Scouting was so popular then that no little league baseball games were scheduled when Troop 12 and the other Tupelo troops were at summer camp at Yocona.

Buddy and Robin took two special trips together when they were in the troop, attending the national jamboree in 1957, which was again at Valley Forge, and backpacking in the mountains at Philmont Scout Ranch. For the trip to Philmont, they ordered bamboo-frame packs inspired by Daddy's tubular-frame military pack. Buddy said Daddy always had the coolest gear and his outdoor skills were unsurpassed, especially cooking. He was deliberate, methodical, and made it look easy. He was always prepared, and the boys learned to be prepared by watching him.

The men talked about lessons in leadership and responsibility they learned in Troop 12. Daddy didn't run everything or do all the teaching. The senior patrol leader led the meetings, and patrol leaders and older Scouts taught younger ones how to tie knots, build a fire, and repeat the Scout law. The boys learned to be teachers. Helping others became a habit.

The Scouts were required to bring their Boy Scout Handbooks to every meeting. If a Scout finished a requirement for advancement but didn't bring his handbook so it could be signed off, he had to repeat the task at the next meeting. Buddy said Daddy wasn't harsh and didn't demand perfection, but the boys had to meet the letter and spirit of all the requirements. Daddy had the patience of Job and remained calm even when things didn't go well. He never acted angry, but you could tell when he was disappointed. And when he asked you to do something, you did it. He was always present, always watching, helping, and encouraging.

Buddy said Daddy was perhaps the best teacher he ever had. He didn't realize until years later all he had learned from his years in Troop 12. One trait that stood out was Daddy's humility. Despite his exceptional talents and many honors and achievements, he never talked about himself. Buddy said Daddy was interested in you. He wanted to talk about you, not about him.

The men remembered only twice when Daddy put his foot down

and gave orders. The first was when they established a secret society in the troop called Brethren of the Fox. When Daddy found out, he declared that there would be no secret societies. The Brethren disbanded. The second was when the Scouts planning to attend the 1957 jamboree wanted to sew Confederate flags onto the sleeves of their uniforms. Daddy said there would be no Rebel flags, and there weren't.

Robin brought up two of their fellow Troop 12 Eagles, Dave Shands and Andy Lawhon, who both suffered from dementia before their deaths in recent years. Even when Dave and Andy could remember little, Robin said they remembered Daddy and Troop 12. They said it was the best time of their lives, and Robin agreed it was the best time of his. He said he had a wonderful time in the troop, learned important values, and made lifelong friends. Andy once told him, "There will never be another man like Paul Eason." Robin agreed with that too. He said Daddy was a great man and left a great legacy, that following in his footsteps would be like following in Bear Bryant's. I said Daddy had now been likened to Bear Bryant in two interviews in a row.

Buddy is retired from a successful career as the head of an architectural firm with offices in Tupelo and Nashville. When I asked what he learned from Daddy that he used in managing the firm, he said he learned the importance of being a good listener. Daddy asked the boys their views about all sorts of things—what to do on campouts, where to pitch tents, what to cook, and how to cook it. Not only did he listen, but he often changed his mind. Buddy said he learned two benefits of listening from Daddy: that better solutions come from collaborating than from dictating and that members of an organization are more committed and productive if they have a say.

Buddy said he also learned the importance of being accurate, doing things the right way, and not cutting corners. He believes his firm was successful because he and his colleagues lived those principles. He said he also benefited from Daddy long before then, when the lessons he learned in Troop 12 gave him the confidence he needed during the year he fought in Vietnam.

I asked Buddy about the summer of 1957, when Daddy trained

him until he could run three-quarters of a mile in less than six minutes. Buddy said he didn't ask for help; Daddy offered it. He would
stop by the McCartys' home on Clayton Avenue every day after
work, pick Buddy up, and take him to Robins Field, where he would
run a mile or two. Sometimes Daddy ran with him; sometimes he
stood on the track and timed him. They talked about how much
faster Buddy needed to run, and Daddy told him he was going to
succeed. Buddy couldn't believe Daddy was interested enough in
him to spend his free time after work every day for weeks helping
one boy earn one merit badge. He said his own father never would
have done it. But Daddy cared. He didn't say he cared, but Buddy
knew he did. And because he cared, Buddy wanted to succeed.
And one day he did.

Nearly a decade after Daddy's death, he was still influencing Buddy.
When I told him I planned to use the story of the training at Robins
Field in the prologue of the book, he decided he needed to verify
that he had the details right. It was sixty-five years ago; he wanted
to be sure. He learned the importance of being sure from Daddy.

Buddy began doubting his memory when he found his son's Boy
Scout Handbook and saw there was no timed-run requirement for
Personal Fitness merit badge. He kept looking, found a 1957 handbook for sale on eBay, and ordered it. The day it arrived, he sent me
a photo of the page containing the timed-run requirement along
with a note that said: "At long last, the Handbook for Boys, 1957
Edition, arrived and confirmed my memory! I had to run 3/4 mile
in under 6 minutes! Thanks to Paul, I trained until I could do it!"

At the end of our time together, Buddy told me Daddy was
like a second father to him and like a first one to the Scouts who
came from broken homes. He then said something I wrote down
verbatim: "We were fortunate to have an American hero like Paul
Eason to guide us during that all-important time when we were
boys learning to be men. I would have done anything for him."

Rob and Lindsey Leake

Buddy McCarty and Rob Leake were both among Daddy's first

Eagle Scouts, but they have something else to be proud of in common. Buddy has two sons and a grandson who are Troop 12 Eagle Scouts. Rob does as well. Buddy and Rob are the only two Troop 12 Eagles whose sons and grandsons are also Troop 12 Eagles.

Buddy's sons Pearce and Richmond became Eagle Scouts in 1985 and 1990; Richmond Jr. received his Eagle in 2020. Rob was in the troop when Daddy became the Scoutmaster, and he earned his Eagle in 1949. A photo of him and five other Scouts who received their Eagles at the same time appeared on the front page of the *Tupelo Daily Journal*. Rob's sons Clark and Lindsey earned their Eagles in 1983 and 1984; Lindsey's son Bob became an Eagle in 2017. The two grandfathers became Eagle Scouts more than six decades before their grandsons did. In the intervening years, more than 400 boys attained the rank of Eagle in the troop.

Rob has lived in Tupelo all of his nearly ninety years. He was born in the old hospital on Main Street three years before the terrible 1936 tornado and grew up on Highland Circle. He knew Daddy long before he joined Troop 12 and thought of him as a father figure, though they were only a dozen years apart in age.

Rob described Daddy as a great Scoutmaster in a quiet way. Rob remembered few details from his time in the troop three-quarters of a century earlier but recalled going to Camp Yocona in early 1947 when Richard Condrey was impaled by a Lucky 13 lure. He also spoke about hiking from downtown Tupelo to camp on Holcomb's Hill, where the new hospital was later built.

Rob worked alongside Daddy for many years on the all-volunteer Tupelo Parks and Recreation Commission. They took turns as chairman, Daddy serving eight years and Rob fourteen. They were both on the commission when the city's parks and swimming pools were desegregated. With assistance from excellent black leaders and support from the board of aldermen, Rob said they were able to complete the task quietly and without fanfare. An article about Daddy years later said he was proud that Tupelo, unlike many other cities in the South, desegregated all of its pools and parks without closing any of them. Daddy never said he was proud of himself, but he took great pride in his hometown.

Lindsey brought notes to our meeting about what he wanted to share and started by saying he got off to a rocky start in Troop 12. On one of his first campouts, to the Current River in Missouri, his brother Clark pitched their tent on a slope. It rained, the runoff soaked their sleeping bags, and they suffered through a cold, miserable night. By the next morning, Lindsey had decided to quit the troop. But Daddy encouraged him to stick it out, and Rob offered a bribe: fifty dollars if he became an Eagle Scout. Lindsey remained in the troop and earned his Eagle, though he said his dad never paid him the fifty bucks. I said it wasn't too late, and he could tack on nearly forty years of interest.

Troop 12 had more than a hundred members during Lindsey's years as a member. It was too many, but Daddy never turned a boy away. He typed a roster, gave a copy to each Scout, and learned all the boys' names. He also did a masterful job of organizing the troop and its meetings and campouts. Though the troop was enormous and the boys hard to control, everything ran on time. Daddy had excellent, devoted assistants, though some of them got rattled and yelled at the boys at times. But not Daddy; he always kept his cool.

Lindsey spoke of some of the lessons he learned during his years as a Scout. When the boys traveled to and from campouts, they were required to wear uniforms. The practice taught them the importance of pride and professionalism, and they were more likely to conduct themselves appropriately. The troop and each patrol had quartermasters responsible for keeping up with all the gear the troop took on campouts, cleaning it, and returning it to the Scout Hut. From this, the boys learned the importance of taking care of property entrusted to them. On a canoe trip, the troop found an abandoned canoe in the river. It would have been an easy matter to load it onto the trailer, bring it back to Tupelo, and keep it, but Daddy and the other leaders found a local deputy and asked him to try to find the rightful owner. From this example and many others, the boys learned to do the right thing.

Lindsey had wonderful parents and learned many of the same lessons at home, but not all the boys were as fortunate. When the troop returned from a campout and parents were waiting in the church parking lot to pick them up, the Scouts were required to unload every piece of equipment and return it to its appointed place in the Scout Hut before they could leave. This taught them that a job is never over until it's over. But some parents were impatient and left with their sons before the job was finished. They didn't set a good example, but Daddy and his assistants did.

Lindsey said Daddy always made sure there was time for fun, both before meetings and on campouts. Lindsey realized later that if Scouting had been all work and no play, boys would have quit the troop and missed out on the enormous benefits of being a Boy Scout.

Lindsey recalled a prank he and three of his buddies played one year on the annual church-lawn campout in February. It was early morning, and his friend Walter Hall was still sound asleep on a cot in his tent. Lindsey and the others seized the opportunity, picked up the cot, carried Walter out to Jefferson Street, and left him there. Then they returned to the campsite and waited. Walter had slept through his journey from tent to street but soon woke up, dazed and confused.

Lindsey's story reminded me of my own misconduct on a church-lawn campout a decade earlier. It was cold, and I wanted to go inside to warm up. The church and Sunday School building were locked, but I knew of one building that wasn't. I walked by myself to the Lyric Theater on Broadway Street, watched an excellent movie, and warmed up in the process. When it ended, I returned to the church lawn. No one had missed me, and I didn't confess until now. The movie, *Sometimes A Great Notion* starring Henry Fonda and Paul Newman, was released in December 1971. I must have seen it in February 1972. I had just become an Eagle Scout and was almost fifteen, more likely to leave the campsite to go to a movie than when I was younger.

I talked to Rob and Lindsey about how Daddy stretched a dollar and made trips as cheap as possible so boys whose families were of limited means could participate. On long trips, when there wasn't time to set up camp along the way, Daddy arranged to stay in National Guard armories. Rob said members of the military treated

Daddy and the troop well because many of them were former Scouts and they respected the institution. The troop also held an annual pancake breakfast to raise money for the big end-of-the-school-year trip, and Rob told me something I'd never heard—that several men in Tupelo regularly contributed to the troop to defray the costs for the boys. I'm certain Rob was one of them, though he never would have said so. After Lindsey grew up and was working at his family's hardware store and lumber yard, Daddy often came in to purchase supplies for the troop. Lindsey would offer to charge them to the Methodist Church account, but Daddy paid for them out of his own pocket.

Lindsey also served on the Methodist Church Bus/Van Committee that Daddy chaired. Daddy didn't ask Lindsey to serve but just notified him that he was now a member. The committee's logs revealed that Daddy took elderly residents of Traceway Manor to shop, run errands, and attend church services several times a week. Lindsey came to realize how much time Daddy spent serving others in addition to the countless hours he devoted to Troop 12.

Long after he was grown, Lindsey and his wife bought a home on Rogers Drive. Daddy volunteered to prepare a list of the residents of the neighborhood just as he prepared a roster of the boys in the troop. He typed up the list of names, addresses, and phone numbers and went door to door distributing it. In addition to mowing the property owned by the city and highway department well into his eighties, Daddy maintained the vacant lot for the children in the neighborhood. They swung on the rope swing Daddy had hung from a hickory tree and played in the same creek my friends and I had played in decades earlier. When the kids were thirsty, they would walk to Daddy's front door and ring the doorbell. He kept a supply of soft drinks in the refrigerator and handed them out.

Lindsey had an entry in his notes about a lesson he learned on a summer campout when he was in the troop. He was preparing the last meal he needed to earn Cooking merit badge. He did a good job and was sure Daddy would sign off on the requirement, but he was wrong. The problem wasn't the food, which was perfectly fine. It was that a hot beverage, coffee or hot chocolate, was required, and Lindsey had made neither one. When Daddy asked why not, Lindsey said it was summer; nobody wanted anything hot to drink. "Maybe not," Daddy said, "but it's required. You'll remember next time." Daddy was right; Lindsey remembered next time. Four decades later, he still does.

DAN PURNELL AND SCOTT REED

I've known Dan Purnell and Scott Reed for as long as I can remember. Dan is four weeks older than I am; we've been friends since kindergarten. Scott is a year younger and was a year behind Dan and me in school. We all grew up within a mile of each other. Dan and I had to walk or ride our bikes through Scott's backyard to get to each other's homes. We made the trip hundreds of times.

Dan and I learned to love the outdoors together. We spent summer days playing in his neighborhood and our vacant lot and the creek beside it. We waded along the bank of the creek, caught every kind of creature that lived there, and swam in the deep swimming hole. Later we camped and canoed together during our years in Troop 12. He became an Eagle Scout shortly before I did. His older brother George and younger brother Kirk are also Troop 12 Eagles.

Scott earned his Eagle less than a year after I did. He and I were rivals in tennis and doubles partners on the Tupelo High School team when I was a junior and he was a sophomore and again when I was a senior and he was a junior. We won nearly all of our matches but lost our last one, the semifinals of the state tournament my senior year. Scott won the tournament the following year with Jeffery Boyd, another Troop 12 Eagle.

The three of us went in different directions for college—Mississippi State for Dan, Vanderbilt for Scott, Ole Miss for me—and rarely saw each other when we were starting our careers and raising children. Dan and Scott ultimately built thriving businesses in Tupelo. They both point to Daddy as a key factor in their success and a role model in how to lead people.

The route to success wasn't a straight one for either of them. Dan struggled with addiction in his twenties and wound up in a rehabilitation facility when he was thirty-one. He was married and had a one-year-old daughter. In a group meeting early in his stay, the director told the patients the road to sobriety is a hard one and only two out of ten would succeed with just one stint in rehab. Dan decided he would be one of the two, became a devout Christian, and hasn't had a drink or a drug since 1988. When his three children turned fifteen, Dan told them about his past troubles and warned them not to follow in his footsteps. He now has a successful business that buys and sells processed meat, mostly chicken. Each year he and his ten employees buy millions of chickens and parts from processors and arrange delivery to customers all over America.

One Friday in the summer of 2022, I headed north on I-55, Dan headed west from Tupelo, and we met in Memphis to ride together to St. Louis to watch the Cardinals play the Phillies. We had become Cardinals fans together in the 1960s when the business owned by Dan's family, Purnell's Pride Chicken, sponsored their games on WELO AM radio in Tupelo and they played in three World Series in five years. All three went to seven games, with the Cards winning two.

Dan spent most of our four-hour drive to St. Louis on the phone, talking to his staff, suppliers, and customers. He had learned how to treat people from watching Daddy, and I learned why Dan is successful from listening to him. He knows the chicken business, but his real expertise is people. He takes an interest in them, treats them well, and his word is his bond. His company is built on relationships.

Scott's road to success was not as bumpy as Dan's, but he made a sharp turn to get there. After graduating from Vanderbilt, he spent a year in an executive training program in Houston before returning to Tupelo to join the family's department store, which has been a fixture in downtown Tupelo for more than a century. Scott planned to spend his career there but after several years decided to do something else. Based on his father's advice, he became a stockbroker and soon opened the first full-service brokerage in north Mississippi. He later started his own firm with partner John Hardy. Though Tupelo is only the seventh largest city in Mississippi,

Hardy Reed is now the largest investment advisory firm in the state, with more than two billion dollars under management.

Their work keeps them busy, but Dan and Scott both contribute time and money to worthy causes in and around Tupelo. Dan is very active in his church and conducts a regular ministry at the Tupelo City Jail. He takes a special interest in those who are down on their luck, some of whom he met when they were behind bars. At the time of our interview, Dan was helping a man who had neither a driver's license nor a car and lived in Okolona, a small town more than twenty miles south of Tupelo. To help the man get back on his feet, Dan was driving to Okolona every morning, bringing him to work in Tupelo, then taking him home every evening.

Scott has carried on the Reed family's long tradition of community service in Tupelo. He has served on the boards of directors of more than thirty non-profits, including North Mississippi Medical Center, the Community Development Foundation, and the Yocona Area Council, and as president of United Way of Greater Lee County, Big Brothers/Big Sisters, and the Tupelo Kiwanis Club. Like Daddy, he received the Julius G. Berry Award for Outstanding Volunteer Service. He has written one book and is working on two more. He's also the lead singer in a band called Two Drink Minimum. They played at my fortieth high school reunion, where I spent too much time dancing and not enough talking to old friends.

While we were in Tupelo, Carrie and I drove to Dan and his wife Robin's home on the outskirts of town. Scott met us there, and we talked about Daddy and Troop 12. We initially focused on Daddy's leadership style. The comments from Dan and Scott followed a familiar pattern. Daddy didn't bark out orders or give detailed instructions. He knew the Scouts would learn more from figuring out how to do things and solving problems themselves. Daddy had complete control but rarely exercised it. He let the boys make mistakes but not dangerous ones. He was always watching but intervened only when necessary. He knew how to do everything, but he didn't do everything for the boys. He would let them stumble but not fall. He was the safety net. He always knew what to do.

Scott offered two examples of Daddy's willingness to put the burden on the boys to solve their problems. It rained one year on the Current River, and the water breached the bank and began flooding the campsite. Scott expected Daddy to give the boys instructions, but instead he told them to figure out what to do. They moved their tents to higher ground, and it all worked out. On another campout, when a bigger, stronger boy wanted to wrestle Scott in the back of the White Elephant, Daddy told Scott he needed to decide how to handle it. In both cases, Daddy would have intervened to prevent anyone from getting hurt, but he wanted the boys to learn to make their own decisions. He was not a helicopter Scoutmaster.

Daddy expected the boys in the troop to work hard and succeed. He expected great things of them. He told Scott there was only one way out of Troop 12, and that was to become an Eagle Scout. Scott said he'd been told that the troop had the highest percentage of Eagle Scouts of any troop in the nation. I don't know if that's true, but Troop 12 undoubtedly has had far more Eagles than most. Nationally, only two percent of Boy Scouts become Eagles. The percentage in Troop 12 during Daddy's years as a leader was far higher than that. When the Scouts saw how hard Daddy worked and all he did for them, they didn't want to let him down.

Because the Scouts held Daddy in such high regard, it often took no more than a hint or a nudge to get them to do what he wanted even long after they were in the troop. Scott managed Daddy's investments, and one day he invited Daddy to his office to go over them. Daddy told Scott he was in another former Scout's office recently and saw his Eagle certificate hanging on the wall. He didn't suggest that Scott should display his certificate, but he didn't have to. Scott went home that night, found his certificate, had it framed, hung it on his wall, and made up an excuse for another meeting so Daddy could see it.

With the story of the airmen and the bowline and others, Daddy emphasized that the skills Scouts learn are important in and of themselves, not just for advancing in rank and earning merit badges. Scott told a story demonstrating that Daddy was right. When Scott was a young man, he was the first on the scene of a serious one-car wreck. The driver wasn't breathing but, using the skills he'd learned for First Aid merit badge, Scott revived him. A doctor soon arrived, then an ambulance came and took the man away. To make sure he'd done the right thing, Scott called his uncle, pediatrician Charles Tharp, who told Scott that what he did was perfect.

I asked Dan and Scott if they follow any practices in running their companies that they learned from watching Daddy run the troop. Scott said he learned to determine the worst-case scenario and take steps to make sure it doesn't happen. Dan said he never asks anyone in his company to do something the employee hasn't seen Dan do first. He told me people reveal themselves in what they do, and their actions speak louder than their words. Daddy's actions spoke loud and clear to Dan. By working alongside the boys, having high expectations but treating them fairly, always being patient, and always doing the right thing, Daddy showed the Scouts in the troop how to lead. When their time came to lead, they knew how.

Scott had recently taught a Sunday School class and talked about those who light the road and show the way. He said Daddy did exactly that. But because he was a humble man, he never viewed his work with Troop 12 as special. He thought of himself as an ordinary man, but Scott said he was wrong. Daddy was an extraordinary man and gave the young men in Troop 12 a priceless gift, not just of his time but of his wisdom, his judgment, and his example. He had a profound impact on them.

Robin was hearing much of this for the first time and declared that Scouting was Daddy's ministry. Daddy would have rejected the characterization, but he would have been wrong about that too. His sixty-year commitment to Troop 12 was an invaluable ministry to three generations of boys he mentored on the road to manhood.

ALICE VIRGINIA DANIEL AND CAREAN DENDY

Daddy had been the Scoutmaster for nearly three years when he married Mama, and his service to the troop continued until long after she died. During their marriage of nearly fifty years, he met with the Scouts every Monday night and left her at home to go camping every month. He couldn't have done it without her support, and he wouldn't have done it without her blessing. When Margie and I were little, if Mama had told him the burden of keeping us while he was gone was just too much, I'm sure he would have stopped, or at least cut back. As strong as his commitment was to the boys in the troop, his commitment to Mama and to Margie and me was even stronger.

But Mama never said it was too much and never complained. She was both generous and wise. She no doubt realized the enormous value of Daddy's contribution to the boys in the troop as well as the sense of purpose it gave him. His commitment to Troop 12 meant extra work for her, but she was happy to do it. It was her contribution to his contribution. Some of Daddy's former Scouts, after they were grown and had children of their own, realized the sacrifices Mama had made and thanked her.

Perhaps she would have objected if he had gone camping one weekend a month and played golf the other three, but Daddy had no hobbies to speak of. Other than listening to Ole Miss football games and occasionally going to one, he did almost nothing just for himself. When he wasn't doing Scout work, he was doing some other kind—in the yard, for the church, or something else to help others. It's little wonder he fell asleep in front of the TV every night.

After Betsy Ann and I left for law school in North Carolina in August 1979, I never lived in the home on Rogers Drive again. Twenty years later, in September 1999, Mama died there. During the two decades when Mama and Daddy were empty nesters, when he wasn't caring for her, he still went camping every month, but in those years he left Mama alone at home with the dog and the cat. There were always a dog and a cat.

Mama and Daddy never had much of a social life. They spent time with Daddy's parents, his sisters, and their families, and they had friends in the neighborhood and at church, but I don't remember a single time when they went to dinner with another couple. If a babysitter ever kept Margie and me so they could go out for the evening, I don't recall it.

Mama had little time for socializing when Margie and I were still at home and she was still working. But after we left and she retired, she had more free time and wanted to spend it with friends. Two of those friends were Alice Virginia Daniel and Carean Dendy, who both worked at the First Methodist Church. When Carrie and I were in Tupelo, I met with A. V. and Carean to talk to them a little about Daddy and a lot about Mama.

Mama had known Alice Virginia and Carean from church for many years, but they did not become close until after Mama retired and decided she needed a new way to get some exercise. She didn't like walking outside in the heat or riding the stationary bike in the living room, but she found something she could do at the church that she loved and was good for her. She drove downtown to the church family life center nearly every weekday, donned her roller skates, put on some big band music from the 1940s, and took off skating. Her routine afterward included stopping by to see A. V. in the church's kitchen and Carean in her office. Both looked forward to her visits and, more than a quarter of a century after the last one, they enjoyed telling me about them.

Alice Virginia said she and Mama had a ball together and talked about everything under the sun. A. V. was responsible for preparing meals to deliver to church members who were shut-ins. Mama helped her decide who needed what and insisted on delivering some of the meals herself. In their many talks, Mama never complained about anything, certainly not about the time Daddy devoted to the Scouts, which had long been a fact of her life. A. V. said Mama was a very accepting person—easygoing, bright, and funny.

Mama was a generation older than Alice Virginia and like a second mother to her. She said Mama would give her tactful advice and remind her if she didn't follow it. They shared a bad habit—smoking—and would go outside for smoke breaks. Mama held her cigarette the old-fashioned way and gestured when she talked. A. V. was afraid she would burn herself when she got worked up about something.

Carean said Mama stopped by her office every day, and they also spent time together on Monday nights when Daddy was at Scout meetings. She told me Mama was a great listener. She once told

Mama she felt bad when her mind wandered during the Sunday sermon. Mama said not to worry, it happened to her too, and she worshipped privately while the choir was singing. Mama and Daddy gave a box of Whitman's chocolates to each member of the church staff every Christmas. Daddy delivered them, but he gave Mama the credit.

Carean said Mama took over responsibility for the church's annual Singing Christmas Tree in the mid-1980s. Each year she designed and ordered sweatshirts for the singers to wear, wrapped empty boxes to make the singing tree look like a real one, and recruited men to assemble the structure the choir stood on. Daddy and Adrian Thompson, who was both Carean's father and the man who called Daddy the Apostle, outworked men half their age. Mama's efforts made the tree a success and reminded me of another creative project she undertook in the mid-eighties. She asked Daddy to bring my old toy chest down from the attic, painted teddy bears and balloons on it, then added Ann Lowrey's name across the lid. The toy chest has been passed down to Mama's great-granddaughter who was born five years after Mama died.

Alice Virginia said she and Mama both loved cats and other animals. After cleaning up following the evening meal at church one night, A. V. told Mama her cat was out of food, but she was too tired to go to the grocery store. The cat would just have to go hungry till morning. Not long after A. V. got home, her doorbell rang. When she opened the door, Mama was pulling out of the driveway. There was a grocery bag on the porch with two kinds of cat food in it, dry and canned. On top was a one-word note that said MEOW.

Alice Virginia told me Mama was her dear friend and always made her happy. She was the one person in the church A. V. wanted to see more than any other, and A. V. missed her terribly after she died. Carean said she missed Mama too. When I sent her a summary of the interview to review, Carean began her response with this: "I just read every word and have a huge smile on my face remembering those two wonderful people who gave of themselves to so many."

Joe Holley

After my interviews in Tupelo, Greg Johnston suggested I talk to Joe Holley and Ken Posey, two Scouts who joined the troop when he did and became Eagles at about the same time. When I told them what I was doing, both said they would be honored to share their thoughts about Daddy and their time in Troop 12. I interviewed them by phone on consecutive days in March 2022.

Joe has had a long, impressive career as a successful physician, but it would have been hard to foresee that when he turned eleven and joined Troop 12 half a century ago. By his own admission, Joe was both impatient and annoying, always in a hurry and pushing others to go as fast as he did. His energy, properly channeled, has been a valuable asset in the decades since, but it was a liability when he joined the troop. He told me he needed to grow up and calm down. During his four years in Troop 12, he said Daddy helped him do both.

Like all the Scouts in the troop, Joe said he learned much more from watching what Daddy did than hearing what he said. He saw that Daddy was a hard worker and the most patient man he's ever known. He was always steady and never upset or out of control. He encouraged boys to step up and do the right thing the right way. If they failed, they learned and did it the right way the next time. Daddy was both a genteel man and a father figure.

Joe had fond memories of camping in the '70s and was delighted when I told him the troop's streak of monthly campouts remains unbroken. When Daddy drove the White Elephant to campouts, Joe often stood beside him and shifted gears. On one campout, Joe took refuge in the driver's seat of the Elephant when there were reports of tornadoes in the area. He fell asleep, his head fell forward and came to rest on the horn, and the noise woke up everybody but him. Daddy had to bang on the door to rouse him and stop the honking.

I have a photo from 1974 of all the troop members standing beside the White Elephant. Joe, who grew to be 6'3", is the tallest in the picture, leaders included. With his height advantage, he learned to love volleyball in the games the Scouts played in the church parking lot before the troop's Monday night meetings.

From watching Daddy, Joe said he learned the importance of patience, service, and mentorship, and his career has exemplified all three. After completing medical school, he chose to specialize in emergency medicine. Since moving to Memphis in 1985, he has devoted his career to training and mentoring students, Emergency Medical Services technicians, and other first responders. He is currently the EMS medical director for the State of Tennessee and serves as the medical director for several schools that train paramedics.

For many years, Joe has also been the medical director of a FEMA search-and-rescue team that has been deployed to disaster sites all over the world. During his tenure, Joe and his team have been sent to more than forty sites, including Oklahoma City after the 1995 bombing, the Pentagon following 9/11, the Gulf Coast in the wake of Katrina, Miami after the condominium collapse in the summer of 2021, and Kentucky in the aftermath of the devastating tornadoes later that year.

The members of the FEMA team include Joe and other doctors and medics as well as specialists trained in search and rescue. The specialists on the team include dogs. Several years ago, Joe took his wife Kimberly to a canine training session. After watching for thirty minutes, she declared that she had a new mission in life. She now trains the dogs on the FEMA team. Joe said he and Kimberly have five dogs. Two are trained to find human remains and one to search for survivors. When I asked about the other two, Joe said they're trained to sleep on the couch. I said our dogs excel at that too.

Joe told me a story that reminded me of another of Daddy's traits. Unless something really needed to be said, Daddy didn't say it. And because he had heart-to-heart talks with Scouts only on rare occasions, they paid attention and remembered when he did.

The story involved one such occasion. In Joe's first years in the troop, Daddy tried to break him of his annoying impatience by teasing him. When Joe said, "Let's go, Eason," Daddy would respond, "Let's go, Holley." But instead of going, Daddy would keep doing what he was already doing. Joe didn't take the hint, and one Monday night Daddy pulled him aside outside the Scout Hut door. It took place fifty years ago and lasted no more than a few seconds, but Joe remembered it well. Daddy told him, "You need to slow down and calm down." When he thought about it later, Joe figured Daddy must be right because he was always right. He took the advice to heart, learned to control his impatience, and dealt with people differently. His relationships changed for the better.

Though Joe may have calmed down, I don't believe he's ever slowed down. When I asked his age, he wasn't sure if he was sixty-two or sixty-three—he has no time to keep up with such trivial matters—but was sure he loved his work and had no plans to retire. Joe's a busy man, but he was delighted to take time out of his schedule to talk about his Scoutmaster.

Ken Posey

Like Joe Holley, Ken Posey has led a fascinating life of service, though unlike Joe, Ken is now enjoying a life of leisure. During the pandemic, Ken took early retirement from his position as a United Airlines pilot. His weeks, he said, now consist of six Saturdays and one Sunday. He and his wife Kathy live in Woodlands, Texas, with their rescue dog Bella, and he finally has time to pursue his passion for bass fishing.

Ken's life, like countless others, was changed dramatically by an unlikely event. He was planning to attend veterinary school, but he wasn't sure it was the right choice. One weekend during his senior year of college, he visited a friend at the Air Force Base in Columbus, Mississippi. While Ken was there, he happened to be invited to take a turn at the controls of a flight simulator. He liked it so much he applied to flight school in the Air Force, Navy, and Marines. When the Navy accepted him, he forgot all about vet school and followed in Daddy's footsteps as a Naval Aviator. Nearly forty years after Daddy trained pilots at the Naval Air Station in Pensacola, Ken enrolled in Officer Candidate School there.

Ken earned his wings in 1983 and spent most of his career as a light attack and fighter pilot, flying the A-7E Corsair and McDonnell Douglas F/A-18 Hornet. He was deployed five times on aircraft carrier cruises and was at sea for approximately six months each time. Ken nearly missed his wedding in 1990 because of one of them. He was on his way home aboard the USS Carl Vinson while Naval commanders debated whether to order the ship to return to the Persian Gulf for Desert Storm. But they decided against it, and Ken made it home and married Kathy as scheduled.

In his time as a pilot, Ken amassed more than 2,800 jet flight hours and landed safely on carriers more than 600 times. He flew eighteen combat missions in Operation Southern Watch as one of the pilots responsible for enforcing the no-fly zone over southern Iraq after the end of Desert Storm.

When he was not in the pilot's seat, Ken served for two years aboard a carrier as Senior Landing Signal Officer. LSOs stand on the fantail of the ship and serve as the last safety valve responsible for safe landings. He said waiting for a jet to land was like waiting for a child to be born. Watch the opening scene of the original *Top Gun* and you'll understand why. A carrier landing is often referred to as a controlled crash. Ken also served as Air Wing Safety Officer for the Commander of Air Wing 15 and Deputy Branch Chief for Operational Plans for U.S. Central Command, and he spent two years in Norway as Tactical Maritime Air Advisor to the Commander of NATO Air Forces in northern Europe.

Ken left active duty in 1996, joined the Reserves, and became an airline pilot. But five years later, after 9/11, he was recalled to duty at MacDill Air Force Base in Tampa, where he assisted the Director of Operations of U.S. Central Command for two years. In addition to personal, unit, and campaign awards, Ken twice received the Defense Meritorious Service Medal. He retired from the Navy as a captain, the equivalent of a colonel in the Army.

Ken reminisced in our interview about fun times in Troop 12 and all the meetings and campouts, but mostly he spoke of his gratitude. He was grateful not only for Daddy but also Assistant Scoutmasters Buddy Miller and Paul Fairley. He said all three had a hand in shaping his character, but Daddy was in charge. Using a

Naval term, Ken called Daddy the skipper. Daddy always did the right thing and always came to the right decision. From watching him, Ken learned the value of hard work, how to treat people, how to lead them, and the many other qualities that made Daddy a great leader. Ken didn't realize at the time all he was learning from Daddy and the others, but he came to appreciate it as he grew older. "To say I'm eternally grateful," Ken told me, "would be an understatement."

So we wouldn't be starting the interview from scratch, Ken sent me a short summary before we spoke outlining what he's done in the nearly fifty years since he became an Eagle Scout. He wrote that Daddy's fingerprints are all over the story of his life, just as they're all over the stories of thousands of other lives. I thought that was a good way to put it. Daddy's fingerprints may not be visible, but he left a mark on all the young men he served as the Scoutmaster of Troop 12.

Jim High

Jim High was born in 1940 and joined Troop 12 in 1951, just in time to go on the very first of the consecutive monthly campouts that August. He achieved the rank of Eagle Scout six years later.

After graduating from Mississippi State in 1962, Jim returned to Tupelo. When his father died unexpectedly the following spring, Jim's only way to support his mother and younger siblings was to take over the insurance agency his father owned and ran. He was just like George Bailey in *It's a Wonderful Life*, thrust by his father's death and a sense of obligation into a career he never planned or wanted.

Like George, Jim made the best of the hand life had dealt him, and in the decades that followed he built the agency into a thriving business. Though running it took most of his time, he also volunteered as an Assistant Scoutmaster in Troop 12. He served in the role for nineteen years, including the years when I was a Scout. He drove a Corvette, which made him cooler than Daddy and the other assistants.

In addition to the campouts Jim attended during his years as a Scout, he went on more than 200 as a leader. One was to Philmont, where he and Daddy took a group from the troop backpacking for a week in the mountains of New Mexico. Jim sat beside hundreds of campfires over the years with Daddy and knew him as well as anyone did. When I interviewed Jim, he said of Daddy, "He was the finest developer of young people I've ever known."

Jim reminisced in our talk about campouts from his years as a Scout and a leader: hiking to Livingston Lake and trips to Ruff's Farm, the battlefield at Shiloh, and other destinations. He still knows the constellations he learned when Daddy taught astronomy on campouts seventy years ago. He also told me something Daddy had learned as a pilot. When planes flew over in the darkness, he said Daddy could identify them by their sound.

Jim said Troop 12 did things other troops didn't do, and the boys knew they were in the best troop in town. He spoke of using ropes to build a monkey bridge that spanned Bear Creek in Tishomingo State Park and erecting towers by lashing long limbs together. Both projects gave the boys a sense of accomplishment. We also talked about the ill-fated canoe trip on Bear Creek in March 1971, when he and Daddy launched before they tied everything down, then watched as their canoe filled up with water and their packs and other gear floated away. Jim said the trip was a learning experience for Scouts and Scoutmasters alike about the importance of being prepared.

Buddy McCarty was not the only chubby Scout who needed help from Daddy to satisfy the running requirement for Personal Fitness merit badge. Jim did too. Robins Field was only a short walk from the Highs' home on Jefferson Street. Daddy met Jim there after work every day for a month and trained him until he could run fast enough. He said Daddy's willingness to spend that much time helping him complete his one remaining requirement to attain the Eagle rank was totally unexpected. Jim and Buddy both became Eagle Scouts in 1957. Jim earned his Eagle first, so Daddy must have trained him first.

Some merit badges were much more difficult than others. Bird Study was one of the hardest. To earn it, a Scout had to identify fifty different bird species in the wild. The first twenty-five, the common ones, were easy, but finding twenty-five more was a challenge. Jim and several other Scouts nonetheless decided to try, and Daddy agreed to help. Every Sunday morning for a year, Daddy would rise before dawn, pick the boys up at their homes, then head out into rural Lee County searching for birds. Time was limited because they had to be home and dressed for Sunday School at 9:30, but eventually all of them identified fifty and earned the merit badge.

Jim talked about the leadership skills he learned from Daddy and employed in making his insurance agency a success. Daddy was a natural leader but was never dictatorial. He didn't give orders. His attitude was "let's get this done," and he worked alongside the boys until it was done. Nobody outworked him, and nothing ever seemed like a chore or a hardship. He was encouraging but not demanding, and he had a way of getting boys to do things for themselves. He knew how to talk to them and would discuss options and problems and listen to their suggestions. The goal was to come up with the best solution, and Daddy didn't claim he always knew the right one. He accepted people for who they were and believed everybody had something to contribute. He treated all the boys the same and never played favorites. And if a Scout needed correcting, Daddy did it quietly and without embarrassing him. Jim described Daddy as a gentleman in every sense of the word.

Jim joined Troop 12 before Daddy turned thirty and served as an Assistant Scoutmaster until after Daddy turned sixty. The span of more than thirty years gave Jim a unique perspective. In all that time, I asked, did Daddy change? He answered without hesitation and with a single word: no.

In my long career as a lawyer, I've conducted countless interviews and depositions and learned that silence is often an effective means of interrogation, that if you don't follow up an answer by asking another question right away, the witness will often start talking again and reveal more. I tried the tactic with Jim to see if he would elaborate on his one-word answer. Five seconds passed, then he said no again. I waited a bit longer to give him another chance, but he said nothing. I gave up and went on to another subject.

I can't say I was surprised by Jim's one-word answer. Interviewing Daddy's Scouts, from his first ones to some of his last, made it clear that he was the same man from beginning to end. For more than six decades, from 1947 to 2008, he was as constant as the North Star. And until near the end, as Jim pointed out, he never seemed to get old.

In November 2011, to honor Daddy on his ninetieth birthday, Jim wrote a column in the *Lee County Courier*. The subject was "the wonderful life of Paul Eason, and the wonderful life given to me and thousands of others by Scoutmaster Paul Eason." Jim recounted memories from his time as a Scout and Assistant Scoutmaster and wrote that Daddy worked with every boy in some special way; he always seemed to know just what each of them needed. Jim said he learned the true understanding of life from Daddy, and he also learned from him to pass that understanding on to others. He ended the column with these words: "If you can make a difference for at least one person, then you have tremendous merit indeed. Paul Eason's wonderful life has made a difference to thousands. Happy Birthday, Paul!"

Several months after the interview, Jim shared another Troop 12 story with me. He'd received a call from Jim Beane, who became an Eagle in the troop in 1969. The younger Jim was calling to thank the older one for saving his wife's life. He said he'd come home and found her on the floor, struggling to breathe. The training Jim gave him more than fifty years earlier while teaching First Aid merit badge came back to him, and he gave her mouth-to-mouth resuscitation. He called 911, the ambulance came, and she was saved. Jim High said he told Jim Beane that his nineteen years as an Assistant Scoutmaster with Paul Eason were some of the best years of his life and had served him in good stead ever since.

WALTER HALL

Walter Hall became Troop 12's 192nd Eagle Scout in 1984. The suggestion that I interview him about Daddy came from Lindsey Leake, who earned his Eagle immediately after Walter did. When Walter and I spoke, I asked him about the church lawn campout when Lindsey and three co-conspirators carried him and his cot to the middle of Jefferson Street and left him there. To my surprise and disappointment, he had no memory of the incident. Maybe it was because the campout was forty years earlier, but maybe it was because he was asleep.

Walter graduated from Auburn, earned an MBA from Ole Miss, and works in the book publishing industry in Nashville. He became a father later in life than most. At the time of our talk in March 2022, he was fifty-three and his children were nine, six and three. He coaches youth sports, which perhaps keeps him as young as Scouting kept Daddy, and has also raised money for the local council of the Boy Scouts.

Walter's father ran the TVA office in Tupelo for thirty-five years, served as an assistant leader in Troop 12, and signed Walter up for the troop when he turned eleven. In the next four years, Walter learned lessons he didn't know he was learning and others that didn't come in handy until decades later.

One lesson Walter mentioned was about structure. The older Scouts ran the Monday night meetings, but they did so based on the military structure Daddy had established. Meetings began and ended with a flag ceremony. Before any business was conducted, the colors were presented, and the boys saluted the flag and recited the Pledge of Allegiance and the Scout Oath. Sometimes Scouts paid attention to the words, but even when they didn't, the ritual calmed them down and made meetings more productive.

There was also structure to the monthly campouts. Boys cooked by patrol on some campouts and individually on others, and the plan was established by the time the date and location of the campout were announced. The time set aside for activities, even playing games like capture the flag, was also set in advance. By the time Walter joined the troop, Daddy had adopted another practice to help the troop run on time. There was no bathroom in the White Elephant, and they would have been chronically late if they stopped every time a boy said he needed to go. Daddy solved the problem by keeping an empty Gatorade bottle in the back of the Elephant that could be emptied when the troop reached the destination.

In 1982 Daddy took the troop to the World's Fair in Knoxville, which was also called the International Energy Exposition. As at many fairs, there were games of chance. One of the Scouts couldn't resist, lost all his money, and had none to pay for his meals. Walter said Daddy didn't give him more money, but he didn't let him starve either. Daddy instead shared his own food with him. What he got to eat was not what he would have chosen, and he learned that beggars can't be choosers.

Walter said Daddy never missed a meeting and was present for every Troop 12 activity. He had old-fashioned common sense and humility; he never wanted the spotlight. He was that way when he served on the Tupelo Board of Aldermen and City Council just as he was when he was leading the troop. Walter said Daddy also had an extraordinary knack for remembering names. There might be a hundred Scouts in the troop, but he knew everyone's name. Daddy led by example. He collaborated; he didn't boss. He rolled up his sleeves and worked side-by-side with the boys.

Walter concluded our talk by telling me that that Daddy helped mold him into the man he is and that he learned more in Troop 12 than in any other organization of which he's ever been a part. He closed by saying, "His impact and reach have been extraordinary. The boys of Troop 12 have grown up and spread the lessons they learned around the world."

JACK REED JR.

Jack Reed Jr., Scott's older brother, became an Eagle Scout in Troop 12 in 1965. The following year, when he was in the tenth grade and I was in the fourth, he coached my flag football team. Jack was very competitive. He wanted to win, and we did. Three decades later, while Daddy was an Assistant Scoutmaster, Jack's only son, Jack III, became the troop's 303rd Eagle. Nearly fifteen years after that, when Jack was Mayor of Tupelo, he presented Daddy with the key to the city on his ninetieth birthday.

I arranged to interview Jack in August 2022 after a book signing event at Reed's GumTree Bookstore, which is part of the department store in downtown Tupelo that Jack has run for many years. Having learned to be prepared nearly sixty years earlier as a member of Troop 12, he brought with him several pages of notes of memories he wanted to share.

Before we talked about Daddy and the troop, Jack briefly mentioned the excellent male role models in his family. I knew all of them other than Jack's grandfather Bob Reed, who built a successful business, served as a civic leader, and was the president of the Yocona Area Council in the early years of the Scouts. Bill and Bobby Reed, Jack's uncles, were fine men and pillars of the community. The one I knew best was his father, Jack Sr., a wonderful man with a delightful sense of humor. Jack Sr. was three years younger than Daddy. They were good friends and shared a common interest in serving the people of Tupelo.

Jack Sr. was a Boy Scout but fell just short of Eagle because Troop 12 lacked effective leadership during his years as a member. After that experience, he decided to become a leader himself. He took a Wood Badge adult training course in the early 1950s and planned to volunteer to serve as the Scoutmaster of Troop 12 when Daddy decided to step down. If he had known that Daddy would not step down for forty-five years, he might not have taken the course. But he found other ways to serve and was presented with the Silver Buffalo Award by the Boy Scouts of America for his outstanding leadership.

Jack Sr. was a moderate Republican and the party's nominee for governor in 1987. Like Daddy, he entered politics late in life to serve others, not because of personal ambition. He was more gregarious than Daddy and comfortable talking to anybody. When he was serving in tennis, he stopped talking only when he hit the ball. He opened a speech to a group of Democrats by saying it was wonderful to be among friends, even if they weren't his. He would have been an outstanding governor, but he lost in a close race.

In addition to the men in his family, Jack Jr. said he had the good fortune to have two wonderful male role models during his formative years, and he had them at the same time. They were Frank Bell Sr., who ran the camp in North Carolina Jack attended during the summers, and Daddy, who ran Troop 12 in Tupelo all year round. Jack said he learned a great deal from both. It wasn't from anything they said, but from observing what they did, how they conducted themselves, and how they treated others. He learned from them through osmosis.

Jack shared some personal philosophies with me. He said what a person does is more important than what he says, and how a person lives is more revealing than what he says he believes. He also said children are only listening part of the time, but they're watching all the time. He watched Frank Bell and Daddy and benefited greatly from doing so. Jack became an Eagle Scout fifty-seven years before our interview, but he could still picture Daddy in his Scout uniform, working with the Scouts to build the monkey bridge over Bear Creek and squatting beside his Dutch oven baking a cobbler to share with them.

I noted that Jack and I were fortunate to have such wonderful fathers and that Daddy must have been especially important to the boys in the troop who came from broken homes or whose fathers were not good role models. Jack said he volunteered many years ago to work with Big Brothers Big Sisters of Mississippi and has served as the Big Brother for a boy who was now a man of thirty-one. The boy's father had no relationship with him, and Jack was the closest thing he had to one. For some boys in Troop 12, Daddy was probably the closest thing they had to one.

Jack said Daddy was not a micromanager. He let boys be boys, and he tolerated horseplay so long as it was neither dangerous nor cruel. Jack said he was the victim on one occasion, that some boys pulled up his shirt, slapped him on the stomach, and gave him a pink belly. He was so angry that he started to pray that the pink-belly ringleader would die. Then he stopped himself, realizing that praying for the boy's death wasn't very Christian. But he wasn't willing to drop the matter with God entirely. He came up with a compromise, toned down his request, and prayed that the boy would move away. His wish was granted when the boy's father was transferred to North Carolina two months later. Jack figured it was a promotion, so he didn't feel guilty. I said he must have been glad he modified the relief he sought.

Jack had especially fond memories of church services on campouts. The troop usually camped on Friday nights, but whenever the campout was on Saturday, Daddy made sure there was time on Sunday morning for church. Jack recalled that the boys led the service, and the troop used old Cokesbury hymnals and sang "Church in the Wildwood," an old hymn that's also a favorite of mine. Jack said he learned on those Sunday mornings in the woods that you don't have to be in a building to be in church. The time Jack spent outdoors, both on Troop 12 campouts and in North Carolina, gave him a lifelong appreciation for nature, as did lessons learned from his mother Frances, the family naturalist.

Another Frances, a schoolteacher named Frances Gregory, taught Jack in the third grade and me in the sixth, both at Joyner Elementary School. Miss Gregory was brilliant, enthusiastic, and as perfectly suited to be a teacher as Daddy was to be a Scoutmaster. On the first day when he was in the third grade, Jack said Miss Gregory announced that she knew all about the students and how they fared in the second grade. They were the smartest class she'd ever had, and they were going to learn great things together.

Jack said Miss Gregory made him want to achieve, and Daddy made him feel the same way. Daddy maintained a high bar to become an Eagle Scout—there were no shortcuts—and that made Jack want to reach it. When he watched an older boy, Bill Patrick, receive his Eagle in front of the congregation at the First Methodist Church, he vowed that he would stand up there too. He wanted his parents and Daddy to be proud of him, and he wanted to be proud of himself. When he received his Eagle a year later, they all were.

Jack said he was grateful to Daddy and Troop 12 for providing his first leadership opportunities. He was chosen by the members of his patrol to be their patrol leader, then was elected by the entire troop to succeed Bill Patrick as senior patrol leader. Jack said he learned a valuable political lesson from that election. He'd been friendlier than the other candidate to the new Scouts, and their votes made the difference.

Daddy entrusted the senior patrol leader with significant responsibility for running the troop. Jack said the opportunity to preside at

Monday night meetings and help plan campouts was very important to him, and it started him out on a lifetime of leadership. In
the decades that followed, Jack was chosen to serve as president
of the student body when he was in law school and to chair many
organizations after he returned to Tupelo, including the Community Development Foundation, United Way of Greater Lee
County, Northeast Mississippi Habitat for Humanity, The Free
Clinic, Kiwanis Club, Downtown Tupelo Main Street Association,
and Mississippi Economic Council.

Jack's many leadership roles prepared him well when he decided
to run for Mayor of Tupelo in 2009. Two decades earlier, he had
encouraged Daddy to run for the board of aldermen and contributed to his campaign. When Jack ran for mayor, Daddy returned
the favor. Jack won in a landslide, just as Daddy did.

Jack talked about the day Carrie and I brought Daddy home
to Tupelo in November 2011 to celebrate his ninetieth birthday.
He said he considered it a high honor to be the mayor then and
to present Daddy with the key to the City of Tupelo. Daddy was
Jack's Scoutmaster and taught him how to lead. Daddy passed the
torch of leadership on to many, including Jack Reed Jr.

Brian Steger

When Brian Steger transferred from Knoxville to Tupelo in 1997
to become the Scout executive for the Yocona Area Council, Daddy
was seventy-five years old and had been a leader in Troop 12 for
fifty years. Sam Agnew had taken over as the Scoutmaster five
years earlier, but Daddy was still very involved as an assistant and
very influential. When he spoke, people listened.

Brian worked in two capacities with Daddy, as the Scout executive but also as a fellow Assistant Scoutmaster. Brian's son Blaine
had been a Scout in Knoxville. He visited several troops when the
Stegers arrived in Tupelo, but after going with Troop 12 to the
Locust Fork River in north Alabama, Blaine told his dad he didn't
need to visit any more. He became the troop's 329th Eagle Scout
in 1999. I understood that it would have been a scandal if the son

of the Scoutmaster did not become an Eagle. I'm sure Blaine, the son of the Scout executive, felt the same way.

Shortly after his move to Tupelo, Brian observed that Troop 12 was participating in very few council-wide activities. Most significantly, the troop wasn't attending summer camp at Camp Yocona but instead was holding its own camp at Pickwick Lake. But Daddy was very supportive as Brian set out to make improvements to Yocona. Daddy shared his concerns, and Brian addressed them. The camp was updated, with new cabins and an expanded lake, and the teaching program was greatly improved. Over the span of just a few years, the number of boys attending summer camp at Yocona doubled. Troop 12 returned.

When Brian first met with Troop 12's troop committee, he was impressed by the quantity and quality of men Daddy had assembled. There were thirty-eight altogether, and they included many of the city's finest leaders. Brian described Tupelo as a city of giants and named several: Jack Reed Sr., Felix Black, Henry Brevard, Rob Leake, and J.C. Whitehead. Those men, along with Daddy, inspired the next generation of leaders, many of whom were alumni of Troop 12. Brian said that Scouting builds leaders. His work with Daddy and other adult Scouters during his years in Tupelo prepared him well when he was transferred to a council in Washington D.C. that was fifteen times the size of the Yocona Area Council.

From observing Daddy work with the Scouts in Troop 12, Brian came to have great admiration for his leadership skills. He was patient and tolerant, and he reinforced the values and principles Brian believed in at meetings and on campouts. During Blaine's time in the troop, he rarely needed to be disciplined. Brian had to say only that he was disappointed, and it had the desired effect. Once when Brian and Blaine were discussing the subject of discipline, Blaine said Daddy didn't even have to say he was disappointed to get the Scouts to do the right thing. He just had to look disappointed. But, Blaine said, Daddy would then lift the boys up. He would let them fall because they couldn't learn without falling, but he didn't let them fall too far or stay down too long.

Another of Daddy's traits that Brian admired was how he dealt with challenging circumstances. Daddy had no fear of challenges and never let them get him down. They were just issues to be faced, analyzed, and resolved and opportunities to learn and grow. Once when Troop 12 was dealing with some difficulty, Daddy said something that summed up his philosophy: "Anybody can camp in pretty weather." Brian said he stole the line and used it over and over for the rest of his Scouting career.

Brian was a Boy Scout but also loved baseball and dropped out of Scouts to focus on the sport when his family moved to Atlanta. His father and stepfather were fine men, but they didn't push him to earn his Eagle. He regrets it to this day. After telling me this, Brian said he was jealous that I was Daddy's son and he wasn't. I said it wasn't always so great being Daddy's son. When Brian gave me a curious look, I explained that there was no way I could ever measure up. I suppose all sons of great men feel that way.

During Brian's tenure as the Scout executive in Tupelo, the council commissioned a painting of a Scout scene each year and gave away prints to significant donors. One of them, entitled "The Gateway to Adventure," features an older Scout leader with gray hair wearing a red coat. I inherited a print of the painting from Daddy, who was one of the donors, and have always assumed he was the leader depicted in it. Brian confirmed that Daddy was the inspiration but said he didn't reveal that when he was the Scout executive. If supporters of other troops wanted to think the man in the painting was their leader, Brian wanted to let them.

In 2003, the year Daddy was chosen to be the grand marshal of the Tupelo Christmas Parade, Brian was in the stands watching when Daddy marched at the front with me and the Scouts of Troop 12. As Daddy walked by in his red coat, the same one the leader is wearing in "The Gateway to Adventure," Brian said he thought to himself, *There goes the Pope of Tupelo.* Perhaps that's an odd title for a lifelong Methodist, but I like it. To Adrian Thompson, Daddy was the Apostle. To Brian Steger, he was the Pope.

Because the Yocona Area Council is a small one, the executive position was not considered a plum assignment. Brian agreed to serve for only four years and planned to move to a larger council at the first opportunity. But with the support he found in Tupelo, he soon realized he was in a wonderful place for Scouting. He didn't want to leave; nor did his wife Sue. They wound up staying for thirteen years and moved back to Tupelo when Brian retired. Like Mama and Daddy, they concluded that there was no better place to live.

REED HILLEN

Tupelo lawyer Reed Hillen comes from a long line of Boy Scouts. Members of four generations of the family, all named Walter Reed Hillen, were Scouts, and three were Eagles. Reed's grandfather and father were Scouts in South Carolina. Reed's father earned his Eagle in Charleston. Reed's son, Walter Reed Hillen IV, who also goes by Reed, is the only one to earn his Eagle in Troop 12. He became the troop's 302nd Eagle Scout in 1997.

Reed III grew up in Starkville, the home of Mississippi State, where Daddy's squadron came under enemy fire on their leaflet mission in November 1946. Reed earned his Eagle under the leadership of Scoutmaster Don Fitzgerald, an engineering professor whose mission was to teach the boys of Troop 27 to love the outdoors as much as he did. During his years as a Scout, Reed climbed his first mountain, explored his first cave, and canoed his first river. The experience opened his eyes to what has been a lifetime of adventure.

In the summer of 1976, when Reed married a young woman from Tupelo after his first year of law school, Mama and Daddy attended the wedding. Two years later, when Reed joined a law firm in Tupelo, Daddy asked around about him. Two canoes leaning against the front porch of the law firm's office confirmed what he was told. Daddy soon appeared at the office, introduced himself, and asked if Reed would help with Troop 12's outdoor program. Reed wasn't planning to get back into Scouting anytime soon, but he knew immediately that he liked Daddy and wanted to spend time with him. He began attending Monday night meetings, teaching merit badges, and camping with the troop.

Reed has spent his entire career practicing law in the same firm in the same office. The name has changed from Holland, Ray & Upchurch to Hillen, Wicker & Tapscott, and Reed has gone from the youngest lawyer in the firm to the oldest. But the office, a converted home on West Jefferson Street less than a block from the Lee County Courthouse, remains the same. Forty-four years after Daddy showed up at the office to talk to Reed about helping with the troop, I showed up there to talk to Reed about Daddy.

Also present for our interview was Bo Hillen, a large, gentlemanly Lab mix Reed rescued from his life as a stray on the campus of Itawamba Community College. Reed and Bo are constant companions, and Bo's behavior is so impeccable that he's welcome in the courthouse. He no doubt has better manners than many members of the Bar.

I learned about another constant in Reed's life in our interview. He was in his mid-twenties when Daddy came calling and is now in his late sixties, but he's never stopped working with Troop 12. He started out helping with the outdoor program, then became an Assistant Scoutmaster, then served on the troop committee, then chaired it, and is now chairman of the board of review, which meets with boys who are eligible for rank advancement to ensure that they've met all the requirements.

While working with the troop committee in the 1980s, Reed accompanied Daddy to a meeting of the administrative board of the First Methodist Church to discuss a proposal to build a new Scout Hut. The old one was being torn down to make way for the church's new family life center, where Mama later roller skated to big band music. Reed said Daddy presented the plan, and the board approved it without asking a single question. Daddy had been the Scoutmaster for nearly forty years by then. The board knew he would ask only if it was essential and that he wouldn't waste a cent.

Other than when his son was in the troop, Reed didn't camp every month, but he camped often and got his wish to spend time with Daddy. He told me about his first campout, to Shiloh in the fall of 1978, a winter trip to the Sipsey Wilderness when all the waterfalls were frozen, and canoe and raft trips on Bear Creek, the Ocoee River, and the Locust Fork.

Reed shared with me the qualities he believed made Daddy a great leader. Even with chaos swirling around him, Daddy was always the voice of calm and reason. He never raised his voice and never needed to. He had a quiet confidence and presence. Reed figured he was that way from the beginning; he couldn't imagine him any other way. He said Daddy was the consummate Scoutmaster and always seemed to know the best solution to every problem.

Daddy's two principal assistants in Reed's early years were Paul Fairley and Buddy Miller. The three men were close friends and worked well together, but Daddy was the calm one. When one of the Scouts hid Fairley's car keys on a campout, he got angry and started yelling, which was no doubt exactly the reaction the boy wanted. Daddy walked to the campfire to speak to the boys. He had a good idea who the culprit was, but he didn't accuse anyone and didn't raise his voice. He just said, "We're going to need those keys. Where do you think they might be?" The prank wasn't fun anymore, and the suspect soon confessed and returned them.

Reed said Daddy kept a special eye out for boys who were socially awkward and didn't fit in well with the others. He often asked one or two of them to share a tent or canoe with him, and he made sure the other boys weren't too hard on them. He wanted all the Scouts to enjoy Scouting, love camping, and keep coming back. Reed said Daddy never gave up on a boy. Some who were homesick on their first campouts and wanted to quit became Eagle Scouts four years later. They entered the next phase of their lives with self-confidence they'd never had before. Daddy once said, "Working toward Eagle, a young man feels he has a goal. When he attains it, he knows that he has accomplished something." Halfway through his tenure as Scoutmaster, Daddy said his goal was for Troop 12 to have 200 Eagle Scouts. By the end of 2022, the troop had 457.

Reed said Daddy was an expert in all camping skills and a connoisseur with a Dutch oven. Reed had Dutch oven experience as well. The troop was large and active, and multiple cobblers baked in Dutch ovens were needed to feed everybody on campouts. I told Reed about the wonderful emails I received from Mike Bush after Daddy died—about Daddy's apple eating and the boys' spoons reflecting the firelight when they gathered round for cobbler. Reed said he could picture Daddy with the firelight reflecting off his pocketknife as he sliced his nightly apple. When Reed stopped by Rogers Drive for a visit during Daddy's last years in Tupelo, he always took Daddy some apples.

Reed was impressed by Daddy's energy and work ethic even in his later years. He was always the first to arrive and the last to leave, and he stayed until everything was in its proper place. He also admired Daddy's willingness to defer to Sam Agnew after Sam became the Scoutmaster. Not many who've led an organization for forty-five years are comfortable in a secondary role, but the boys came first for Daddy. His ego didn't matter. And his commitment to serve others inspired Reed to follow in his footsteps. In addition to his many years of service to Troop 12, Reed has chaired the United Way and Downtown Redevelopment Agency, served on the board of the Red Cross, and participated in many other volunteer activities.

Reed and I became friends when I returned home to Tupelo in the 1980s to canoe with Daddy and the troop. All three of us were on the canoe trip on Bear Creek when a deer was swept over the waterfall to its death. I also canoed with Reed and the troop on the Locust Fork, where he and some paddling buddies own a rustic cabin on a cliff overlooking the river. The cabin, which they built during an icy February four decades ago and repeatedly expanded, has no gas, no electricity, and for many years had no running water. Yet they still managed to have a hot tub. They filled the tub with water by running garden hoses from a stream on the slope above and heated it with charcoal. After a cold day on the river, it was sublime.

Reed and I were also together on the 500th campout in 1993 and the trip to the Middle Fork of the Salmon River in Idaho the following year. He had forgotten that I was the one who suggested the Middle Fork, but he remembered the enthusiasm when the trip was proposed, approved, and announced. Dads who had never camped with the troop in the usual sites around Tupelo were excited about going to Idaho, and they were right to do so. It was a magnificent trip.

When Daddy was asked to run for the board of aldermen, Reed counseled against it. He told Daddy he didn't need the headache. But Daddy rejected his advice, won easily, and Reed said he soon became the board's leader. He listened carefully, said what he thought was best for the city and why, and the other members deferred to him. Scott Reed told me nobody seemed to know or care whether Daddy was a Republican or a Democrat. He was a member of the Tupelo party. Daddy did such a fine job that Reed later encouraged him to run for mayor. Daddy rejected his advice again.

While he was serving on the board and city council, Daddy often stopped by Reed's office for coffee when he was downtown on city business. One occasion was shortly after Reed and his wife of many years had separated. Daddy didn't mention the separation, but he obviously knew about it. He told Reed, "Take a deep breath, you'll get through this, it will be okay." Daddy was right; Reed got through it and is now happily married to Mary Jane Meadows. Daddy's advice to Reed could just as well have been one of the principles he followed in leading Troop 12. *No matter the challenge, take a deep breath, we'll get through this, it will be okay.*

A Scout is usually awarded his Eagle badge in a ceremony in his own church, but many non-Methodists in Troop 12 chose to receive theirs in the First Methodist Church because it sponsored the troop and was Daddy's church. The ceremony has always been a special occasion and a rite of passage, with all the Eagle Scouts in the congregation asked to stand.

The Hillens are Episcopalian, but young Reed chose to have his Eagle ceremony in the Methodist Church. Reed arranged it so he would be on one side of his son with Daddy on the other. He has a photo of the three of them together. There are no doubt hundreds of similar photos spanning Daddy's six decades of service to the Scouts of Troop 12. Each one includes a proud parent or two, a boy on the path to manhood, and the Scoutmaster who helped him along the way.

Months after interviewing Reed, I came across the email he sent me after Daddy died. He wrote: "One of the best, and I mean best, things that ever happened to me was that day in June 1978 when he knocked on my office door for the first time. Within ten minutes, I had either volunteered or been drafted into Troop 12's ranks—you just couldn't say no to him—and have never regretted the adventure for a moment. And to have Reed IV as one of his Scouts and a Troop 12 Eagle was just icing on the cake."

BILL MURPHREE

I interviewed Troop 12 Eagles Will and Jim Murphree in February 2022. Six months later, I spoke to their father, Bill, who became the troop's fifty-ninth Eagle Scout in 1962. When I interviewed him in his office in downtown Tupelo, Bill had just turned seventy-five and was at the end of a long, successful career as a trial lawyer in the largest firm in northeast Mississippi. Half a century earlier, he served in the Marines during the Vietnam War. He reached the rank of first lieutenant, then served more than two decades in the Mississippi National Guard. He retired as a lieutenant colonel.

Like many of the men I've interviewed, Bill began our talk with memories of campouts. He remembered his very first one, to Tishomingo State Park in the fall of 1958. Some of the older boys tricked him into going on a snipe hunt, and he helped build the monkey bridge across Bear Creek. Two years later, also at Tishomingo, he listened on his transistor radio to the 1960 World Series, the one when the Pirates beat the Yankees on Bill Mazeroski's home run in the bottom of the ninth in the seventh game. I told Bill about the troop's campout to Tishomingo nine years later, when Daddy and I listened by the campfire while the rest of America watched as Ole Miss lost to Alabama 33-32. Bill said he was one of those watching. He was in Officer Candidate School in Quantico, Virginia, at the time.

Bill also remembered a winter campout at Ruff's Farm when the temperature dropped to far below freezing. Campfires were useless because of the high wind. He said it was the coldest he's ever been in his life. I told him about my first cold-weather campout, when six of us piled into a three-man tent to keep each other warm. As Daddy told Brian Steger, anybody can camp in pretty weather. Daddy could have added that you remember it when you camp in weather that's not pretty. From campouts when Bill was a Scout and those he attended when his sons were in the troop three decades later, he said he was certain that Daddy thoroughly enjoyed camping.

Bill echoed what others told me about Daddy's leadership style. He wasn't heavy-handed; he expected the senior patrol leader to lead the troop and the individual patrol leaders to lead the patrols. They learned by watching Daddy, but they learned even more by doing it themselves, often by making mistakes. Daddy let boys be boys, but he didn't let things get out of hand. There were no fights. He treated everyone the same and didn't play favorites.

When Daddy taught the boys how to tie knots and other practical skills, he used stories to illustrate why the skills were important. Bill recalled the story of the airmen who saved themselves by tying bowline knots when the wind lifted the blimp they were holding. Daddy told the same story to Bill, to me, and to Bill's sons, and all four of us remembered. I wonder how many times Daddy told the story over the span of six decades.

Because of the respect the Scouts had for Daddy, he could get them to do things they may not have wanted to. They did them for Daddy, and they rarely told him no. Bill offered two examples, one involving Ken Kirk, whose suggestion started the monthly campout streak in 1951, the other involving Bill. Ken was a celebrated All-American football player at Ole Miss when Bill was in the troop. Every year Ken made time to come home from Oxford to talk to the Scouts and show them an Ole Miss game film. It was an exciting night and increased the boys' enthusiasm for Troop 12. In Bill's case, after he began practicing law in Tupelo, Daddy asked him to teach Citizenship in the World merit badge, one of those required for Eagle. Bill was busy and the merit badge boring, but he taught it every year for nearly a decade because Daddy asked.

Bill told me about incidents when two Scouts needed discipline and guidance. The two were Bill and his son Jim. The first occurred in the summer of 1959 when Bill was at Camp Yocona. Instead of spending the week working to meet the requirements to advance to First Class, he hung out at the trading post and the lake. Daddy summoned him, addressed him by his last name, and said "Murphree, you need to get to work and quit goofing off." Like the bowline story, the incident made an impression. He said Daddy never screamed or hollered, but he got his point across.

More than three decades later, when Daddy was in his last year as the Scoutmaster, Jim said he wanted to skip a campout and hang out with friends who weren't in the troop. Bill said he needed to go, that the other Scouts and Daddy had placed their trust in him by choosing him to be the senior patrol leader. When Jim protested, Bill told him he could stay home, but first he had to call Daddy and tell him he was resigning as senior patrol leader. That ended the discussion. Jim went camping, just as I camped in the Sipsey Wilderness when I wanted to stay home with my girlfriend. Daddy taught me, and Bill taught Jim, that if you say you're going to do something, you do it.

I asked Bill about lessons he learned from Daddy that he used later in life, and he mentioned two. One was how to lead people and know when they need a pat on the back or a kick in the rear, as he needed at Camp Yocona in 1959. The other was to be prepared, always. Bill said he applied the lessons both in the military and in his law practice. He might lose a trial on occasion, but it was never from lack of preparation. He said Daddy demonstrated the importance of being prepared by always being prepared himself.

Whenever a new preacher was transferred to the First Methodist Church, Bill said Daddy would meet with him to enlist his support for Troop 12. Daddy had better luck with some than with others, and he had the best luck with Bo Holloman, a wonderful man who was the preacher when I was in the troop. Brother Bo supported the troop with enthusiasm; he even attended the Monday night meetings in a Scout uniform. Some may have thought of Daddy as the Apostle or the Pope, but I'm sure having an actual preacher there improved the Scouts' decorum. When the troop was leaving to go on a campout, Brother Bo would meet us at the Scout Hut and pray for our safety before we headed into the wilderness. We always made it back.

Bill's firm represented the city when Daddy was an alderman and city councilman. He said Daddy was considerate of other people's opinions and cared deeply about the job he was doing. After Daddy stepped down, a lawsuit was filed under the Voting Rights Act claiming that having an at-large position diluted the rights of black voters. When the court ruled against the city, Bill's partner Guy Mitchell told the judge he understood the ruling, but he wanted him to know that the best city council member Tupelo ever had was an at-large member, Paul Eason.

When I mentioned what Daddy must have meant to boys who didn't have good fathers at home, Bill became the second man to bring up Andy Lawhon, who was Bill's cousin. Andy's father was killed on Saipan in World War II when Andy was less than a year old. He told Bill there were five wonderful men in his family who cared for him—two grandfathers and three uncles—but that nobody meant more to him than Paul Eason. Andy said he tried all his life to be like his Scoutmaster. When he died in 2021, his obituary said his fondest childhood memories were spending days with cousins and friends and being a member of Paul Eason's Boy Scout Troop 12.

At the end of our talk, Bill spoke of Daddy's innate decency and said he always did the right thing. He was a wonderful man, thoroughly honest, morally straight, and a perfect example for boys. He never heard Daddy brag or thump his chest and never heard anyone else say a bad word about him. He never knew anyone who was more comfortable in his own skin. Bill concluded by saying, "He was the most principled man I've ever met. People like your dad don't come along every day. He was one in a million."

Phil Ruff

Phil Ruff is my first cousin. Daddy's sister Puddie and her husband, Guy, were his parents. Phil became Troop 12's eighty-sixth Eagle Scout in 1967. Daddy had three nephews who earned the rank of Eagle in the troop—Phil, his brother David, and Eason Leake—and one great-nephew, Phil's son Adam, who became the 367th

Eagle in 2005. That was fifty-eight years after Daddy became the Scoutmaster, but he was still coming to meetings and camping.

Phil began our talk with memories of campouts. The troop went every month, rain or shine, hot or cold. Cold-weather campouts were a challenge for Phil because he had chronic asthma. He had trouble sleeping in the cold, but he never missed a campout. When Puddie dropped him off at the Scout Hut, she would tell him, "If you need anything, Bubba will be there." Daddy's sisters and their children called Daddy Bubba. Nobody else did.

Phil talked about riding to Tishomingo in the back of a U-Haul truck the troop borrowed from a Tupelo dealership. Someone always supplied a case of moon pies for the ride. The back door was kept open for ventilation, and a net made by lacing ropes back and forth across the opening kept the boys from falling out. Some sat with their legs dangling over the edge. A Scout leader would probably get arrested for letting boys do that now. On the way back to Tupelo on Sunday, the older Scouts convened a Kangaroo Court in the back of the U-Haul for younger ones who'd misbehaved. Daddy allowed it because punishments were mild, and it was another way for the boys to learn to govern themselves.

Phil described building the monkey bridge that spanned Bear Creek. There were two long ropes that were used for handholds, a long, thick one for walking on, and many short thin ones that were attached to the three to keep them the right distance apart. Timbers were erected and lashed together on the banks of the creek, and the long ropes were tied to them. Daddy had a knack for coming up with projects that were fun and educational but also helped the boys earn merit badges. A Scout could meet some of the requirements of Pioneering merit badge by working on the monkey bridge.

Phil talked about three canoe trips from his time in the troop. On a trip to Bear Creek, the weather and water were bitterly cold. Three boys who kept turning over abandoned the trip and called their parents to retrieve them. I told Phil I was surprised Daddy let them go home. Phil said they were scared and cold, and Daddy probably decided it was no longer a teachable moment. That night, the remaining boys, all exhausted, sat by the campfire trying to get warm. Daddy told them a story that must not have been his best because they started dozing off. Daddy kept talking, and more of them fell asleep. Finally, when Daddy had outlasted them all, he ended the story with a blood-curdling scream. The startled boys rose and shuffled off to their tents.

A second trip was in east Mississippi on the Tombigbee River, long before there was a Tenn-Tom Waterway. The troop stopped paddling the Tombigbee before I was a Scout, and Phil explained why. The current was so slow that the boys tied their canoes together, then tied the lead canoe to a jon boat equipped with an outboard motor. The boat towed them down the river like a string of barges.

Phil and David talked their dad into joining the troop to paddle the Current River one year. The trip included two full days on the river and three nights of camping. The last night's campsite was at the take-out point where they'd left their vehicles. When it was time to turn in, Phil and David couldn't find their dad and asked Daddy where he was. Guy wasn't much for camping and was tired of sleeping on the ground. He had left his sons behind, driven into town, and was staying in a hotel room. The story of Guy's slipping off to check into a hotel reminded me of the church-lawn campout when I went to a movie at the Lyric Theater, and I told Phil about it. It turned out I wasn't the first to have the idea. He said he and some other Scouts saw a Boris Karloff movie one year at the church-lawn campout.

We also talked about the tapping ceremony for the Order of the Arrow, which we called OA, that was held one night during the week the troop spent at Camp Yocona in June. All the boys from every troop at camp gathered in an amphitheater in the woods at the narrow end of the lake. The ritual had a Native American theme, with beating drums and headdresses worn by the Scouts leading the ceremony. Each Scout elected by his troop to join OA learned he had been chosen when an arrow was broken over his shoulder. The highlight was a huge bonfire by the lakeshore lit by a flaming arrow sent sliding down a wire from high in a tree on the opposite side of the lake. The wire ended in a tall pile of timber. The wood had been soaked with kerosene and burst into flames when the arrow reached it. The ceremony was a highlight of the week at camp.

A water carnival on Saturday morning with troops competing against each other marked the end of the week at Yocona. The carnival had been a fixture of summer camp since the Yocona Area Council was established in 1926. One event was called the canoe exchange. Two boys in a canoe raced around a series of buoys, swapping places when a whistle blew one time and jumping into the lake and climbing back in when it blew twice. Phil and David won the race when they were at camp, and Dan Purnell and I won it when we were there. There was also a greased watermelon event in which boys competed in shallow water to see who could pick up a watermelon covered in grease and bring it ashore. Troop 12 always won the water carnival.

Phil said Daddy and his assistants, James Byrd, W.E. Plunkett, and Jim High, imposed few limits other than those necessary to prevent injuries to Scouts and damage to equipment. Part of learning leadership was discovering what was acceptable and what wasn't. Daddy let boys learn by making mistakes. He also knew that boys loved fires and would let them build big ones as long as they took precautions to keep them from burning out of control. I told him of a campout when some of us found a fallen tree that was too big to saw into logs. We dragged it into camp and fed it into the campfire four feet at a time. By midnight, it was gone.

Phil said the Scouts were expected to do the work and be responsible. Daddy and the assistants didn't inspect patrol boxes to make sure they contained everything needed for a campout. They told the boys that was their job. They could do it well or do it poorly. The older Scouts helped and taught the younger ones. When a new group of boys joined the troop, the older ones served as their role models. When a Scout had been in the troop two or three years, he wanted to be a role model too. The culture of Troop 12 was not one of bullying or pulling rank as in some organizations.

Phil said the culture came directly from Daddy. He was the head teacher. He stressed the principles embodied in the Scout Law and Oath as well as the Scout Slogan to do a good turn daily.

With the basic principles and processes in place, Daddy adopted a hands-off approach to managing the troop. The boys learned and became leaders and teachers themselves.

Phil, his wife Norma, and their two children moved back to Tupelo from Tampa in 1998, the year before Mama died. In the years that followed, he and Daddy began attending events together, including meetings of the Community Development Foundation and the Kiwanis Club. Later, after Daddy gave up driving, Phil became his principal caretaker. He recalled the day Daddy asked for a ride to an appointment with his neurologist. When Daddy failed several of the tests used to diagnose dementia, Phil realized he needed to play a bigger role. They developed a weekly routine. Every Friday Phil picked Daddy up and took him to Kiwanis, and every Sunday after church, Daddy treated Phil to lunch and they went to the grocery store. He said Daddy's weekly list included a single roll of toilet paper and seven pints of ice cream but no green bananas.

When Daddy and Phil were at lunch, at least one person in the restaurant who knew Daddy, and often more than one, would come over to speak. Daddy might not remember them, but he was always gracious and glad to see them. They included former Scouts, people who worked with Daddy on the city council, and fellow employees he'd hired and worked with at FMC. Phil said they often pulled him aside to share things just with him, perhaps because they were too embarrassed to say them directly to Daddy. Phil remembered some of their comments: "He stood up for me." "He was the best boss I ever had." "He did more for me and my career than anybody."

CHRIS RILES

The ranks in Scouting between Tenderfoot and Eagle are Second Class, First Class, Star, and Life. When Chris Riles moved to Tupelo and joined Troop 12 in 1991, he was already a Life Scout and close to becoming an Eagle. He worked on the few merit badges he still needed and began camping with the troop. He said he was impressed by Daddy, the assistant leaders, and the dads who joined the troop on campouts. One of his first campouts was a backpacking trip in the Sipsey Wilderness. Chris had already signed up to go to Philmont with his old troop in Brandon, Mississippi, and the trip to Sipsey was a good warm-up.

Chris said Daddy was already a legend by the time he joined Troop 12. Daddy wore vintage uniforms from the '60s and '70s that looked newer and nicer than the ones the Scouts wore in the '90s. Several boys who were in the troop with Chris were the sons of men who had become Eagle Scouts under Daddy's leadership. The second-generation Eagles who were Chris's contemporaries included Will and Jim Murphree and Britt Rogers Jr. Daddy was not only a legendary Scoutmaster, but he also volunteered at the Methodist Church and elsewhere and was an elected official in the Tupelo city government. Chris said attending a city council meeting to fulfill a requirement for Citizenship in the Community merit badge was special because Daddy was there as the councilman-at-large and vice mayor.

To become an Eagle Scout, a boy must plan a service project to benefit a church, school, or community and lead others in completing it. When Chris asked Daddy for suggestions, he said the Tupelo Garden Club wanted birdhouses, and he could ask Gravlee Lumber Company to donate the materials. With help from his parents and fellow Scouts, Chris built forty birdhouses that were placed all over town. He completed his Eagle project in the spring of the tenth grade and finished all his Eagle requirements by the time school ended. Daddy scheduled a board of review, and Chris became Troop 12's 261st Eagle Scout that summer. He was one of the last Scouts to become an Eagle before Daddy stepped down as Scoutmaster and became an assistant.

Most boys end their time in Scouting when they become Eagle Scouts, but Chris remained active through his eleventh-grade year, teaching young Scouts and acting as the senior patrol leader when he was needed. He also served as a troop officer at the 500th campout, when Troop 12 alumni living all over America gathered at Camp Yocona to honor Daddy. Chris said it was a weekend he'll never forget. Leaving his friends in Brandon and moving to Tupelo in high school was difficult, but the opportunity to spend time with Daddy was a silver lining.

During his senior year of high school, Chris worked part time in a grocery store. Once a week or so, Daddy would come in with residents from Traceway Manor. He always took time to visit with Chris, and the two of them would assist the residents with their shopping. Daddy helped the residents just as Phil Ruff helped Daddy fifteen years later.

Chris was a member of Phi Delta Theta when he was in college at Mississippi State. He returned to Tupelo after graduation, became a banker, and began working with the troop again. Daddy was almost eighty, but he still came to every Monday night meeting. Chris wore a Phi Delta Theta tee shirt to one of them, and Daddy told him they were fraternity brothers. Chris was delighted to learn they were Brothers in the Bond. There are many great men who were members of Phi Delta Theta—Lou Gehrig, Neil Armstrong, and William Winter among them—but whenever Chris recruits high school seniors to join the fraternity, especially former Boy Scouts, he always tells them about Daddy.

Chris said Daddy gave Troop 12 a tradition and a brand, that boys still join because of his legacy. Fathers want the same experience for their sons that they had when Daddy was their Scoutmaster, and those who were not in the troop have heard about Daddy and Troop 12. Chris was forty-six at the time of our talk, and his son had just earned the rank of Life in Troop 12, the same rank Chris held when he joined the troop three decades earlier. I expect his son will soon be added to the roster of Troop 12 Eagles.

Chris and I closed our talk by discussing the extraordinary length of Daddy's service. Chris said most men give less than a decade as a volunteer, and I told him Daddy gave six decades to the Scouts of Troop 12. Daddy was awarded the Silver Beaver for his outstanding contribution to Scouting in 1959, when he'd been the Scoutmaster for a dozen years and had two young children to raise. Margie was four, I was two, and Daddy was the plant manager at Milam Manufacturing. He could have decided he'd given enough, but he kept giving for five more decades. Chris told me he was blessed to spend time with Daddy during one of those decades and is a better man because of it. He wanted to be like Daddy then, and he still does.

ELNA BARBER

Two years after I left for college, Elna and Eddie Barber bought the house on Rogers Drive across the street from the creek where my friends and I spent our summer days. The Barbers' two children, Lauren and Griff, were born not long after. When our children were young, they played with Lauren and Griff on their trips home to Tupelo to see Mama and Daddy.

When I interviewed Elna about her time living on Rogers Drive, she started with a question: "Did he ever once lose his cool?" I said maybe a time or two, and she said she couldn't imagine it, that Daddy was the calmest, most even-keeled person she's ever known. By the time the Barbers moved into the neighborhood in 1977, Daddy had been the Scoutmaster for thirty years. A man has to be calm and even-keeled to do that.

Elna said Mama and Daddy were wonderful neighbors and recalled that Daddy maintained the property on the east side of the creek even though it was owned by the city. If something needed doing, unless a Scout needed a lesson in responsibility, Daddy didn't worry about whose responsibility it was. He just did it.

Elna enjoyed singing with Mama in the annual Singing Christmas Tree at the Methodist Church and said Mama and Daddy were always helping at the church. She told me about being tricked by Mama on Halloween. Mama would wear a costume, mask, and wig, get down on her knees, ring the doorbell, and wait. When the Barbers opened the door, Mama would say trick or treat in a child's voice and hold out her bag. She somehow managed to keep from laughing until they forked over the candy.

When Megan and Shannon, Margie's two daughters, traveled from Florida to see Mama and Daddy, we would take Ann Lowrey up from Jackson to spend time with her cousins. Elna said Daddy would load up his three granddaughters and Lauren, sometimes Griff too, and take them in the White Elephant to get ice cream. In my day it was cones from Bill Bates's gas station. A quarter century later, it was cups from the Company Store. Ice cream was the constant.

Daddy would also entertain Griff and the girls by using a string and raw bacon to lure crawdads from their holes alongside the creek and by taking them to play on the swing set at City Park. With Daddy in the lead, they would march down the hill through the woods to the railroad tracks behind the park. When they heard a train coming, he would give each of them a penny to place on the tracks. After the train passed, they searched for the flattened pennies. The story of the pennies reminded me of the years before we had central air on Rogers Drive, when I would lie in my bed with the windows open and listen to the trains as they rolled through Tupelo.

There were few boys for Griff to play with in the neighborhood, and he would often walk across the street to spend time with Daddy. After Daddy retired in 1986, he was usually working on some project in the yard or his workshop. Griff would watch and learn, and they would talk. Daddy was good at talking to children without talking down to them. Griff also liked to ride with Daddy when he ran errands for Troop 12 in the Elephant. They were two generations apart, but they were friends.

The Barbers sold their home on Rogers Drive and moved to another neighborhood in 1991. When Griff turned eleven two years later, he joined Troop 12. Daddy had stepped down as Scout-master, but he was still active in the troop. Elna said he taught Griff and some other young Scouts how to cook breakfast on a campfire. Before then, Griff didn't know you could cook the bacon first and use the same pan and some bacon grease to fry or scramble your eggs.

Griff became the troop's 310th Eagle Scout in 1997. Daddy was seventy-five and Griff fifteen when they had their photo taken together at the Eagle ceremony. Elna told me she was amazed by Daddy's patience and willingness to devote so much of his time and his life to other people's children. He did it for thousands of them.

ANN LOWREY FORSTER

Ann Lowrey Forster, my only daughter, has much in common with her grandfather. Like Daddy, she's a natural leader, a gifted teacher, and a role model for young and old alike. But there are differences. Unlike Daddy, Ann Lowrey has never been accused of being reserved or soft-spoken.

Ann Lowrey became a single mother when she was twenty and founded a school before she was thirty. The school, St. Augustine, is a classical Christian school in a Jackson suburb that works on a hybrid model. The younger students attend classes two days a week, the older ones three. Parents home school the younger ones on the off days. The older ones have assignments they're expected to complete on their own. St. Augustine started from scratch and had fewer than sixty students its first year. Now it has more than 300. Ann Lowrey, whose title is Founder and Head of School, has been the driving force. While performing her duties as an educator, she has also been raising four of my five grandchildren.

One weekend in January 2023, Ann Lowrey made time in her schedule to talk to me about Daddy. When our children were young, we started calling him Big Paul to distinguish him from our son Paul. She said the times she spent with Mama and Big Paul in Tupelo are among her fondest early memories. Sometimes all five of us made the pilgrimage, but she and her brothers would often go without us, transferring from our vehicle to Daddy's at the McDonald's in Kosciusko. Ann Lowrey described Mama as bright, feisty, and efficient, Daddy as easygoing, reserved, and low maintenance. Neither was sugary or overly affectionate. They loved her and her brothers but didn't spoil or indulge them. They treated Margie and me the same way.

Ann Lowrey and the boys played in the creek and vacant lot with the neighborhood children, including Lauren and Griff Barber, and Daddy took them to the Ruffs' house to swim and pick blueberries. It was obvious to Ann Lowrey that he loved Puddie and loved spending time with her. He pushed them in the rope swing hanging from a huge oak in the Ruffs' front yard and the one hanging from the hickory in the vacant lot. He would say, "One for the money, two for the show, three to get ready, and four to go" as he gave them four pushes and ran under the swing on the last one. Ann Lowrey thought as he pushed her that I did the exact same thing. It must be something else I learned from Daddy without realizing it.

Ann Lowrey saw how thrifty Daddy was and concluded that I learned that from him too. They rarely went out to eat, and he handed them an apple when they wanted him to buy them a snack. On the rare occasions when they went to McDonald's, he wouldn't buy them Happy Meals. I know what he was thinking; he wasn't going to waste an extra dollar on a box and a toy that wouldn't last an hour. But while Daddy was scrimping on fast food for his grandchildren, he was also making significant contributions to their college funds. He also enclosed a five-dollar bill in each letter he sent Ann Lowrey when she was at summer camp and told her to buy something at the camp store or put it in the collection plate. Daddy was both thrifty and generous. Being the former enabled him to be the latter.

Daddy also took them to City Park, which was beside Joyner School, and to the graves of his parents in the cemetery beside City Park. Ann Lowrey has a vague memory of Momie, who died when Ann Lowrey was four. Daddy gave the children coins to place on the railroad track behind the cemetery, and they searched for them after a train rolled past. Ann Lowrey initially said they were pennies and quarters, but we decided they must have been pennies and nickels. A man who wouldn't buy a Happy Meal wouldn't let a train ruin a quarter. When he wasn't doing something with the children, Daddy was always mowing or working around the house. He rarely hired anyone to do anything. He was too thrifty and self-reliant.

Ann Lowrey remembered studying all the plaques and certificates hanging on the wall in the den on Rogers Drive and thinking Daddy must have received every award there was. I said displaying them was probably Mama's idea, but she said maybe not. Daddy was never one to call attention to himself, but he might have thought that putting plaques in a drawer or behind a cabinet door would show a lack of gratitude.

We talked about the 500th campout and the wonderful trip on the Middle Fork of the Salmon the following year. Ann Lowrey was only ten, but even then she thought the trip must have been fancier than anything Daddy had ever experienced. Sitting by the campfire on the trip, she listened to stories told by former Scouts and was surprised to hear that Daddy enjoyed playing pranks. She remembered hearing about a practice I witnessed first-hand involving one of Daddy's favorite beverages. Daddy loved apple juice. In the days before juice came in individual cartons, he would pour some into a jar and take it on campouts. If one of the boys asked what he was drinking, Daddy would take a sip, wipe his mouth, grin, and say, "cool specimen."

On most Sundays during her years at Ole Miss, Ann Lowrey drove to Tupelo and met Daddy for lunch. Mama was gone by then, and Daddy had overcome his aversion to eating in restaurants. But there was still nothing fancy. His three favorites for lunch were IHOP, Olive Garden, and Danver's. Ethnic food was out of the question. She talked him into going to a Mexican restaurant once, and he ordered a cheeseburger. We took him to a Greek place after he came to live with us, and he ordered a cheeseburger then too. Ann Lowrey said he was middle class to the core. After lunch, they went to his house, where she spent the afternoon doing laundry and visiting with him. She tried to get him to talk about himself—his childhood, the Navy, and courting Mama—but she didn't get much out of him. He would give a short answer and return to the crossword puzzle.

In her junior year, Ann Lowrey began taking Ada Brooks and Paul Forster on the Sunday pilgrimages to Tupelo. She told me Daddy soon became Paul's biggest fan. He was not only a candidate to become the father Ada Brooks needed, but he and Daddy were cut from the same cloth. Both were men of duty with simple tastes and no interest in finery. Paul was thrilled when Daddy treated him to a stack of pancakes at IHOP. Once when Daddy was late meeting them for lunch, he apologized and said he'd been driving the old folks back to Traceway Manor after church. Ann Lowrey and Paul gave each other a look. Daddy turned eighty-five the year they graduated and married.

Ann Lowrey reminded me that she and Paul considered moving to Tupelo after graduation. Daddy rode around town with them and showed them affordable neighborhoods, but he put no pressure on them. He would have loved to have them in his hometown, but Ann Lowrey said he didn't try to influence them. Where they lived and what they did were up to them. He just wanted her to be honorable. He got his wish.

Paul, Ann Lowrey, and their children came to our house often after Daddy came to live with us, and they stayed with him for a week so we could take a vacation. She remembered a time when I asked Daddy if he knew who his great-grandchildren were. He said he knew they were connected to him somehow.

Ann Lowrey was fifteen when Mama died in 1999. While we were in Tupelo for the funeral, she made a point of keeping an eye on Daddy to see how he was doing. She said he was somber but not the least bit undone. We agreed that he was never the least bit undone. Like John Prine's grandfather in "Grandpa Was A Carpenter," Ann Lowrey's grandfather was level on the level.

Lynn Bryan

Like Ann Lowrey, Lynn Bryan has a great deal in common with Daddy. Daddy was born more than forty years before Lynn was, but both were Eagle Scouts in Troop 12, both served as the troop's Scoutmaster, and both were elected to three terms on the Tupelo City Council.

Lynn became the troop's 164th Eagle in 1978. His younger brothers Hamp and Locke are also Troop 12 Eagles, as is his son George. When I spoke to Lynn in February 2023, he had just stepped down after serving as the troop's Scoutmaster. He's now in his third term on the city council but is running for Lee County Tax Collector, and he decided the campaign would leave him with too little time to continue leading the troop. Sam Agnew, who stepped up to serve as the Scoutmaster in 1992 and stepped down in 2005, has stepped up again. Lynn is now chairing the troop committee.

Lynn remembered when his mother dropped him off for his

first campout after joining the troop. It was raining so hard he could barely see. She said, "I'll see you Sunday," and he raced to the Scout Hut with his gear. The campout had not yet begun, but he was already soaking wet.

Lynn told me stories of misbehavior and mistakes on campouts from which he learned. On Bear Creek one year, he and some other boys didn't follow Daddy's instructions about the route to take. They ultimately had to turn back. When they finally caught up, Daddy and the rest of the troop had been waiting for two hours. Daddy said nothing, but punishment was swift and sure when they stopped to make camp.

On a trip to the Naval Air Station in Pensacola, Lynn and his buddies discovered there were more than just soft drinks in a vending machine in the barracks. Schlitz and Old Milwaukee were also available. The boys bought and drank their first beers, got caught, and again got punished.

On the Shiloh campout one year, the temperature was in the twenties. With Daddy at the wheel of the White Elephant, they came upon a large, perfectly shaped hornets' nest hanging from a limb. They assumed it was abandoned and decided to take it back to Tupelo and display it in the Scout Hut. A boy climbed the tree, sawed off the branch, and they put the nest in the back of the Elephant. But the nest was not abandoned, the heat was on in the Elephant, it roused the hornets, and soon they were flying everywhere. The boys flung the nest out the passenger door and vowed never to make that mistake again. I'm sure Daddy did too.

Lynn joined the Army after college and served as an officer in Germany and in the Gulf War. He and his wife returned to Mississippi when he was discharged in 1994 and a few years later moved back to Tupelo, where he owns and manages a successful construction company. When he began helping with the troop in the late nineties, Daddy was still active but couldn't attend some of the campouts because he needed to be home with Mama.

Lynn said he learned many things from his years in Troop 12 that still come in handy: first aid, how to put up and take down a tent, tie knots, build a fire, and stay warm and dry. When I asked what he learned from Daddy, he said the main thing was commitment. More than half a century, camping every month, and Daddy rarely missed one. Lynn also spoke fondly of Daddy's assistants, Paul Fairley, Buddy Miller, Jim High, and Rob Coates. They rarely missed a campout either. When Daddy was there, they were too, and he couldn't have done it without them.

Lynn said he's also learned how valuable it is to be an Eagle Scout. Eagles are sought after in the business world because earning the highest rank in Scouting is a sign that a young man will make a commitment and see it through. Lynn's son George was able to enlist in the Coast Guard at a higher rank than others because he was an Eagle. There are numerous scholarship programs for Eagle Scouts as well. Many institutions of higher learning, including all the public universities in Mississippi, provide scholarships for Eagle Scouts. The National Eagle Scout Association offers scholarships of up to $12,000 a year. Eagle Scouts also make up a high percentage of each class at America's service academies and more than twenty percent at West Point. Congressman Trent Kelly told Lynn he likes to nominate Eagle Scouts for appointments to the academies because he knows they will stick it out.

One of my favorite Eagle Scouts, though not one of Troop 12's, is Jonny Drake, a full-bird colonel in the United States Army. Johnny earned his Eagle in Troop 8 in Jackson and lived with us his senior year of high school after his parents moved to Montana. He graduated from West Point, served combat tours in Iraq and Afghanistan, and now holds a high-level position at the Army War College in Carlisle, Pennsylvania. Patriotism and duty to country are virtues a Boy Scout learns.

Daddy once said Scouting was the only game in town during his early years as the Scoutmaster. At its peak during his tenure, the troop had 120 members. But there is now far more competition for boys' time than there was then, and the number of boys in Troop 12 dwindled to thirty in the years after Daddy stepped down. But thanks to Lynn, Sam Agnew, and others, Troop 12 is now on sound footing again. To make the troop an attractive option, they've taken the boys to national and world jamborees and on high adventure trips to Minnesota's Boundary Waters and elsewhere. Thanks to their efforts, the troop is now back up to fifty-five members. Lynn said two boys showed up at the Scout Hut for the most recent Monday night meeting wanting to join the troop. The legacy begun by Daddy continues.

GLENN MCCULLOUGH

Glenn McCullough has had a long and successful career in the public sector. He served as Executive Director of the Appalachian Regional Commission, Mayor of Tupelo, Chairman of the Board of Directors of the Tennessee Valley Authority, and Executive Director of the Mississippi Development Authority. He now chairs a European company, serves on the board of directors of a Mississippi bank, and consults on energy and economic development matters. Despite all these successes, when I spoke to Glenn in February 2023, he told me his aspiration was to be more like Daddy.

Glenn's two significant experiences with Daddy were thirty years apart. In the first, Daddy was the Scoutmaster of Troop 12, and Glenn was a member of the troop. In the second, Daddy was the at-large member of the Tupelo City Council, and Glenn was the mayor.

Glenn is thirty months older than I am, and I didn't know he'd been in Troop 12 until we spoke. He must have left the troop shortly before I joined it. He said he was interested in sports, pursued them instead of Scouts, and didn't stay in the troop long enough to advance to Eagle. More than fifty years later, he still regrets it. But though he wasn't in Troop 12 for long, he has fond memories of Daddy's quiet leadership and his commitment to the boys in his charge.

When Glenn was elected mayor in 1997, Daddy had already been on the council for two terms and was a recognized leader. Glenn said Daddy was a skilled listener and observer, a doer, not a talker. Daddy did his homework and made things happen. He was an excellent sounding board for Glenn. Daddy didn't do a lot of talking, but when he did, the other members of the council and Glenn listened.

Glenn told me of three of the city's successes that Daddy was

instrumental in achieving. One involved the acquisition and development of fifty acres on the east end of downtown on the old site
of the Mississippi–Alabama Fair and Dairy Show where Elvis
Presley performed. The project, which was named the Fairpark
District, required the city to issue bonds in the amount of $23
million, which was a huge debt for a city the size of Tupelo. Daddy
studied the options, listened to what others had to say, and decided
on the best one. The other council members quickly agreed. Since
then, Tupelo's Fairpark District has become a national model for
urban renewal. The district includes a new Tupelo City Hall, two
hotels, four restaurants, the Cadence Bank arena, the Community
Development Foundation headquarters, a business incubator, office
buildings, and a residential development.

The second success involved construction of a huge pavilion
at Ballard Park on the west side of town, the site of the Paul
Eason soccer field. Tupelo has been recognized many times as an
All-American City by the National Civic League. Every Fourth of
July, the city hosts an All-American City picnic in Ballard Park with
fireworks and entertainment by the Tupelo Symphony Orchestra.
It's the only opportunity many have to see and hear the symphony.

One of the principal expenses of the annual picnic was $30,000
to rent and assemble a stage large enough for the orchestra. Daddy
decided there had to be a better way and, working behind the scenes,
persuaded private citizens to underwrite the cost of construction of
a huge pavilion in the park. The pavilion is now used for events year-
round, and the city no longer needs to rent a stage for the picnic.

The third project was securing approval of a new City of Tupelo
Transportation Plan that included a four-lane northern loop connect-
ing Gloster Street, the city's principal north-south thoroughfare, to
Interstate 22. The plan was important to the city's future, and Glenn
said Daddy was instrumental in obtaining the council's approval.

I learned about all these achievements for the first time from my
talk with Glenn. When he was mayor and Daddy was on the city
council, I lived three hours south of Tupelo. I was busy practicing
law and raising children, and Daddy didn't tell me about his work
on the council. Glenn said Daddy never called attention to himself

and never wanted any recognition or applause. He just wanted to get things done and make his hometown a better place.

Daddy replaced Glenn briefly as mayor in the third year of Glenn's term. I knew part of the story but not all of it. I learned from Glenn that Daddy became the mayor thanks to Senators Thad Cochran and Trent Lott and President Bill Clinton.

Glenn was in his office one day, and his assistant said Senator Cochran was on the phone. Unlike many bigwigs, Thad placed his own calls. Glenn answered, and the senator said he and Trent had a new job for him. When Glenn said he already had a job, Thad asked how many people lived in Tupelo. Glenn knew the exact number and told him: 32,684. Senator Cochran asked if he would like to serve 10,000,000 people instead. That was the number of residents in the Tennessee Valley who received electricity from the TVA. Mississippi's two senators wanted to request President Clinton to nominate Glenn to serve on the TVA's three-member board of directors.

After discussing the opportunity with his wife Laura, Glenn decided he couldn't turn it down. President Clinton nominated him, the Senate approved him, and two years later President Bush chose him to become the chairman of the board. After Glenn took the position with the TVA, Daddy served as the acting mayor until a permanent replacement could be chosen in a special election.

Glenn told me that serving with Daddy was one of the most cherished experiences of his life. He said Daddy improved everything he touched. But it was clear that Glenn admired Daddy more for who he was than what he achieved. He described Daddy as a humble man who was totally devoted to his faith, his family, his country, and his hometown. Daddy wanted to know about other people and had no interest in talking about himself. He was calm, soft-spoken, and made you feel comfortable. He was a man with his life in order.

DAVE AND CLARK BURNETT

Dave Burnett became Troop 12's forty-ninth Eagle Scout in 1959, his brother Clark its seventy-first five years later. They learned to be leaders during their time in the troop. Both were elected by their peers to serve as the troop's senior patrol leader and were chosen for induction into the Order of the Arrow. I interviewed them in February 2023.

Before talking about Daddy and their years in the troop, I asked the Burnetts to tell me what they've done with their lives in the six decades since they were Scouts. They both joined Naval ROTC when they were in college and, like Daddy, served as active-duty officers after graduation. Dave was a Nuclear Submarine Officer on the USS Spadefish, a fast attack submarine. Clark was a Deck Officer on the USS Long Beach, the first nuclear-powered surface ship ever built, and fought in the Vietnam War.

Before joining the Navy, Dave studied Chemical Engineering at Georgia Tech. While in the Navy, he went to Nuclear Power School, served in many leadership positions on the Spadefish, and earned a master's degree in Nuclear Engineering from Rensselaer Polytechnic Institute in upstate New York. After his discharge, he obtained a second master's degree, this time in Business Administration from Harvard. He then had a successful career in the private sector, mostly in California, before retiring in 2013. In the decade since then, he's enjoyed hiking and backpacking in the mountains near his home in Santa Clarita. Dave was seventy-seven at the time of our talk, but Clark said he can't keep up with him on the trail.

Clark said Dave got the brains in the family, but he got the looks. I said he definitely got the hair. Neither has much, but Clark has more. Clark went to Ole Miss and returned home to Tupelo after Vietnam to work with his family. Their father Cy owned and operated the Rex Plaza, a hotel and restaurant on North Gloster Street where we often ate Sunday dinner. Clark spent his mornings working in the hotel, his afternoons helping on his grandparents' farm. He enjoyed the farm work, and his grandmother enjoyed watching him. His dad wanted him to take over the hotel, but Clark said the hotel business was not for him. He accepted a position with a large cotton merchandising company in Memphis and worked there until it went out of business in 2008. He spent ten

more years in the cotton business before retiring in Wimberley, a
small town in the Texas Hill Country.

Neither of the Burnetts' parents was interested in the outdoors,
but Dave and Clark both came to love it during their time in Troop
12. They credit Daddy for what has been a lifelong passion. Dave
put outdoor activities on hold for most of his career, but he resumed
them in 2005. The trip that renewed his interest was climbing Mt.
Whitney with his seventeen-year-old son and his son's friends. The
boys were too young to get a permit, so they recruited Dave to
join them. He was sixty, but he reached the summit of the highest
mountain in the lower forty-eight states. The trip reminded him
how much he loved the outdoors and hiking, and he's been doing
it at every chance since then.

Clark has never taken a break from the outdoors. He said he's
been on too many trips to count—hiking, backpacking, mountain
climbing, and whitewater rafting all over the country. He's climbed
Mount Rainier and the Tetons and, like Daddy and me, rafted the
Grand Canyon and the Salmon River. He still takes his family
hiking in Colorado every summer. After talking about all of his
adventures, Clark said of Daddy, "He gave me that." He gave me
that too.

Both Burnetts shared fond memories of their years in the troop.
Clark said, "We were THE troop" and always won the water carnival on the last day at Camp Yocona. Dave spoke of the games
the Scouts played after Monday night meetings, great times on
campouts at Tishomingo and Shiloh, and a canoe trip on the
Tombigbee River when they had a ball. He recalled that Assistant
Scoutmaster W. E. Plunkett was on the canoe trip. Plunkett always
wore his life jacket because he never learned to swim.

Dave recounted the February when he was the senior patrol
leader. The troop's campout was scheduled for early in the month,
but the weather was terrible, so they agreed to postpone it. The
next weekend was just as bad, so they postponed it again. It came
down to the last weekend of the month, and the forecast called
for miserable weather again. No matter how bad it was, Dave and
Daddy agreed they would camp out to keep the streak alive even if

it was just the two of them. They wound up with Daddy and a half dozen boys, though the troop was more than ten times that size.

Clark told three stories of his time in the troop, one when he disappointed Daddy, a second when Daddy was proud of him, and a third when Daddy helped him become a leader by making him lead. On the first occasion, Clark was working on Cooking merit badge on a campout. Preparing a hot cereal was required. Clark had forgotten to bring oatmeal, grits, or cream of wheat, so he improvised. He heated some milk and poured it on some corn flakes. It was cereal, and it was hot. Daddy asked him, "You really think that's what hot cereal is supposed to mean?" and walked off. Clark said Daddy didn't say a lot, but you always knew how he felt.

Clark did better in the second story. While they were building the monkey bridge across Bear Creek at Tishomingo in his last year in the troop, one of the younger Scouts slipped off a rock into the water and was carried downstream by the swift current. Clark jumped in, grabbed the boy by the arm, and pulled him to shore. Daddy arrived seconds later and told Clark how proud he was. Clark said it made him feel wonderful.

Clark's third story was from a Monday night meeting, his first as senior patrol leader. The boys had just come in from outside and were loud and wild, as boys tend to be. Clark was standing by Daddy and asked him what to do. He was expecting advice on how to get the boys to calm down, but Daddy gave him different advice. It's been sixty years, but Clark remembers Daddy's exact words: "You're the leader now. Take charge." So he did.

Dave and Clark said they used the leadership skills they learned from Daddy in the Navy and their careers that followed. Clark said Daddy had a subtle way of teaching leadership and didn't tell the boys how to lead. He led by example, and the boys learned by watching. Dave said they also learned honesty, integrity, and steadfastness from Daddy. He was always encouraging in a quiet way, and you always wanted to please him.

Both Burnetts came back to Camp Yocona for the 500th campout in March 1993. Dave and Stuart Worley came from the longest distance, both from California. Dave remembered sitting around a campfire with old friends on Friday night and gathering for the banquet on Saturday. He said the dining hall was packed wall-to-wall with Eagle Scouts. The Burnetts' father, who was nearly ninety, drove over from Tupelo for the banquet. He was the only one at their table who was not a Troop 12 Eagle.

When their father could no longer drive, Daddy picked him up every Friday and took him to the Kiwanis Club. Years later, when Daddy could no longer drive, Phil Ruff picked him up and took him to Kiwanis. Whenever Dave came home to Tupelo, he made a point to stop by Daddy's house and spend time with him. When Daddy was in his late eighties, Dave wasn't sure Daddy knew who he was, but he was always glad to see him.

Dave and Clark both said Daddy was one of the three most important men in their lives. The other two for Dave were their father and grandfather. For Clark, they were their father and Coach Jerry Clayton. Clark said Daddy was a great man, and Dave agreed. When I mentioned that Daddy stuck with it for sixty years, Clark said he was a saint.

At the end of the interview, I told the Burnetts how much I was enjoying writing the book and what a treasure it was to talk to some of the many people who loved Daddy. Clark said, "We sure did. Lots of people did."

Brad Tackett

I've seen Brad Tackett one time in my life. It was at a Halloween party in 2021 in Seagrove Beach, Florida, at the home he shares with his wife Rebecca and their daughters Taylor and Harper. Carrie and I didn't know the Tacketts but were invited to the party because we were visiting the beach with Rebecca's mother and stepfather. I had no idea Brad had ever lived in Tupelo, much less that he was a member of Troop 12.

After introducing ourselves to Brad and Rebecca, Carrie and I were on their patio talking to some other people we'd just met. Brad was in another group ten feet away. Carrie overheard him say he was from Tupelo. She told him I was too, that Eason Boulevard was named for my family. Brad looked from her to me, and his eyes widened. "Paul Eason?" he asked. I said he was my father.

Brad abandoned his group and marched over with his hand extended. I'd shaken it when we arrived minutes earlier, but I shook it again. He spent the next ten minutes telling me about his time in Troop 12 and how much Daddy meant to him. He shook my hand twice more while we talked. He said Daddy and I were legends. I corrected him. Daddy was the legend, not me.

Sixteen months later, I called Brad so he could tell me more about his life, his time in Troop 12, and his memories of Daddy. Brad studied landscape architecture at Mississippi State, and after graduating accepted a job on Hilton Head Island with Wood and Partners, a large landscape design firm. He and Rebecca had a great time there, but they ultimately came back to Mississippi, where he became a contractor and built houses. After nearly a decade, which included the housing crash of 2008, Brad began working for Wood and Partners again, this time remotely. An opportunity then took the Tacketts to Seagrove Beach, where he spent the next few years overseeing large commercial projects for the firm. But his passion is residential landscaping, and at the end of 2021 he took a leap of faith and opened his own firm. It's been going like gangbusters ever since.

Brad wasn't a member of Troop 12 for very long. Like Glenn McCullough two decades before him, his time in the troop was derailed by a passion for sports, and in his case a family tragedy. Most of the men I've interviewed for the book were Eagle Scouts. Glenn and Brad are reminders that Daddy had a positive impact on thousands of boys who did not make it to Eagle. It has been thirty-five years since Brad was a member of the troop, but he said Daddy is etched in his mind and has never left his memory. When I showed up at his Halloween party, the memories came flooding back.

Brad had no family members in Troop 12 and no connection to the First Methodist Church, but a friend, Clay Short, invited Brad and another of their buddies, Pip Pipkin, to come to a meeting to learn about Troop 12 and Scouting. They liked what they heard, signed up, bought their uniforms, and began attending Monday night meetings. Brad said he loved the meetings and loved being in the troop.

Not long after he joined, Brad went to summer camp. It was 1985, one of the years Daddy decided the troop would have its own camp at J. P. Coleman State Park. Brad said the week camping on Pickwick Lake was one of the greatest times of his life. It was a boy's dream, exploring the wilderness, learning to shoot a bow and arrow, playing with the other boys. He called home on a pay phone during the week to tell his parents he was having a great time and had learned to water ski and loved it.

Brad shared a tent with Pip at J. P. Coleman. Like many new Scouts, Brad said he and Pip were dumb and dumber. When they pitched their green canvas tent, they looked like two cats fighting in a paper bag. They put the tent on a slope with the door facing uphill and did nothing to prepare for rain. That was fine the first two nights when the weather was clear, but not the third. It started raining, Brad realized he was getting wet, and sat up and turned on his flashlight. Water was rushing in through the door. So much water came in that the tent collapsed. Some older boys came to their rescue, and everything dried out the next day. They did better the second time they put up the tent.

On the next to last day of camp, Brad and Pip got busted for violating the buddy system. If one of them was swimming, the other one was required to be in the water too, but Pip stayed in and Brad got out. Their punishment was having to wear wet life jackets to dinner. It was just unpleasant and embarrassing enough to ensure they would never do it again. When Taylor and Harper go swimming now, Brad reminds them to use the buddy system.

The boys had ridden to camp on a bus, but their parents were to pick them up on the last day. Brad's parents were coming to get him and Pip, but Daddy said they were running late. This was before cell phones, and Brad wondered how Daddy could know. While the boys waited, Daddy asked them to walk down to the pier to make sure the troop had left nothing behind.

Waiting for them there, in a brand-new ski boat, were Brad's parents. Brad stopped in his tracks, stared at his parents and the boat, then turned and looked back up the hill. Daddy was standing there, watching and smiling. Daddy waved; Brad and Pip waved back and jumped into the boat. The Tacketts were not well-to-do by any means, and it was the last thing Brad expected. He said it was one of the best moments of his life.

They spent a wonderful afternoon skiing and exploring Pickwick Lake, and Brad and his dad had many great times on the boat the rest of that summer and the next. They returned to Pickwick and went skiing on the Tenn-Tom Waterway and elsewhere.

But in August 1986, Brad's world came crashing down. He and his parents were out on the boat. His mother was driving. His dad was skiing and took a nasty fall. On the drive home, he started coughing up blood. They rushed him to the hospital, where he was diagnosed with Stage 4 lung cancer. He never came home and died before Christmas.

Brad was not yet twelve. He and his mother had to make it on their own and figure out how to get by. Brad was in Troop 12 and played baseball and soccer. His mother worked, they lived out in the country, and getting him to and from meetings, practices, and games was a constant challenge. She decided he couldn't keep doing it all and needed to decide what was most important to him. Brad loved Troop 12, but he was very competitive and very good at soccer. He chose soccer over Scouts and baseball. He never formally quit the troop, but he went to fewer and fewer meetings as the months went by, then stopped going altogether.

Brad's time in Troop 12 had ended, but Daddy's influence on him had not. He told me Daddy was his first real mentor and role model other than his parents. Daddy was sweet, gentle, and easygoing. When you accomplished something, he made you feel proud of yourself. Brad's parents thought very highly of Daddy, but he didn't know if they knew him or just knew of him. He said everybody in town knew Daddy was a great man and a great leader. Brad remembered watching Daddy and thinking, *There are really good people out there*. He said kids watch adults. They listen and learn. Brad watched Daddy and wanted to be like him.

When I asked Brad what he learned from Daddy that is still with him, he thought for a few seconds and answered with one word: integrity. Daddy always did the right thing. He mentored Brad and showed him the right path. He treated others with kindness, helped them, and did things without expecting anything in return.

The Tupelo soccer organization established a select team called the Tupelo Titans in 1988. Brad tried out and made it. They traveled around the state and played other elite teams. The Titans were good, and Brad loved it. Though it was their first year, they won the regional and made the state tournament. The semifinal game was at Ballard Park in Tupelo on Paul Eason Field. Brad said it was the premier field in the soccer complex. The turf was better, the goals better, the bleachers bigger. Only big games were played there. Brad had never played a game on it before. When he walked onto the field, he said he looked at the sign with Daddy's name on it. He felt bad about dropping out of Scouts and thought about how much Daddy meant to him.

The game was tied late in the second half, then Brad scored a goal at the end to win it for the Titans. He told me he stayed on the field for forty-five minutes soaking it all in, not wanting to leave, not wanting it to end. He thought of all the people who'd helped him and all the people who would be proud of him. And he thought of Daddy.

At the end of our interview, Brad said he was honored to talk to me about Daddy and grateful that I asked him to contribute to the book. As for me, I'm grateful that I was invited to the Tacketts' Halloween party and that Carrie heard Brad say he was from Tupelo.

Kirk Purnell

Camille Purnell, the leader of my Cub Scout den in the mid-1960s, loved the Boy Scouts, Troop 12, and Daddy. When her sons were in the troop, she bought their gear, took them to meetings and campouts, and pushed them to earn merit badges and advance in rank. Over the span of three years, all three of them—George, Dan, and Kirk—became Eagle Scouts.

In March 1971, when we had to cut the Bear Creek trip short because of high water, Camille was part of the rescue team that came to pick us up. I remember watching as she helped carry a canoe through the muddy cow pasture up to the waiting trailers. She was never one to stand around when there was work to be done. I was helping carry the canoe behind her. She and I were both on the right side of the canoes. I was using my left arm because my right one was in a cast. Camille's canoe tilted her way because she was barely five feet tall.

I interviewed Camille's youngest son, Kirk, in February 2023. It was the first time I'd spoken to him since July 1994, when we parted ways at the end of our wonderful trip on the Middle Fork of the Salmon River with Daddy, Ann Lowrey, and all the rest. Kirk reported that his mother is still active, driving like a bat out of hell to deliver Meals on Wheels to the elderly three times a week. She is ninety years old but still a force of nature.

Kirk moved to Texas not long after graduating from Mississippi State and accepted a job with Ben E. Keith Foods, a food-and-beverage distribution company headquartered in Fort Worth. Though he had a degree in marketing, his first job with the company was driving a forklift. He advanced quickly from there and held positions in sales and purchasing before moving into management. Kirk is now in his thirty-ninth year with the company and serves as the General Manager of its Oklahoma Division, which has often been chosen as one of the best places to work in Oklahoma. He has a total of 580 employees who work under his supervision.

Kirk told me his boss says you get promoted by showing that you're promotable. Kirk attributes his promotions to having a strong work ethic, which he in turn attributes to the hard jobs his father gave him in the family chicken business when he was growing up and to his time in Troop 12.

Kirk worked on a company farm in his teens baling hay, and he spent a summer mowing grass at the company's facilities. One night a group of us, including Kirk and Dan, volunteered to work on a chicken-catching crew. Wearing surgical masks to ward off the dust, we walked back and forth into chicken houses all night, bringing out seven chickens at a time to be loaded onto trucks and taken to the processing plant. We would reach under the chickens and grab them by one leg, four in one hand, three in the other. It was a grand adventure the first half hour but miserable the rest of the night. Kirk said the physical labor he did growing up was good training for supervising employees who do physical labor.

All the Purnell boys were small and had to learn to be tough. Camille viewed Scouts as one way to accomplish that. Troop 12 went camping come hell or high water. The weather didn't matter. Kirk remembered camping in the snow on the church lawn the last weekend in February one year to keep the streak alive. He went with the troop on grueling hikes and difficult canoe trips. It wasn't always easy, but it wasn't supposed to be. And it built character.

But all of Kirk's memories of his years in the troop, even the hard times, are fond ones. He recalled playing capture the flag at Shiloh and listening to the Ole Miss–LSU football game by a campfire later that night. On a cold winter campout, he and three other boys decided to unzip their sleeping bags and put one under them and the other three on top. Daddy discouraged them and suggested that two boys climb into one sleeping bag if they were cold. They didn't listen and suffered through a miserable night. Kirk learned his lesson. He's camped many nights since then and knows how to stay warm.

Kirk was also on the trip to Pensacola and got busted along with Lynn Bryan when they discovered a vending machine with beer in it. The violation in Kirk's case was buying and drinking a Falstaff. He remembered jumping out of the White Elephant at red lights and running around it until the light turned green. One year he had stitches in his head when the troop went to the Current River. The doctor sprayed some sort of wax on the wound to keep it dry and ordered Kirk not to let his canoe turn over. He didn't.

For Christmas in 1972, Kirk's parents gave him and Dan a trip to the 1973 National Boy Scout Jamboree in Farragut State Park in northern Idaho. More than 34,000 Scouts from all across America attended. Bob Hope was the featured entertainer. Scouts from throughout the Yocona Area Council, some who later went to

Mississippi State with the Purnell brothers, rode thousands of miles together on a bus. The trip included stops in three national parks—Rocky Mountain, Yellowstone, and Glacier—and Kirk got his first taste of the mountains of the West.

Kirk and his brothers returned to Camp Yocona for the 500th campout in March 1993. The following summer, two decades after his trip to the jamboree, Kirk returned to Idaho for the raft trip on the Middle Fork of the Salmon. He asked me about Richard and Mike Condrey from the trip, and I told him I'd interviewed Richard and learned that Mike was sailing around the world. I talked to Kirk a year after talking to Richard, but Mike was presumably still at sea.

Kirk and his wife Shannon married late. He was forty-two; she was thirty-five. They live in Oklahoma City and have one child, Sam, who became an Eagle Scout the year before our interview. Kirk was very active with Sam's troop and camped often with them. Times had changed from when we were Scouts. The adult leaders in Sam's troop always had a separate campsite and campfire so they could enjoy an adult beverage or two. The adults' site was called North Korea, the boys' South Korea, and the senior patrol leader was the only Scout allowed to cross the DMZ between them.

Other than vending-machine beer in Pensacola, there was no alcohol on Troop 12 campouts. But there are far more rules now than there were then, and Kirk said the boys don't have to be as tough or endure as much. He told me Sam's troop would cancel a campout if the forecast was for a low below forty. But Kirk made sure Sam experienced grand adventures. The two of them went to all three of the Boy Scout high-adventure camps, sailing at the Sea Base in the Bahamas, hiking in the mountains of Philmont, and canoeing in the Boundary Waters. Kirk told me he's also taken several camping trips to the Grand Canyon with a group of friends, hiking from the rim down to the Colorado, along the river, then back up to the rim. Of the seven men who went on his most recent trip, five were Eagle Scouts.

When I asked Kirk what he learned from Daddy, his answer was similar to what many others told me. Daddy was always positive.

He was a good listener and teacher. He didn't talk a lot, but you listened when he did. He led by example, and Kirk learned to lead by watching him. He saw that Daddy was ethical, calm, and patient. His patience, Kirk said, was unmatched. Kirk also grasped the importance of practicing what you preach and never asking anyone to do something you wouldn't do yourself. He said Daddy also made him realize that having fun is part of good leadership. Daddy had a great sense of humor and loved to have fun with the boys. Like many others, Kirk said he didn't realize how much he benefited from his time in Troop 12 with Daddy until long after he was grown.

Kirk now serves on the Board of Directors of the Last Frontier Council of the Boy Scouts. He enjoys telling others about his Scoutmaster and said his fellow board members and hiking buddies know all about Daddy and Troop 12 and are envious of Kirk's experiences when he was a Scout. He asked when the book would be published and said he wanted ten copies to give away. When Daddy died, Camille sent him the obituary, and he sent it to many of his friends. He knew about Daddy's service to the Scouts but had no idea he had done so much else for so many others. Kirk told me times may have changed, but the principles Daddy taught have not.

At the end of our talk, Kirk and I vowed to camp together again in November 2034 if we're both still able. I'll be seventy-seven, he'll be seventy-five, and it will have been forty years since we camped together in Idaho. The occasion will be Troop 12's thousandth consecutive monthly campout. We'll share a campfire like we did when we were members of the troop more than sixty years earlier, and this time we'll offer a toast to Daddy and Troop 12.

HANK BARGER AND STAN BYRD

Hank Barger and Stan Byrd both became Eagle Scouts in Troop 12 in 1967. At the time of our interview, they were seventy years old and enjoying retirement after long, successful careers. Each of them had just one employer as an adult. Hank was an executive at Exxon, Stan a professor at the University of Tennessee at

Chattanooga, UTC. They haven't lived within 500 miles of each
other since college, but nearly five decades after going their separate
ways, they are still close friends.

Hank went to work for Exxon after graduating from Mississippi
State. He spent forty years with the company, holding positions in
revenue, financial and production accounting, accounting systems
development, and training. His career took him to Houston, Los
Angeles, Houston again, then Fort Worth, where he and his wife
Jean now live.

Stan earned three degrees in math—bachelor's and master's
degrees at Mississippi State and a Ph.D. from Florida State. He
arrived at Florida State the same year as legendary football coach
Bobby Bowden and joined the faculty of UTC in 1980. He taught
math there until his retirement thirty-seven years later. He said he
knows nothing other than math, but I didn't believe him.

Stan said his career choice was inspired by another Troop 12
Eagle. When he and Hank were in the troop, Daddy invited Eugene
Worley to a city-wide Eagle Scout banquet to talk about his work in
NASA's space program. Stan was fascinated, became more interested
in math and science, and the interest led to his decision to become
a math professor. Stan said Eugene was instrumental in establishing
and maintaining hiking trails around Huntsville, and I told them
about my discovery that Eugene's brother Stuart hiked in Patagonia.
They recalled another Troop 12 Eagle Scout, Gary Moore, who
spent a year hiking from Argentina to Texas in the 1970s.

Stan told us another story involving Troop 12 and NASA. In
1961 or '62, several years before Eugene Worley spoke at the Eagle
Scout banquet, the troop traveled to Huntsville to see the Redstone
Arsenal and a Mercury rocket. Stan was still a Cub Scout but was
allowed to go because his dad James had recently become an Assistant Scoutmaster in the troop. Stan had his Brownie camera, pulled
it out, and began snapping pictures. A NASA official spotted him
and confiscated the camera. Photos, even taken by a nine-year-old,
weren't allowed.

Hank has remained active in Scouting as an adult and now serves
as his church's institutional representative to the Boy Scout troop

it sponsors. He advised an Explorer post in Houston during his first stint there, and an older man who was the Scoutmaster of a troop in Los Angeles asked Hank to serve as an assistant shortly after he moved there. Just as A. P. Bennett turned Troop 12 over to Daddy as soon as he saw that it was in good hands, the leader of the troop in Los Angeles bowed out after a month and turned it over to Hank. He served as the Scoutmaster until he was transferred back to Houston.

Hank and Jean have two daughters. He was very active with them in the YMCA Indian Princess program during his second stint in Houston and camped as often as when he was in Troop 12. He and one of his daughters spent a night aboard the USS Lexington, an aircraft carrier that was converted into a museum in Corpus Christi Bay after it was decommissioned. Hank has two pictures of him sitting in the captain's chair on the Lexington, one on the trip with his daughter, the other when he boarded the ship in Pensacola thirty years earlier with Daddy and Troop 12. I told them the troop was planning to spend a night aboard the USS Alabama in Mobile Bay on the next campout.

Stan told us of meeting a professional Scout executive named Connie Hay at a Mississippi State alumni event in Chattanooga. Connie was a World War II veteran and former coach, and before that he played college football. He weighed only 150 pounds, but he started on the Bulldogs' offensive line alongside future comedian Jerry Clower. Connie was similar to Daddy in many ways and, though he and Stan were a generation apart, they became close friends. Connie lived a long, productive life and died when he was ninety-four.

Hank and Stan compared notes before our interview to recall all the places Troop 12 camped when they were members. The first two they mentioned were Tishomingo and Shiloh, the two favorites where the troop camped every fall. They loved riding to Tishomingo in the back of the Hertz truck, and both remembered listening to Ole Miss–Alabama games on the campout, though they were no longer in the troop in 1969 when Alabama won 33–32. Stan also recalled listening to the 1964 World Series at Tishomingo, and he

said the battlefield at Shiloh was one of his favorite places in all
the world. He's bought old patches on eBay commemorating the
hikes the troop took there. They listed other Troop 12 campsites:
the church lawn; Davis Lake; Boggan's, Kelly's, and Ruff's farms;
the Nettleton Clubhouse; the Pensacola Naval Air Station; and
the Tombigbee River, which they canoed every year. They cherish
their memories of camping with Daddy and the troop.

But they also recalled incidents when Scouts misbehaved and
suffered the consequences. Two were at Ruff's farm. One time the
problem was fire, the other time cows. Hank was one of the delin-
quents in the first incident. He and some other Scouts, displaying
the wisdom for which adolescent boys are known, decided to throw
burning sticks into the area where some younger boys were camping. They managed to set two sleeping bags on fire. In the second
incident, a boy left a gate open, and cattle escaped and had to be
rounded up. If Puddie had not been Daddy's sister, that probably
would have been the end of the annual campout at Ruff's farm.

On another occasion, Hank, Stan, and Phil Ruff were walking
on the Natchez Trace, taking one of the ten-mile hikes required
for Hiking merit badge. Litter was more of a problem than it is
now, and hundreds of beer cans were strewn along the roadside.
The boys began stomping on the cans with their heels and walking
with them stuck to the bottoms of their shoes. When a can fell
off, they would find another one and repeat the process. A trooper
pulled over, pointed to the trail of cans behind them on the road,
and read them the riot act. Hank said they often learned the hard
way, but at least they learned.

In 1969, two years after he earned his Eagle, Hank went to the
national jamboree in Idaho. Stan's dad was one of the leaders on
the trip, but Stan was in summer school at Mississippi State getting
a head start on college. Hank said a huge television was set up in
the middle of the jamboree site, and Scouts from all over America
gathered around it and watched Neil Armstrong walk on the moon.

Hank's dad Henry was a fine man and was always willing to help
when Hank was in the troop. When Troop 12 canoed the Tombigbee, Henry piloted a jon boat full of supplies and camped with the

boys. He continued helping when Hank's brother David and I were in the troop. Henry was an Army tugboat captain during World War II and piloted houseboats on the troop's Tennessee River trips.

Stan said his dad loved mine and thoroughly enjoyed serving as an Assistant Scoutmaster. He began several years before Stan joined the troop and continued for several years after Stan earned his Eagle, stopping only because his career took him to Long Beach on the Mississippi Coast in 1970, the year Stan graduated from high school. Three decades later, Daddy attended a conference on the Coast while serving as Tupelo's acting mayor. He made a side trip to Long Beach and had a great visit with his old friend and former assistant, who sent Daddy home to Tupelo with a sack full of vegetables from his garden.

Near the end of our talk, I asked Hank and Stan what they learned from Daddy. Hank said he and Stan carry a lot of Daddy with them and that Daddy's leadership style rubbed off on him. Daddy led through his assistants and the older Scouts. He was the unflappable conductor of the orchestra, delegating tasks to others and staying on the sidelines unless things got out of hand. Stan said Daddy could be stern, but he never saw him get mad. They agreed that Daddy's talents and demeanor were perfectly suited to be a Scoutmaster and that serving in the role was his passion. Both said it was an honor to know him.

Stan said Daddy was like a second father to him and, after his own father, the second most influential man in his life. When Hank was asked to become an elder in the Presbyterian Church, he was required to write a paper about the men and women other than his parents who had the greatest influence on him. He put Daddy at the top of the list and said Stan's dad and W. E. Plunkett were on it too.

I told Hank and Stan that the three of us were fortunate to have such wonderful fathers and told them about Brad Tackett, whose father died when he was eleven. "As much as Daddy meant to the boys who had fine fathers who raised them to adulthood," I said, "just imagine what he meant to those who didn't."

Channeling Richard Condrey, Hank said, "Amen."

BARRY PLUNKETT

W. E. Plunkett always went by his initials or his last name, never his first or middle names. His full name was not even revealed in his obituary. He was just W. E. Plunkett, 86, of Tupelo. Like Mama, he died in September 1999. In a span of less than ten days, Daddy lost his wife and a dear friend.

If you had been given the names W. E. was given, you would go by your initials too. The W was for Welmer, the E for Elbert. When asked how he came to have such unfortunate names, W. E. would say his mama hated him. But he didn't mean it, she didn't hate him, and she raised him well. He was a fine man with a keen sense of humor, a stalwart member of the First Methodist Church, a longtime Assistant Scoutmaster of Troop 12, and the leader of Explorer Post 12. I interviewed his son Barry and grandson Jeff Pruett in February 2023. Barry became an Eagle Scout in Troop 12 in 1962, Jeff in 1979.

Barry is seventy-four and "retired" from a long career as a hospital executive. I put retired in quotes because Barry and his wife Barbara own and operate a boutique in Jackson, and he has an active healthcare consulting practice. He evaluates grant applications for states all over the country, performs health needs assessments for hospitals, and leads leadership retreats for healthcare executives.

When Barry was in Troop 12, if he wasn't at home or in school, he could almost always be found somewhere in the city block in downtown Tupelo bounded by Main, Church, Jefferson, and Green Streets. His dad worked for the TVA in the Professional Building on the southwest corner, his grandmother lived in the northeast corner, and he attended Sunday School, church services, and Scout meetings in between. He recalled a memorable weekend on the same city block. It was Valentine's Day and the troop's annual church-lawn campout. He slept soundly, poked his head out of his tent in the morning, and the world was white. Five inches of snow had fallen in the night. Many of the boys' tents had collapsed under the weight, but Barry's was still standing.

Barry told a story of another campout that had nothing to do with Daddy or Troop 12, but I liked the story, so here it is. When his son was a Scout, Barry and a friend took a group of boys to Fort Pickens on the Florida Panhandle. A storm rolled in, blew down their tents, and soaked everything. They went into town searching for hotel rooms, but there were none to be found. They settled for buying sheets and pillows from Wal-Mart, returned to the campsite, and all piled into the largest, driest tent. In the middle of the night, Barry's friend said the tent was leaking again. Barry turned on his flashlight and saw no sign of it, but his friend insisted. He said there was water running down his back. Barry pulled up his buddy's shirt, where he found a tree frog clinging to his back and peeing on him. Now, when it's only sprinkling, they say it's just a tree frog.

Barry went on two grand adventures during his years in the troop, one to Colorado, the other to New York. The first was to the 1960 national jamboree in Colorado Springs, where President Eisenhower made an appearance and rode in a parade. More than two decades later, Barry's father-in-law, a stern German-American doctor named Hans Carl Stauss, mentioned that he had also been at the Colorado Springs jamboree. Dr. Stauss was devoted to the Boy Scouts and volunteered to go to Colorado and give the boys at the jamboree routine physicals. Barry realized for the first time that his future father-in-law had examined him in 1960.

Several years later, Barry was selected to spend a summer working in the Boy Scout Pavilion at the World's Fair in New York. He and other Scouts from around the country served as ambassadors for the Scouts and conducted flag ceremonies. Barry was chosen from among them to make a presentation to the Shah of Iran. The boys would sit around the fire at night, play guitars, and sing. He said the summer in New York was an extraordinary growth experience and his first opportunity to see that there are good people all over America. He told me he was chosen to go only because of Daddy's efforts and those of the Yocona Area Council.

I asked Barry what he learned from his years with Daddy in Troop 12, and he first mentioned something no one else had. He said wearing a proper Scout uniform was part of the troop's culture, and Daddy set the tone. He was fit and trim and always looked sharp, his shirttail tucked in and a crease in his pants. Barry later learned a saying—*look good, do good*—and thought of Daddy when he heard it. He said Daddy was an example of the principle that appearance carries over into character.

Barry also came to realize long after his time as a Scout that he learned keys to success in business from his time in Troop 12, including leadership, teamwork, and organizational skills. Not all boys were interested in becoming leaders, but Daddy provided opportunities for those who were. He said Daddy was a servant leader. His mission was to make sure the boys had what they needed to succeed, both while they were in the troop and long after.

JEFF PRUETT

Jeff Pruett, who was sixty-one at the time of our interview, is an accomplished photographer, a Methodist preacher, and a cancer survivor. He was diagnosed with cancer nearly fifteen years ago but survived thanks to five surgeries and chemotherapy dispensed every twenty minutes through a port in his chest. Since then, he's had a series of health problems, some that were side effects of the cancer treatment. He's now on medical leave from preaching but grateful to be alive. His grandchildren call him Happy. He said it's funny when they sing Happy Birthday to him.

Boys who were athletic, outgoing, and popular benefited greatly from their time with Daddy in Troop 12, but boys who had none of those traits may have benefited even more. For many, learning skills and advancing in rank gave them their first taste of success. They felt good about themselves and pride in their accomplishments for the first time.

Jeff told me he was one of those boys. He said he was uncoordinated, overly serious, and socially awkward. He was also tiny. On his fifteenth birthday, four years after joining the troop, he was still only 5'2" and weighed just ninety-eight pounds. He was an easy target, and older, bigger boys picked on him. Daddy kept an eye out for him but intervened only when it was essential. He realized Jeff had to learn to look after himself.

And he did. After several years in the troop, Jeff was elected by the members of his patrol to serve as their leader. Daddy also entrusted him to teach merit badges, including First Aid and Photography, as well as a class for new Scouts. Jeff also recovered from being tiny. Between his fifteenth and sixteenth birthdays, he grew eleven inches. He was still skinny, but he got over that by eating fried chicken.

Jeff was a member of Troop 12 for a long time—like Daddy, he did not become an Eagle Scout until he was nearly eighteen—and he had many fond memories of his time as a Scout. Jeff didn't realize it at the time, but his parents couldn't afford a backpack when he joined the troop, so they created a makeshift pack for him. His dad built a frame out of steel conduit, and his mother found a green canvas bag and sewed it onto the frame. It was functional but heavy, and Jeff struggled to carry it. On a campout at Yocona, the boys backpacked a mile into camp the first day and a mile out the second. On the way in, Jeff labored under his heavy load and fell behind. Daddy was following in the White Elephant and asked if he was going to make it. Jeff said, "I got to," and he did. Jeff's mom had packed a heavy cast iron skillet for him to cook breakfast. Having served its purpose the next morning, Jeff tossed it into a cotton field on the hike out.

When the troop went hiking at Shiloh and elsewhere, many of the boys raced ahead and turned the hike into a contest. I recall doing that at the Brice's Crossroads campout one year. Jeff said he preferred to stay close to Daddy, to listen and learn. Daddy told stories and gave advice, including simple things such as making sure your socks are dry. Jeff learned from Daddy that you don't have to walk in the front or be in the spotlight to be a great leader.

When Jeff started his senior year of high school, he was still attending meetings and teaching merit badges, but he was not yet an Eagle Scout. As he approached his eighteenth birthday, the deadline for becoming an Eagle, Daddy said he better get it done or he was going to miss out. Jeff completed the requirements in April 1979 and received his Eagle badge in a ceremony at the First Methodist Church in May, the same month he graduated from high school.

Jeff chose not to enroll in college right away but instead became a professional photographer. He soon opened a studio in Aberdeen, a small town thirty-five miles south of Tupelo. He joined the First Methodist Church there, learned that its Boy Scout troop was inactive, and decided to reactivate it. He was only twenty-one, had gone from Scout to Scoutmaster in only three years, but they handed him the keys to the church bus and told him to have fun. He assumed Scouts were supposed to go camping every month because that's all he knew, so that's what his troop did. Jeff moved back to Tupelo after several years, but the troop in Aberdeen, now led by his former assistant, was still going strong the last time he checked.

After returning to Tupelo, Jeff joined the church his fiancée attended, a Methodist Church ten miles south of Tupelo in Verona. He soon discovered that the Boy Scout troop his new church sponsored was also inactive. Jeff was only in his mid-twenties, but he became a Scoutmaster for the second time. He asked boys in the church to join the troop but also recruited from the local school. No predominantly black church in Verona sponsored a troop, and more than half the boys who joined Jeff's troop were black.

Not long after returning to Tupelo, Jeff felt the call to enter the ministry. He completed his undergraduate degree by correspondence and was admitted to the Master of Divinity program at Emory. In his first years there, he pastored two churches in rural north Georgia a hundred miles from Atlanta. His family lived so far out in the country, he said you had to go toward town to hunt. Four days a week, Jeff left home at 5:30 in the morning to drive to Atlanta for classes. He prepared sermons in his spare time and preached every weekend.

After graduation, Jeff became a Scoutmaster for the third time. This time he started a troop from scratch and was also involved in starting the church that sponsored it. He was the second minister of the Diamondhead United Methodist Church on the Mississippi Gulf Coast and the first Scoutmaster of Boy Scout Troop 316. The troop could camp only on Friday nights because Jeff had to preach on Sunday mornings.

When I asked Jeff what Daddy meant to him, he said, "I attribute any success I have achieved in life to my time with Mr. Eason in Troop 12." Jeff has often wondered where he would be without Daddy as a mentor and told me that learning from him was the closest thing to osmosis you could know. Daddy didn't lecture. He just conducted himself the way a man should, and the boys watched and imitated. Daddy knew he was teaching the boys how to tie knots and build campfires, but whether he knew it or not, he was also teaching them how to live, how to lead, and how to serve.

Jeff told me he often mentions Daddy in his sermons and talks about his great gift to the boys of Tupelo. He describes Daddy's long tenure as the Scoutmaster of Troop 12 as "a ministry without a pulpit." He said Daddy had a unique ability to touch boys' lives, and he did it for three generations. Daddy believed in boys even when nobody else did, and he believed in Jeff. He said good leaders find a way to help others grow and become successful. That's what Daddy did. He gave the boys room to learn, fail, and learn some more.

Jeff believes encouragement has the power to give a child direction in life and a passion for living he will carry with him all of his days. He said Daddy was always encouraging. He devoted his life to shaping and forming lives, and those lives have branched out all over the world. Jeff has preached in Georgia, served as a missionary in Louisiana building homes for victims of Hurricane Katrina, and pastored churches in Mississippi from the Tennessee line to the Gulf of Mexico. Daddy, he said, has been with him every step of the way.

Near the end of our talk, Jeff told me a story I'd never heard. Daddy never would have told me because it would have been bragging. When Jeff was at Emory and he and his wife lived in north Georgia, they struggled financially. His annual salary for pastoring the two small churches was only $15,000. In those hard times, Jeff told me he received an envelope in the mail from Daddy every month. Inside there was always a check for a hundred dollars along with a note of encouragement. The money made all the difference in what Jeff and his family could afford to eat. He said he loves peanut butter and jelly sandwiches, but they sure taste better when you don't have to eat them.

One day Jeff walked out to the mailbox to check the mail. His son, who was three or four, tagged along. When Jeff opened the envelope from Daddy and saw the check and the note, he started to cry. His son asked what was wrong. Jeff told him nothing was wrong and why he was crying, and his son said, "But don't you practice what you preach, Daddy? You said the Lord would provide and take care of us." When his son asked who had sent the money, Jeff said, "It's from Mr. Eason; he's my Scoutmaster."

Eason Leake

Exactly twenty years after Elizabeth Leake interviewed Daddy about his life and his tenure as the Scoutmaster of Troop 12, I interviewed Elizabeth's father about his years in Troop 12 and about Daddy.

Eason Leake, my first cousin and Daddy's nephew, is now seventy-six and nearing the end of a very successful career in insurance and finance. He and his wife Ellen married on Super Bowl Sunday in 1973. I remember sneaking into the kitchen at the reception and watching on a tiny black-and-white television as the Dolphins beat the Redskins. The following year, Eason joined Ross & Yerger, a commercial insurance agency in Jackson. He's worked there for nearly half a century and served as chairman of the board for many years. He is still a member of the board but is winding down and has an eye on retirement. I told him it was about time. He is now focused on the coverage needs of a handful of large banks, mentoring younger agents, and delegating responsibilities to them. He said he first learned to delegate when he was a member of Troop 12 more than sixty years ago.

Since he was very young, Eason has also taken an interest in banking and finance. While his mother was in a sanatorium for two years suffering from tuberculosis, he lived most of the time with our grandparents on Highland Circle. Cliff, who became the president of People's Bank when Eason was eight, taught him about banking and was a major influence on him. Eason's other grandfather was a successful entrepreneur and gave him silver dollars on his birthdays, one for each year he'd been alive. When Eason turned nine, he told his grandfather he wanted to deposit the nine dollars right away so it would start earning interest. His grandfather was so impressed he doubled the gift. In addition to handling the needs of banking clients at Ross & Yerger, Eason is chairman of the board of the holding company of the bank from which Carrie recently retired and serves on the board of another one.

Eason and Ellen have also contributed their time and resources to many educational and charitable endeavors. Eason served as a trustee of his alma mater, Millsaps College, for twenty years, but their principal focus in recent years has been on the fight against diabetes. After Elizabeth was stricken with juvenile diabetes, they became deeply involved with the Juvenile Diabetes Research Foundation. Eason served on the board of the Mississippi chapter of JDRF, and Ellen was its president. She was later chosen for the international board of JDRF, which she chaired for two years.

The Leakes are also part of a small group that donated $50 million to establish the T1D Fund, a venture philanthropy fund formed for the purpose of encouraging investment and research needed to cure Type 1 diabetes. They and other philanthropists were also instrumental in raising $150 million to fund Civica, a company that manufactures insulin and charges a fraction of what major pharmaceutical companies have customarily charged. The monthly cost of insulin manufactured by those companies has ranged from $200 to $800 compared to $35 for Civica, whose new facility for producing insulin is scheduled to come online in 2024.

Eason and Ellen also purchased 650 acres west of Oxford, which they developed into Splinter Creek, a lake house community that includes three spring-fed lakes and miles of hiking trails. They split their time between their lake house there and their home in Jackson. They have more irons in the fire than most couples who've been married fifty years.

Eason told me he loved everything about being a Boy Scout in Troop 12. He was small and not much of an athlete, but he loved camping, hiking, canoeing, swimming, and sitting around a campfire with friends. His favorite campouts involved water, either canoeing on it or swimming in it. He described the lake at Camp Yocona as a nasty snake pit but said he had a ball swimming in the muddy water. He also enjoyed earning merit badges and learning skills and subjects he never would have learned otherwise. He became Troop 12's fiftieth Eagle Scout in 1959.

Eason remembered walking on a railroad track for Hiking merit badge and spending a night alone in the woods when he was initiated into the Order of the Arrow. He also recalled hiking through Civil War battlefields, Shiloh and others, and noted that you can see much more on foot than looking out a car window. That reminded me of a passage by outdoor activist and author Edward Abbey, who wrote that walking "stretches time and prolongs life. Life is already too short to waste on speed. . . . Walking makes the world much bigger and thus more interesting. You have time to observe the details."

Because he was a member of the family, Eason said Daddy kept him at arm's length when he was in the troop and was not overly protective. As in my case, there was no favoritism. Eason said leading a Scout troop is like herding cats, but Daddy had a gift for it. Some of the boys who were in the troop when Eason was a member were wild and some were bullies, but Daddy was still able to maintain discipline in his own quiet way. He never raised his voice and never threatened to report a boy to his parents. He counted on the boys to correct their mistakes and learn from the experience.

Eason said Daddy seemed to know innately how to use the Boy Scout program and path of rank advancement from Tenderfoot to Eagle as a platform to teach leadership and build maturity. From his time in the troop, Eason said he learned not only leadership skills and how to delegate but also what he could and couldn't do. He pushed himself to try new things, discovered he could do them, and grew in confidence and self-discipline. He said his years in Troop 12 were an important part of growing up and that Daddy was a very significant influence in his life.

When he was in college, Eason said he could tell who had been a Boy Scout and who hadn't based on differences in maturity and competence. But he told me about one exception. One of the wilder Scouts when Eason was in Troop 12, a boy named Carl, later joined Eason's fraternity at Millsaps. One Saturday night, Carl and two friends, their judgment impaired by beer and testosterone, drove from campus to the Jackson Zoo, broke in, caught a small alligator, and brought it back to campus. I don't know how they kept it from biting them, but they managed. When they returned to the fraternity house, they took the gator upstairs and released it in the bathroom. Then they found a hiding place nearby, cracked open more beers, and waited for the entertainment sure to come. Other fraternity brothers, also under the influence of strong drink, soon arrived and went into the bathroom, where a surprise awaited them.

Eason did not suggest that anyone was hurt in the incident. Nor he did say how long the alligator stayed in the fraternity house, how it was removed, or where it was taken. How the saga ended thus remains a mystery, at least to me. But whatever became of the reptile, the tale is a useful reminder that those of us who had the good fortune to spend time in Troop 12 with Daddy became better men as a result, but we did not become perfect ones. Most of us, however, never absconded with an alligator.

PAUL EASON

My son Paul has the honor of being named for his grandfather. And he and Daddy, who was called Big Paul by my children, share more than a name. Like Daddy, Paul is calm and quiet. He doesn't like being the center of attention and doesn't show his emotions. He loves Ole Miss football, the outdoors, and sharing a campfire with friends.

On a Sunday afternoon in March 2023, Paul came to our house to talk about Daddy. His wife Chris and their sixteen-month-old daughter Evelyn, my youngest grandchild, came with him. I recorded the interview so I could listen to it later. Some of it was hard to make out because of the background noise. Like Daddy, Paul is soft-spoken. Like me when I was her age, Evelyn jabbers.

Paul followed in my footsteps and graduated from law school, but he announced during his last year that he didn't want to practice law. I told him I didn't either—I was tired of the stress—but I didn't have much choice. But Paul still had a choice, and he held several jobs after graduation while figuring out what to do for a living. The most interesting was farming marijuana in Oregon for a close friend of Willie Nelson, a good person to know if you want to grow and sell pot. Paul came back to Jackson after that adventure and now works at a company that performs a valuable public service. He's the Operations Manager for Mississippi Logos, the company that erects and maintains the blue signs on interstates that identify restaurants, gas stations, and lodging at each exit.

Paul told me about the good times he and his brother Cliff had when they went to Tupelo. Big Paul was not a helicopter grandparent by any means. When Paul was born, Daddy had already been the Scoutmaster for more than forty years. He knew both that boys need adventure and that they're not as fragile as most parents think. He cut Cliff and Paul loose to explore the creek and sat on the front porch with an ear open. He would loan them a flashlight, and they would walk the full length of the underground culvert that ran nearly 300 yards along Rogers Drive, from the far end of the vacant lot to their great-aunt Marjory's house.

Daddy sometimes put the boys to work on minor projects and, when he finally bought a riding lawn mower, let them mow the vacant lot. He also took them to play at City Park and swim at Puddie's, but they were happiest in the creek. Daddy had a sweet tooth, and he indulged it when they came to visit, and not just with the ever-present ice cream. He also shared Pop-Tarts and chocolate milk with them.

Shortly before Paul was old enough to join the Scouts, Daddy found a used Scout uniform for him and took him to Washington, D.C., with Troop 12. They went by train. Fifty years had passed since Daddy's train to Valley Forge was commandeered by the Army when the Korean War began. Booking sleeping berths for the trip to D.C. was too expensive, but Daddy managed to sleep sitting up for two-thirds of the ride while Paul and the other boys went stir crazy.

Daddy was serious and respectful when they toured the memorials and monuments on the Washington Mall, and Paul said Daddy's explanation of the Marine Corps memorial and the flag-raising on Iwo Jima had a powerful effect on him. Congressman (now Senator) Roger Wicker rolled out the red carpet when he met with the troop. Paul said it was obvious that Representative Wicker had tremendous respect for Daddy. After explaining the role of the House and Senate, the congressman took Daddy and the Scouts to the basement, where they rode the private underground trolley to the Capitol, and he gave them a grand tour.

While they were in Washington, both Paul and Daddy discovered that their wallets were missing. Daddy was the victim of a pickpocket. Paul may have been as well, but he may have just lost his. After all, who picks the pocket of a ten-year-old? Paul is calm by nature, but he said he was anything but calm then. He didn't know what they were going to do, how they were going to eat, how they were going to get home. They were penniless. But Daddy put his hand on Paul's shoulder and said it was all going to be fine. By then, it had all been fine for more than fifty years. Paul said Daddy had the most calming presence of anyone he's ever known. He never once heard Daddy raise his voice.

When Paul was at Ole Miss beginning in 2008, he went to Tupelo two or three times a semester to see Daddy, whose health was declining by then. Paul would ask Daddy about the war and flying, but Daddy didn't go into much detail and changed the subject. In November of his senior year, Paul drove over to Tupelo for Daddy's ninetieth birthday. He remembered thinking there were far more people at the party than he expected for a person's ninetieth birthday. He watched as Daddy sat patiently, greeted everybody who came to see him, and was glad to see them whether he remembered them or not.

While Daddy was living with us, it took him a few seconds to recognize Paul when he came to see us, but then they were able to carry on a normal conversation. He remembered that Daddy loved Mollie and shared his ice cream with her and said it was hard to watch him decline.

Daddy went with us a few times when I took Ann Lowrey, Cliff, and Paul camping when they were young. I camped often with Paul's troop when he was a Scout, and one summer we canoed the Boundary Waters on the Minnesota–Ontario border. Since then, he and I have gone on many wonderful trips together, canoeing the Missouri River in Montana and the Allagash Waterway in Maine and backpacking in Glacier National Park, the Sawtooth Mountains of Idaho, and on Mt. Rainier and the Olympic Peninsula. Paul said he traces his love for the outdoors straight back to Daddy. At the time of the interview, he and friends were planning a canoe trip on the Buffalo River in Arkansas as a sendoff for a buddy in the Army who is being deployed to Syria.

I told Paul about building the deck behind Daddy's house not long after Mama died, that he was seventy-eight years old but worked alongside me until it was finished. Paul said Daddy was definitely a tortoise, not a hare. He didn't get in a hurry, but he finished every job.

I said being Daddy's son wasn't always easy because I could never measure up and asked Paul if being named for Daddy was a burden for him. He said it wasn't, that the distance from Jackson to Tupelo kept it from being an issue. And he told me there's been a benefit from having the same name as Daddy. When he introduces himself to people from Tupelo, he enjoys seeing their faces light up and hearing that his grandfather was a fine man.

When I asked what he learned from Daddy, Paul said he couldn't imagine that Daddy ever lied to anyone, not even a white lie to make things go easy. With Daddy, what's right was right; what's wrong was off the table. He didn't even consider it. Paul said he tries to be like Daddy, but he falls short in terms of patience. He doesn't like camping or canoeing with a man who hasn't learned how to do it right, much less with dozens of boys who haven't, much less for sixty years.

Paul said he learned another thing from Daddy that nobody

else had mentioned. He learned to accept and appreciate silence. He realized that it's possible to enjoy someone's company without talking all the time. For Paul, being in the same room with his grandfather was enough.

MARION WINKLER AND JIM LEAKE

Marion Winkler, called Wink by his friends, is a year older than I am, Jim Leake a year younger. Wink and I were on the tennis team together in high school; Jim and I were in the same fraternity in college. Though the two of them live more than 2,500 miles apart, they still manage to get together to camp, hike, and climb mountains.

Instead of interviewing them separately, I suggested a conference call with the three of us. After we scheduled a time, it occurred to me that we might be the first three Troop 12 Eagle Scouts whose fathers were also Eagles in the troop. I reviewed the list and confirmed that we were. Our dads became Eagle Scouts from 1939 to 1944; we earned our Eagles in 1971 and 1972.

Of all the Troop 12 alums I've interviewed, Marion has led one of the most interesting lives. Many of Daddy's former Scouts wear suits and work in tall buildings, but not Wink. Not long after graduating from Ole Miss, he headed to the West and never looked back. He and his wife Jean lived in Colorado for many years but recently moved to Selah, Washington, outside Yakima, so they could be near their granddaughters. Marion said one of them takes after him and is adventurous and loves rock climbing.

Choosing location over money, Marion began his life in Colorado tending bar and waiting tables in Snowmass Village. A few years after his arrival, he spotted a want ad seeking applicants for the position of musher. He wasn't sure exactly what a musher does, but he knew he loved dogs and the outdoors, so he applied. He began training sled dogs and after a year was promoted to kennel master.

To become better at taking care of the dogs he trained, Marion completed a two-year veterinary technology program at Colorado Mountain College, finishing first in his class. He also trained at a clinic in Potomac, Maryland, with an emphasis on small-animal

BROOKS EASON

anesthesia, and worked in an after-hours trauma center in D.C. When the owner of the kennel where he worked raced in the Iditarod in Alaska, Marion accompanied him and participated on the veterinary team, examining dogs to make sure they were fit to race. He served as the Chief Certified Veterinary Technician for the race in 1996.

Wink also competed professionally in sprint races in Colorado and surrounding states with his own dogs. He had a six-dog team that stayed together for five years and never lost a race. He and Jean had sixteen dogs at one point. When their son Hayden was growing up, Wink would load up his gear, his dogs, and his son and head into the mountains to sled and camp in the snow. He said they had a blast.

When the veterinary clinic where Marion worked in Colorado shifted its focus from dogs to horses, he decided to try something new. He found another outdoor job working as the certified greenskeeper at Aspen Glen, a Jack Nicklaus-designed course in Carbondale. He stayed there for two decades, then retired to Selah to become a full-time grandfather.

Jim Leake has spent his entire career in sales and marketing, which is no surprise. Everybody likes Jim. He worked for two companies in Tupelo, selling office supplies and equipment for the first one and fabric to furniture manufacturers for the second. When the plant where the fabrics were made burned down, he asked if he could have his old job back, and the owner invited him to return.

In 1997 fellow Troop 12 Eagle Jim Williams recruited Jim to move to Georgia to work for Ashley Furniture. It was an offer he couldn't refuse, but it made him unpopular with his parents, Mem and Ann. Jim and his wife Charlotte had a son, J. T., who was Mem and Ann's first grandchild. J. T. was only eight months old when Jim took him away from them and moved to Georgia.

Jim and Charlotte first lived in Atlanta, then moved to Newnan, where they've been ever since. He's been with Ashley for more than twenty-five years and is now a sales and marketing executive. When J. T. was in Scouts, Jim served as an Assistant Scoutmaster. He said he hoped Daddy's influence helped him be a good leader.

215

Wink said he was sure it did. When J. T. earned his Eagle, Mem and the rest of the family traveled to Newnan for the ceremony. Jim is convinced that being an Eagle Scout made the difference in J. T.'s being admitted to the University of Georgia.

Jim shared memories of Daddy and his time in Troop 12 that he said will always be special to him. He remembered sitting on the floor of the Scout Hut with other new Scouts, Daddy patiently teaching them how to tie knots on the leg of a chair. He recalled marching to the front during Monday night meetings, making precise military turns, and reporting his patrol's attendance to the senior patrol leader. He pictured Daddy standing at attention, a little off to the side, dressed perfectly in his proper Scout uniform, everything in its place, down to the tassels on his socks, staring straight ahead but not missing a thing.

In his first summer at Camp Yocona, Jim was homesick and tried to sneak into the office to call his mother to come get him. He failed and returned to the troop's campsite, trying to hide the fact that he'd been crying. Daddy spotted him and pulled him aside. He doesn't remember what Daddy said, but the next thing he knew, he was learning how to do something—sharpen an axe, weave a basket, or build a campfire. He was no longer homesick and loved every minute the rest of the week. Jim recalled that the troop had so many boys at camp that there were three Troop 12 teams in the water carnival, and they finished first, second, and third. Four years later, his homesickness long forgotten, Jim went to the 1973 national jamboree in Idaho and shared a tent with Kirk Purnell.

Marion said one of his responsibilities as the troop's quartermaster was issuing tents to the Scouts before campouts. The troop had two models; both were made from canvas and used wooden poles, but one was far better than the other. The Voyager was a newer model with a floor; the Baker was floorless and little more than a lean-to. Wink remembered asking Daddy and James Byrd what tents he should give the older boys. He didn't recall what they told him, but he laughed when he considered what would have happened if he had tried to give the lousy Bakers to the Scouts who were older and bigger than he was.

Marion and Jim shared memories from campouts, some that all three of us attended. Jim recalled the boys' rushing in the rain to fill the back of the White Elephant with patrol chests and other equipment, then climbing atop the pile for the ride to the destination. As always, Daddy was at the wheel. Marion was on the aborted Bear Creek trip with me in 1971, and Jim talked about a Current River trip—perhaps the Beefaroni trip—when the river was above flood stage, his canoe turned over, and he spent a cold, miserable night in a wet sleeping bag. Both recalled touring the USS Lexington on a trip to Pensacola. I don't recall the Lexington. I must have been in the emergency room with Daddy, waiting for a doctor to check on the stitches in my foot.

Jim said he didn't play sports and was perhaps a little nerdy when he joined the troop. To prove the point, he said he was one of the few Scouts ever to earn Rabbit Raising merit badge, which was later discontinued for lack of interest. Jim didn't set out to raise rabbits. His parents bought two that the seller said were both males, but the seller was only half right. A litter was soon born, and Jim took care of them and earned the merit badge. As if to out-nerd Jim, Wink demonstrated that he could still perform a skill he learned in the troop: He spelled Marion in Morse Code.

Marion and Jim trace their lifelong love for the outdoors to their time in Troop 12. Both have gone on many grand adventures in the five decades since then. When Jim was at Ole Miss, he rafted the Nantahala in North Carolina and the Rio Grande in Big Bend National Park. He and Jim Williams worked in Tupelo the summer after graduation, saved their money, sold their cars, and flew to Europe, where they spent the fall backpacking and exploring the continent with Eurail passes. In November they found themselves in Vienna. It was cold, they wanted to be warm, so they boarded a train and headed south. They found the perfect spot, a nude beach on a Greek island. They camped on the beach for two weeks and celebrated Thanksgiving by roasting a chicken over their campfire.

Jim also attended the 500th campout at Yocona where Scott Reed and Jim Williams joined him in performing old songs with new lyrics they'd written about Daddy and Troop 12. Jim remembered that one of them was to the tune of "You Can't Always Get What You Want" by the Rolling Stones. He said the campout was a wonderful gathering for men and boys of all ages.

In the years after he moved to Georgia, Jim returned to Tupelo three more times to honor Daddy. The first was for the 600th consecutive campout in July 2001, when he and Scott and I stayed up talking until after midnight hoping it would cool off enough so we could sleep. The last two trips were for Daddy's ninetieth birthday party in 2011 and his funeral two years later. As Jim told me, when you have such love and respect for someone, you make the time, and you show up. I thanked him for coming.

In addition to training and racing sled dogs, Marion has spent countless days and nights hiking, camping, and climbing mountains all over the West. He's summited thirty-seven of the fifty-four 14,000-foot mountains in Colorado, many more than once, and he climbed the Grand Teton in Wyoming with Jim's brother Med. Wink, Med, and other friends host an annual "fourteener" trip. They set up base camp on a 14,000-foot mountain, share campfires, drink beer, and play disc golf, then try to reach the top. Marion is the group's tarp guru. He takes pride in using tarps to protect the camp from bad weather, climbing high into trees to hang them. He calls the finished product the Tarp Mahal. Jim has flown to Colorado for several of the trips but told me he'd made it to the top of only one fourteener. "Me too," I said, "Daddy drove us to the top of Pikes Peak in 1965."

When I asked what Daddy meant to them, Marion said Daddy was an unbelievably special human being—warm, kind, patient, and easygoing. He told me he will always be thankful to be one of the thousands of lives Daddy touched and that the love of nature and adventure he learned from Daddy permeates his very essence. He listed Daddy as one of the five most influential men in his life. The others included Jim's dad, Mem, and the head of Mondamin Camp in North Carolina, Frank Bell Sr., whom Jack Reed Jr. talked about when I interviewed him. Wink said Daddy and Frank Bell had very different personalities but the same goal:

turning immature boys into responsible men who work hard, love adventure, and treat people with respect.

Marion credited a practice he follows to watching how Daddy treated people and gave them his full attention. He said he always speaks to everyone he meets, no matter who they are or what they look like. He takes an interest in them and loves to hear their stories. He said everybody has a story.

Jim spoke of Daddy's dedication, spending week after week, month after month, year after year giving thousands of young men a solid foundation for the future. He was never in the boys' faces telling them what to do, but he was always present, teaching the Scouts by his example to do their best and do the right thing. His patience, kind discipline, and guidance were ever-present. Jim said he learned from Daddy to stick with a task until it's complete and deal with situations the best way he knows how. Marion said those who needed the most guidance as boys may have accomplished the most as men. That made me think of Joe Holley, who needed to slow down and calm down when he was a Scout and is now the medical director of a FEMA search-and-rescue team.

Wink said he'd done some research before our call and determined that Daddy spent more than three years of nights sleeping on the ground in a tent. He and Jim laughed when I said Daddy had told Elizabeth Leake that he joined the Navy instead of the Army so he could sleep in a berth and not on the ground.

When I thanked Marion and Jim for their time, they thanked me for the opportunity to talk to me and contribute to the book. In his research, Wink had read that Daddy died on July 1, 2013, and he asked if I was timing the publication of the book for the tenth anniversary of Daddy's death. Just weeks earlier, Mike Parker of WordCrafts Press had agreed that it could be released that very day.

EPILOGUE

Decisions made early in life can have enormous and lasting consequences. A page is turned, and there's no turning it back.

Daddy said he never used his accounting training in any job he ever held, but the degree qualified him for one he turned down. To become an FBI agent in the 1940s, an applicant was required to have a degree in either law or accounting. When I listened in the summer of 2018 to the recordings Elizabeth Leake made when she interviewed Daddy fifteen years earlier, I learned for the first time that he applied for a job with the FBI before accepting the one at Milam. Why he chose Milam over the FBI, she didn't ask, and he didn't say.

In the five years since I listened to the interview, I've often wondered how things would have turned out if Daddy had chosen a career in the FBI, how his life and mine and many others would have been different. The opportunity with the FBI came before he married Mama. If he had taken it, he probably would have been unable to stay in Tupelo. Had he and Mama already started dating? Would they still have married each other? Would they still have adopted Margie and me?

A friend recommended that I give this book the title of my favorite Christmas movie, *It's a Wonderful Life*. The movie was released in 1946, the year Daddy was discharged from the Navy and returned home to Tupelo, and I've watched it at least a dozen times. Whenever I do, I think about the parallels between Daddy's life and the life of George Bailey, played magnificently by Jimmy

Stewart. Daddy and George both had the talent and drive to succeed in big companies in big cities, but they instead spent their lives serving others in the small towns where they grew up.

In the movie, Clarence the Guardian Angel gives George a remarkable gift, the ability to see what the world would have been like if he had never been born and how the fictional town of Bedford Falls and the people who knew and loved him would have turned out. It's a brilliant way for Clarence to show George all the good he has done and what a wonderful life he has.

Seeing how Bedford Falls was different without George makes me wonder how Tupelo would be different without Daddy. What if Daddy had joined the FBI and never come back home? What of the thousands of boys who became better men because of Daddy's leadership and example? How would they have turned out if he had not been their Scoutmaster? And what of all the others who loved Daddy and benefited from his service? What if they had never known him?

The last scene of the movie, which I cry through every time, concludes with the arrival of George's younger brother, Harry, who has flown home to Bedford Falls in a blizzard. When Harry was nine years old, George saved him from drowning. Harry is now a war hero, having saved all the American soldiers aboard a transport ship. As George now knows, all the soldiers on board would have gone down with the ship if he had never been born and Harry had drowned. Someone hands Harry a glass of wine, and he offers a toast: "To my big brother George, the richest man in town."

I listened to the last of the four tapes of Daddy's interview with Elizabeth while lying in bed on Sunday night, July the first. After the tape ended, I told Carrie all the new things I'd learned about Daddy, things I should have known but never asked. Then something else occurred to me that I told her: Daddy, the richest man in a real town, died exactly five years earlier.

Five more years have now passed, but Daddy's legacy and influence live on. When I consider his extraordinary lifetime of service—his tireless patience and commitment, the thousands of meetings and hundreds of campouts, and all the boys who became responsible young men under his leadership—I couldn't be any prouder. And when I look at my favorite picture of him—the one where he's dressed in his Scout uniform, fast asleep in his recliner, an empty bowl of ice cream in his lap—I think of the first words from a verse in the Book of Matthew: "Well done, good and faithful servant."

ACKNOWLEDGEMENTS

Interviewing a small sample of the many people who loved and admired Daddy, learning what he meant to them and how they benefited from knowing him, has been very special for me. Daddy gave generously of his time to them, and they gave generously of their time to talk to me about him. I'm grateful to all of them.

I am also grateful to those who reviewed the manuscript and offered helpful suggestions, including my wife Carrie, my grand-daughter Ada Brooks Forster, and my dear friend Michael de Leeuw. Michael has now given of his time to review the manuscripts for all five of my books and has improved all of them.

I thank my publisher, Mike Parker of WordCrafts Press, who as always has done a splendid job of turning my manuscript into a book. He also granted my request to expedite the process so we could release the book on the tenth anniversary of Daddy's death.

Finally, I thank Daddy. He was what a man should be. As Mike Bush wrote, we should all be more like Paul Eason. My hope is that this book will help us do that.

About the Author

Brooks Eason loves stories—reading and writing them, hearing and telling them. He has three children and five grandchildren and lives in Madison, Mississippi, with his wife Carrie, three rescue dogs, and an orange tabby cat named the Count. When he's not writing or walking the dogs, he and Carrie host house concerts and dance in the kitchen. *The Scoutmaster* is his fifth book.

Also Available From

WORDCRAFTS PRESS

Country Music's Hidden Gem: The Redd Stewart Story
by Billy Rae Stewart & Gail Kittleson

An Introspective Journey: A Memoir of Living with Alzheimer's
by Paula Sarver

Deployed with My Mother
by David Weill & Tammy Chandler

Lean In: Chasing the Sunset
by April Poynter

Confounding the Wise: A Celebration of Life, Love, Laugher & Adoption
by Dan Kulp

Suddenly Stardust
by Joanne Brokaw

www.wordcrafts.net

www.ingramcontent.com/pod-product-compliance
Lightning Source LLC
Chambersburg PA
CBHW070918120626
46546CB00001B/319